POLITICS
& Feminism

Barbara Arneil

First published 1999

2 4 6 8 10 9 7 5 3 1

Blackwell Publishers Ltd
108 Cowley Road
Oxford OX4 1JF
UK

Blackwell Publishers Inc.
350 Main Street
Malden, Massachusetts 02148
USA

British Library Cataloguing in Publication Data

A CIP catalogue record for this book is available from the British Library.

Library of Congress Cataloging-in-Publication Data

Arneil, Barbara.
    Politics and feminism : an introduction / by Barbara Arneil.
      p.   cm.
    Includes bibliographical references and index.
    ISBN 0-631-19812-1 (hardbound). — ISBN 0-631-19813-X (pbk.)
      1. Women in politics.   2. Feminism—Political aspects.   3. Women's rights.   I. Title.
    HQ1236.A76   1999
    305.42—dc21   98-29203
                                                                  CIP

Typeset in 10½ on 12½pt Palatino
by Graphicraft Limited, Hong Kong
Printed in Great Britain by TJ International, Padstow, Cornwall

This book is printed on acid-free paper

Contents

Acknowledgements

I would like to begin by thanking Simon Prosser and Jill Landeryou at Blackwell Publishers, who have provided both guidance and support through the process of writing and editing this book. I am grateful to the Faculty of Arts at the University of British Columbia for giving me time off from teaching to write, and both my under-graduate and graduate students (who are mentioned in various notes in the book), who opened up new ideas and challenged my thinking. My special appreciation goes to Doug Reimer for his unwavering support throughout, but most particularly at the out-set of this project. Finally, to my family, who have sustained me throughout all of my intellectual journeys, and in particular to my father, who did the proofreading of this manuscript, I owe, once again, the greatest debt of gratitude.

Barbara Arneil
Vancouver, BC

1

Politics and Feminism: an Introduction

Pick up any newspaper in any major western city. In it you will find a daily snapshot of the political world around you. It will be filled almost certainly with images of conflict and the people who are trying to resolve those conflicts. It will have the words of politicians and political pundits. And there will be advertisements, editorials and cartoons. And if you pause to consider it, you will find almost universally that the majority of these images, words and their authors will be men. We must ask ourselves: why? How do we explain the gender imbalance in nearly every aspect of western political life? In search of the answer we must go beyond the headlines and front pages of our newspapers to the roots of western thinking about both politics and gender.[1]

Both western politics and feminism are terms full of ambiguity and loaded meanings. We will begin with some preliminary definitions from which we may launch into our exploration of how each individual term intersects with, responds to and grows out of the other. As we delve into the early origins and evolution of each term, it is critical that we never lose sight of the snapshot contained in the newspaper. Revealing the theoretical and historical underpinnings of how we define both politics and gender will help us to explain the realities of our own daily existence.

Politics

In Ancient Greece, politics was originally defined as how a people governed themselves; that is, the laws they lived by, the constitutions they lived under, and the nature of the rule to which they were subject. Many today believe that this definition remains essentially unchanged. The *Oxford English Dictionary* defines politics as the 'science and art of government'.[2] Politics is thus still the process of 'governing', but it is often defined by a particular set of geographical boundaries, be they local, regional or national, and therefore politics resides in the city council, the provincial or state government, or the national assembly, respectively. But can today's notion of 'politics' be contained within the walls of these institutions? For example, one often hears terms such as 'office politics' or 'political correctness', or statements like 'that was a political decision', or 'there must be a political solution to the problems in Bosnia'. How are we, as political scientists or theorists, to understand these phrases? Is the 'politics' referred to in the above examples simply a colloquial use of the term or does it reflect something more profound about the current meaning of the term 'politics' itself?

In reality, the term 'politics', as it is now used, goes beyond government, encompassing instead nearly every human grouping where individuals conflict over collective goals and the means by which they resolve those conflicts. Lying at the heart of this struggle and therefore of politics itself is the concept of power. The current understanding of 'politics' in the west can only be understood as something which has been constructed through history. Most importantly, from Greek syllogistic thinking onwards, as shall be discussed, any concept in western philosophy has been understood as demarcated from what it is not. This demarcation has been a fluid process, constantly in flux. In arriving at a definition of politics in the tradition of western philosophy, one must recognize the constructed meaning of that term in opposition to what it is not; therefore one must examine politics in terms of the dualities created by its evolving boundaries.

I will suggest, as a preliminary definition of politics, as constructed through western political theory and practice: '*the exercise of power, through reason and language, to achieve a particular outcome within a group of people*'.[3] With this definition one can incorporate not only what occurs in the House of Commons or City Hall but also a broader sense of politics in society as a whole. 'Office politics', for example, concerns the exercise of power in a given office, and how individuals in that context achieve certain outcomes. 'Political correctness' similarly concerns the exercise of power through language either to include or to exclude certain groups of people or ideas, depending on your perspective.

'Politics' is demarcated within given boundaries. There are three boundaries created by this definition which should be noted. The first is that politics can only occur within a group of people. As Vicky Randall comments: 'Politics is recognized to be social; it has little meaning for the solitary inhabitants of a desert island.'[4] As we shall explore more fully, this recognition of the social nature of politics has from the beginning been transformed into a division between public and private, and hence the demarcation of a first and primary boundary.

The second aspect of this definition of politics is the role of reason and language. Beginning with Aristotle, politics represents the capacity for human beings, unlike animals, to resolve their conflicts through collective negotiation and decision-making, rather than yielding to 'natural' instincts and physical struggle. Even today many would argue that politics entails, by definition, a struggle for resolution through reason rather than brute force: thus the reference one often sees to the search for a 'political solution' in Burundi or the Middle East, meaning a negotiated end to the conflicts occurring in those regions. Language incorporates the notion of persuasion through rhetoric. Thus politics and political decisions are associated with the capacity for language and reason.

Finally, at the core of politics is the exercise of power. In early modern texts on politics, power was first defined as the exercise of an individual's, group's or state's will over people or objects.[5] Latterly, power has also been perceived as existing within the underlying structure of our economy or society or as constructed through language and texts.[6] Each of these aspects will be considered in much greater depth when we turn to examine the dualities which create the boundaries around politics as it has developed. We turn first to consider the meaning of feminism.

Feminism

Feminism is an equally difficult term to define. No definition is completely satisfactory because the term is amorphous and ever changing and because there are so many schools of thought with widely varying views. However, a preliminary definition of feminism might be: *The recognition that, virtually across time and place, men and women are unequal in the power they have, either in society or over their own lives, and the corollary belief that men and women should be equal; the belief that knowledge has been written about, by and for men and the corollary belief that all schools of knowledge must be re-examined and understood to reveal the extent to which they ignore or distort gender.*[7]

In second wave feminism, spanning the 1960s to the 1980s, a great debate emerged between different schools of feminist analysis as to what the goal of feminism should be. First, liberal and socialist feminists argued for political and economic equality within a capitalist or socialist economy, respectively. In both cases, it is assumed that men and women are essentially the same; either the rational citizen of liberal democracy, or the revolutionary proletariat of Marxism.

The early, first wave feminists, from the seventeenth century through to the nineteenth century, rooted in the liberal tradition of rights and freedoms, struggled for a formal equality for women within the existing system of rules and laws. That tradition, often referred to as liberal feminism, can still be seen in many of the debates of today. In essence, the objective of this form of feminism is the formal legal and political equality of men and women. It is assumed that men and women are essentially the same when it comes to the rational self-interested individual who lies at the heart of liberal theory. It is only that they have been socialized in different ways. Similarly, socialist feminists have also argued that the real objective of feminism must be equality, but a radical economic rather than political equality, which can only be achieved in conjunction with fundamental changes to the capitalist economy.

Both liberal and socialist feminists were challenged in the 1970s and early 1980s by other feminists, who argue that men and women are fundamentally different, in their natures, their experience and their history. The real problem, therefore, is that most texts reflect the reality of only one gender. The goal of equality does not fully recognize the extent to which every aspect of the western societies within which we live are masculine, and therefore alienating to women. Until we uncover the gendered nature of language and knowledge and make the changes necessary, equality will only result in women having to continue to fit into a world alien to themselves. Second, feminists argued that second wave feminism had failed to recognize differences among women based on anything other than class. The goal of feminism, therefore, should be a respect for difference and with it a recognition that our language and body of knowledge will need to change if it is to include and reflect the diverse reality of both genders.

Having provided preliminary definitions of these two terms, we must now attempt to understand their relationship to each other.

Many books have been written on both political and feminist thought. In most cases they are written as histories independent of each other. The purpose of this book is to understand not only what these two terms mean but their relationship to each other. I have chosen to examine both gender and politics through a 'history of ideas' approach; that is, examining how western conceptions of both these terms have evolved through the history of political thought. Furthermore, at the heart of western political thought, and therefore my analysis of both concepts, are foundational opposites or dualities. The two specific dualities which will underpin the analysis of both politics and feminism are culture versus nature and public versus private. Using these two dualisms to frame the analysis allows us not only to bring together traditional, feminist and postmodern arguments into a single cross-cutting analytical framework, but to get at the heart of, rather than the superficial, exclusion of women from western politics.

Dualities in Western Political Thought

Political theory is subject to the duality of western thinking. If we return to the definition of politics that we began with – 'politics is the exercise of power through reason and language within a group of people to achieve a particular outcome' – we can extrapolate two dualisms, two boundaries which have demarcated what politics is from what it is not. The first is that politics belongs to the world of culture (language, reason, science and arts) rather than nature (instinct, intuition and chaos). Second, politics, as it has been traditionally understood, exists in the public realm – that is, among groups of people – rather than the private sphere of the individual or family. Such dualities are critical not only to reveal the parameters within which our understanding of politics has evolved but to uncover the often hidden nature of gender in political theory. For inherent in the dualisms as they have been constructed by successive western political thinkers is the close identification of men with one side of the dyad and women with the other. Before we explore this intersection of gender and politics, let us first take a closer look at each of the two dualities mentioned above.

The identification of politics with culture rather than nature is first drawn in Ancient Greece between *nomos* and *physis*, when politics are associated with the rule of reason and the philosopher kings over the sphere of natural appetites and the common mob. In both individuals and city-states, a fundamental distinction is drawn between the order, authority and laws of human reason on the one hand and natural chaos or anarchy on the other. For both Plato and Aristotle, politics is the exercise of the former over the latter. The modern period transformed this duality into the distinction between mind and body, and with it the Cartesian distinction between subject and object (or self and other). In modern political thought, the stark dichotomy between culture and nature is reflected in the opposition between the pre-political state of nature and civil society. The transcendence of the latter over the former, by virtue of industry and reason, is central to the foundation of any contractarian political state. Thus, early modern theorists like Thomas Hobbes and John Locke argue that civil society inevitably supersedes the state of nature. This leads in the thought of Jean-Jacques Rousseau and Georg Hegel to the attachment of freedom and choice to culture and the world of politics versus the slavery and lack of freedom in the natural world, and eventually to Karl Marx, who believes that the history of the world is the extent to which culture has overcome nature. Thus we must explore the distinctions drawn between culture and nature as they evolve.

The second dualism inherent in the definition of politics lies in the boundary between public and private. Politics belongs to the public realm (of assemblies, city squares and office blocks) rather than the private sphere (of individual or family). Where, in ancient Greece, ethics was the study of how to order or govern one's soul, politics was a similar application of reason to the good governance or ordering of one's community. From Aristotle's first societies, politics has always been constructed as a public practice, to be distinguished from private life. The public/private divide is transformed in the modern world by a growing interest in the individual. Thus Hobbes in the seventeenth century is the first to speak of the natural rights of an individual. Private property, its preservation and protection, will become for John Locke and the fathers of the American constitution the chief end of government. For J. S. Mill, the private sphere will be the sphere of freedom: in terms of the individual and all of his private associations. Marx will argue for the eventual abolition of the private sphere, of both the family and property, as contrary to the inevitable will of the people, as a whole, in history. The evolution of the public and private and the changing boundary between them will also be analysed fully.

What is critical to understand about the nature of the boundaries is that they are constructed in such a way that if one side collapses, the other is either meaningless or utterly changed. Thus, if one eliminates the 'private sphere', the public sphere has either no real meaning (as is the case in liberal thought; for the preservation of the private sphere – in terms of either freedom or property – is the whole purpose of creating a public authority) or it is utterly changed (as is the case in Platonic and Marxist thought, where the public world becomes all that exists). In a fundamental way, western political theory and its understanding of politics depends on these two spheres remaining relatively constant, even if the boundaries are contested. Similarly, without the *physis*, what is the *nomos* in Ancient Greek political thought, or without the 'nature' upon which the rational and industrious agrarian farmer can labour in Locke's *Second Treatise*, can private property and by extension civil society have any meaning? Thus western political thought may have changed or adapted its understanding of what constitutes either 'private' or 'nature', but it cannot collapse or eliminate them without simultaneously collapsing 'public' and 'culture', and thereby fundamentally changing our understanding of what constitutes politics.

Examining the dualistic nature of western political thought will provide us with the tools to uncover the profound, but often silent, role of gender in politics. Inherent in the dualisms described above is the close identification in political theory of men with the world of reason, order, culture and public life, and women with the world of nature, emotion, desires and private life. Rousseau's citizen, Marx's proletariat, even Plato's guardians, despite some fine words, are ultimately men. When one combines the gendered nature of these dualities with the understanding that politics cannot exist without a private and natural world against which it is constructed, then the task cannot simply be to move women from the worlds in which they exist – that is, the private and natural spheres – into the world of politics. Rather, it will be necessary to rethink the nature of 'politics'. Thus, if one is to understand how politics excludes women by the very manner in which it is constructed, it is necessary to examine these dualities and how they have developed to see how this has occurred historically, and how the way in which we conceptualize 'politics' can continue to exclude women.

The exclusion of women from the political sphere, so that they may literally exist only within the private sphere, may help us to begin to explain how William Blackstone, in his famous commentaries on English law, could argue that for public purposes a woman is completely subsumed by her husband or how a country like

Canada, at the beginning of the twentieth century, could be seized by such a seemingly absurd question as whether women were 'persons' before the law. In private life, no one would question whether a woman was a person, but in public life, the Supreme Court of Canada's finding that women were not in fact legal 'persons' was simply falling in line with the entire history of political thought, which had, by its very definition of politics, created a world in which women quite simply could not exist.

Finally, central to the construction of politics within the boundaries described is the concept of power. Power lies in one half of the bifurcated discourse of political theory. Power lies in civil society over the state of nature, of the guardians over the auxiliaries, of reason and order over chaos, and of the masculine over the feminine. As language and reason bring order and authority to all bodies of knowledge, so too language and reason bring order to the chaos of people living together in nature. Analysing how this power is constructed within the dualities described above is the study of both politics and feminism.

This book is divided into eight chapters. The basic premise throughout the first five chapters is to try to examine both western politics and feminism historically and at their most fundamental levels: to understand how the former has been constructed through the history of ideas, and how the latter has in turn responded to that construction. Thus chapter 2 begins with a 'history of ideas' approach, in order to explore the evolution of western political theory in terms of the changing boundaries and definitions of the two dualities described above: culture versus nature and public versus private, within the specific contexts from which they have emerged. Beginning with ancient Greek thought and continuing through to the twentieth century, this chapter analyses key political thinkers' uses of these dualities in the construction of their own visions of politics and civil society, and the implication of such dualisms for both men and women. Chapters 3 and 4 provide the feminist critique of the culture/nature and public/private dualities, respectively, in western political thought. These chapters adopt a 'history of ideas' approach, in order to examine the evolution of feminist critiques of the ideas described in chapter 2. Included in both these chapters are sections of analysis, based on work done largely by women of colour and lesbians, which raises questions about perspectives and identity, for both western political theory and the 'mainstream' second wave feminist critique of those theories. On the basis of this in-depth analysis of politics, at the level of demarcating boundaries, chapter 5 examines three major theoretical frameworks in western political science (liberalism, socialism and communitarianism), providing, in turn, the feminist critique of each theory's key tenets. Chapter 6 is the first of two chapters on the history of feminist thought in its own terms, and includes the main ideas and writers of both first and second wave feminism. The penultimate chapter, chapter 7, develops the argument that second wave feminism, which has depended in large part on theoretical frameworks outside of itself, has given way to 'third wave feminism(s)'. Third wave feminism(s) are characterized by a commitment to beginning one's analysis from womens' own perspectives; that is, a recognition of 'differences' in perspective, both between women and men and among women. The final chapter is the conclusion which attempts to square the circle begun in this introduction.

2

Demarcating the Boundaries

Culture versus Nature

Beginning with the Ancient Greeks, the distinction between nature and culture is first expressed in political philosophy in the opposition between *nomos* and *physis*. The distinction between them, and the need for the former to control the latter as the basis of politics, is articulated by an Athenian orator in a famous speech:

> Be the *polis* in which they have their abode great, or be it small, men's lives are all controlled by nature (*physis*) and by *nomos*. Nature is something unordered, something uneven, something peculiar to each man; *nomoi* are something common, something ordered, something identical for all men. Nature, if it be evil, often wishes for evil things; and you will therefore find men of that type doing wrong. *Nomoi* wish for the just, the good, and the beneficial; this is what they seek . . . This is *nomos*, to which it is proper that all men should render obedience.[1]

Ernest Barker argues that the distinction between nature and culture underlies Greek political thought from the time of Socrates. At the same time, the basis of the *polis* was hotly contested in Greek society as to whether it was 'natural' or a product of culture or convention:

> A distinction between institutions existing by nature and those which existed 'by convention' had been drawn by popular teachers in Greece for a century before Aristotle's times. Some of them had regarded the state, in the form of the civic republic, as merely a conventional

thing . . . [others saw] the polis entirely and perfectly natural, be-cause it was the natural home of the fully grown and natural man.[2]

Within these two quotations, one finds the two basic meanings of 'nature' to be found in ancient Greek thought. The first is some-thing which exists prior to human reason and convention, a sphere in need of the order and control of convention; the second defini-tion of 'natural' is the sense of something which is existing as it should be, for its purpose. To put it simply, the Greeks, in using the term 'physis' or nature, are referring to a 'natural' object in the sense of something untouched by human convention, as our Greek orator notes above, and/or to the 'nature of' an object or some-thing existing in accordance with its own inherent nature, as Barker notes of some theories of politics in the second quotation. The notion of 'nature' as either 'function' or 'biology' will be part of western political thought through to modern times. Needless to say, culture is defined in relation to the definition of nature chosen. In the case of disordered biology, culture, through reason and lan-guage, must transcend and transform or rule over nature; in the case of purpose or function, culture (for example, the laws of the *polis* or civil society) must reflect or follow the dictates of nature. In both cases it is reason which lies at the heart of the western notion of 'culture', allowing the rulers either to transcend nature or to discover and embrace natural laws.

The duality between culture and nature first emerges in Plato's *Republic* with Thrasymachus's defence of natural law, where he combines both definitions of nature in a spirited defence of the principle that 'might is right'. Thrasymachus argues that the *polis* is mere convention, and we should reject it in favour of nature which provides us with the best principle for the resolution of conflict in a group of people; that is, the strongest, physically and intellectu-ally, should rule over all others in the way they see fit.[3] Any consti-tution or law introduced to counter this law of nature is simply an attempt by weaker members in society to control these natural born rulers through artifical convention.

The *Republic*, in many ways, is a response to Thrasymachus's challenge. What Plato through Socrates eventually concludes, after creating an ideal state, is that there are three different but corres-ponding parts to both a human being and a state. In the indi-vidual it is the appetites or desires, ambition and reason. In the ideal state, it is three classes: the common people, the auxiliaries and the guardians. Plato argues that in both the individual and state reason must rule over nature for the best possible life. In the state, the guardians must rule over the common people; in the individual, the reasoned mind must rule over appetites and ambition. Thus, in response to Thrasymachus's argument, it is those who would rule by reason, rather than those who would rule by strength, who are the best to govern. This is the very foundation of political life or the 'good life' of human beings, rather than the chaos and anarchy of animals. Through reason, the right constitution and laws may be developed to allow the state as a whole and the individuals within it to live the good life; that is, to be political. Those who lack reason must be excluded from politics and from citizenship, and ruled by those who do.

Plato makes clear, for example, that slaves, both male and female, are to be ruled because they lack reason and their masters have it. Contrary to Thrasymachus's argument that slaves are ruled by virtue of force, Plato argues that slaves are ruled because it is in their own best interest to be governed by reason:

> Don't we say that he must be the slave of that best man who has the divine rule in himself? It's not that we suppose the slave must be ruled to his own detriment, as Thrasymachus supposed about the ruled; but that it's better for all to be ruled by what is divine and prudent.[4]

Plato's cave provides another version of the same argument. Those who are governed by reason (that is, the philosopher or guardian) have the ability to see things as they really are in the full light of philosophical inquiry, whereas those living in the shadow of the cave are able to see only what the dim light allows them to see. Knowledge is thus associated with lightness, where the metaphor for the ultimate good is the sun outside the cave; ignorance and the majority of people are associated with darkness. As the guardians or philosophers must rule over the people, so must reason conquer passion and ignorance and light overcome darkness.

The link between darkness, irrationality and disorder and the need to control them through reason, light and order, as first articulated in the cave parable, is reinforced by Plato in gendered terms in the *Laws*: 'Women are accustomed to creep into dark places and when dragged out into the light they will exert their utmost power of resistance, and be far too much for the legislature.'[5] Plato goes on to say, 'They have no similar institution of public table in the light of day, and just that part of the human race which is by nature prone to secrecy and stealth on account of their weakness –

I mean the female sex – has been left without legislation by the legislator which is a great mistake.'[6] The role of power here is unmistakable. As Plato had argued in relation to the philosopher and those left in the darkness of the cave, the resistance of the ignorant must be overcome and the order of reason and light imposed on women.

Plato also explicitly contrasts male rationality and virtue with female biology and emotion in his proposals regarding the education of the guardians. In his discussion of what must be censored in drama and literature, Plato argues that the model for the guardians must be one of 'courage, self-control, independence and religious principle'.[7] His first example of poor moral conduct for young men would be to allow them to play roles or read literature which represents 'women, young or old . . . abusing their husbands or presumptuously quarreling with heaven when they imagine themselves happy or crying and complaining in misfortune. Far less can we permit representation of women in sickness or love or childbirth'.[8] Plato's conclusion is that women, particularly those weighed down by biology (sickness or childbirth) or passions (love), are the exact opposites of rational virtue, as he wishes to see exhibited in his guardians.

The implications of this line of argument for women as opposed to men is made explicit by Plato himself. Woman's association with nature makes her less suitable for the life of philosophy and, by extension, politics than men, associated with reason and culture. In this statement from the *Republic*, Plato makes clear that women, as both wives and slaves, are more closely associated with irrationality and appetites: 'The greatest variety of desires and pleasures and pains is generally to be found in children and women and slaves, and in the less reputable majority of so-called free men.'[9] On the other hand, Plato goes on to say, 'The simple and moderate desires, guided by reason and judgment and reflection, you will find in a minority who have the advantage of natural gifts and good education.'[10] What is critical here to Plato's argument is that *nature* as well as culture plays a role in who can become philosophers or rulers. Natural passions must be controlled by reason, and women by nature are less capable of doing it. It follows that women cannot now or ever be 'philosopher-*kings*'.

On the other hand, in his discussion of the education of the guardians or rulers, Plato explicitly argues that women are equal to men in their capacity to reason and govern, and therefore should be trained and educated in the same manner as men. Plato is almost unique as a political philosopher (excepting some second wave feminist thought) in arguing that there are no natural distinctions between men and women, and that given the right education and training men and women can be equally good rulers. How can we reconcile these two sides of Plato's thought: one in which he explicitly claims that men and women are equally capable of becoming philosopher-monarchs, the other in which he seems to associate women with nature? Feminists, as we shall see in the following chapters, will argue that ultimately Plato, and therefore the roots of political theory, is about the need to find order amidst the chaos and disorder of nature, *nomos* over *physis*, and the formal requirement of equality by Plato, while significant in its own right, must be examined in the context of this overall theory.

Aristotle, who adopts a functionalist view of politics, defines 'nature' by function or purpose as well as biology. The first definition of 'nature' is that which occurs due to *biology untouched* by culture, reason or language. Nature in this sense is seen as a sphere which exists prior to culture, but *can be controlled*, shaped, even transcended, by the cultural realm. A secondary meaning of nature is that which is innate, the purpose of a given thing, which therefore *cannot be changed* by culture, reason or laws. What Aristotle means by 'nature' here is not merely that we are political animals by biological passion or instinct, but that we are political animals by virtue of who we are and our purpose. R. G. Collingwood writes in *The Idea of Nature* that Aristotle's definition of nature is 'the essence of things which have a source of movement in themselves'.[11] Thus nature is fundamentally about movement, growth or development, but in accordance with an essential purpose. Accordingly, Aristotle's philosophy is functionalist: what is a person or object's purpose within the *polis*, which is itself natural, and how does each fulfil its natural functions. The extent to which culture can or should shape, overcome or transcend nature is a tension in Aristotelian political philosophy.

Under the first, biological, definition of nature, Aristotle claims that the first 'natural relationship' is the one between men and women for reproducing the species. Reproduction, according to Aristotle, is the same for human beings as it is for animals or plants, deeply rooted in biological instinct or impulse: 'Male and female must unite for the reproduction of the species – not from deliberate intention, but from the natural impulse, which exists in animals generally as it also exists in plants.'[12] Similarly, the family is a biological unit, a 'natural unit' in the sense of meeting the basic biological needs of that smaller unit – thus the family is barely distinguishable from animal families in this sense. 'The first form of association naturally instituted for the satisfaction of daily recurrent needs is thus the family.'[13] Under the second definition of 'natural', Aristotle believes that the *polis* also exists 'by nature', but in this sense he does not mean biologically but by purpose or function. Thus he says: 'man is by *physis* an animal intended for life in the *polis*'.[14] Aristotle also believes, unlike Plato, that one can and must differentiate between men and women on the basis of their 'natural' purposes or functions. Aristotle concludes that men and women have different purposes depending on the degree to which they are ruled by reason or bodily functions. Within the classification of men and women, there are also male and female slaves, who have an even greater ratio of bodily function or biology to reason then either free men or their wives, as shall be seen.

Culture over nature in Aristotle, like Plato, finds expression in the grounding of politics in the rule of the rational over the irrational, beginning with the individual soul. 'The soul has naturally two elements, a ruling and a ruled, and each has its different goodness, one belonging to the rational and ruling element and the other to the irrational and ruled.'[15] This principle is true for the individual, the family unit and the state. 'What is true of the soul is evidently also true of the other cases (the household and state) and we may thus conclude that it is a general law that there should be naturally ruling elements and elements naturally ruled.'[16] The *polis*, properly constituted through the right laws, would control the irrational and natural side of man. Indeed, Aristotle argues that an individual outside of the *polis* is 'a poor sort of being . . . clanless, lawless and heartless'.[17] Likewise, in the family there need to be those who rule and those who are ruled.

The distinction between culture or reason and nature or lack of rationality is explicitly linked to gender by Aristotle, and related to both definitions of 'nature'. Women are 'by nature' – that is, in accordance with their purpose – to be ruled over by men. Women are also closer to the 'natural' or biological functions of reproduction, food and shelter. Finally, women have less or an inconclusive reason compared to men and must not, therefore, be part of the rational order within the *polis*. The disconnection between women and culture (reason and language) manifests itself both in the *polis*, where women simply do not have the reason to be full citizens, and within the family, where free men rule over their wives or slaves owing to their superior reason. Thus Aristotle concludes: 'It is clearly natural and beneficial to the body that it should be ruled by the soul, and again it is natural and beneficial to the affective part of the soul that it should be ruled by the mind and the rational part; whereas the equality of the two elements . . . is always detrimental. What holds good in man's inner life also holds good outside it . . . the relation of male to female is naturally that of the superior to the inferior – of the ruling to the ruled.'[18] Wives, Aristotle makes clear, are not without reason, but rather have an imperfect rational faculty. This limitation justifies the particular type of rule exerted over them, as opposed to slaves or children in the family unit. 'The rule of the freeman over the slave is one kind of rule; that of the male over the female another . . . the slave is entirely without the faculty of deliberation; the female indeed possesses it, but in a form which remains inconclusive.'[19]

Thus the distinction is made by Aristotle between what he calls 'female' and 'slave'. One must immediately ask: what of 'female slaves'? They are almost entirely erased by Aristotle and much subsequent political, including feminist, commentary, but it appears that Aristotle would argue that among those people lacking rationality (that is, barbarians), female slaves fall into the category of slaves, as opposed to wives, and their husbands equally are slaves rather than husbands.

> Among the barbarian, however (contrary to the order of nature), the female and the slave occupy the same position – the reason being that no naturally ruling element exists among them, and conjugal union thus comes to be a union of a female who is a slave with a male who is also a slave.[20]

Ernest Barker comments: 'The argument is that among the barbarians the female is slave (as well as mate) for the simple reason that all alike are slaves, men as well as women, and the emergence of a true *consortium* of marriage, distinct from the nexus of slavery is thus impossible.'[21] This distinction is critical. There are many critiques by feminists of colour on how 'woman' or female is defined in most second wave feminist texts from a perspective of white middle-class women. In much of the feminist analysis of western political theory, women are seen as almost synonymous with 'wives' in these texts, whereas many black women in the United States, to give just one example, could perceive their historical role as more closely associated with 'slaves' in Aristotle's analysis. Thus, in the

Politics, 'wives' have some limited rationality and therefore some power, whereas 'slaves' and 'barbarians', who must include both men and women, are defined as 'without reason', closely associated with nature and animals. This hierarchy, Greek men, Greek women, and then slave men and women underpins western political theory and thus from its inception there are differences among women and their relationship to power, culture and the public sphere.

Aristotle makes the argument that slavery is based in nature not convention, using the second definition of 'natural' as the inherent purpose of something, rather than something created by society. He recognizes that there are those 'who regard the control of slaves by a master as contrary to nature. In their view the distinction of master and slave is due to law of convention . . . the relation of master and slave is based on force'.[22] As we shall see, this will be the view of some modern writers (slaves are taken by force in a just war). Aristotle argues, however, in a series of famous paragraphs that some people are naturally suited to slavery and this is based on their lack of rationality and strength in body rather than mind. 'We must thus conclude that all men who differ from others as much as the body differs from the soul, or an animal from a man . . . all such are by nature slaves, and it is better for them . . . to be ruled by a master.'[23]

Aristotle transforms the duality between nature and culture in a profound way in his thinking, which will have enormous implications for philosophy generally and gender specifically. Aristotle adds the notion that man is, through his capacity for reason, the active element in a natural world which is perceived as inert, empty and passive. Man, in other words, is the subject of this world, actively working on and transforming the objective, natural world around him through culture; that is, through knowledge, arts and sciences. The origin of this theory is to be found in Aristotle's views of conception. His distinction between active and passive is introduced here in a gendered context:

> The female always provides the material, the male that which fashions it, for this is the power that we say each possess, and this is what is meant by calling them male and female. Thus while it is necessary for the female to provide a body and a material mass, it is not necessary for the male, because it is not within the work of art or the embryo that the tools or the maker must exist. While the body is from the female, it is the soul that is form the male, for the soul is the reality of a particular body.[24]

Aristotle makes this most fundamental distinction between matter which is inert and to be acted upon, identifying that with the female, and the active subjective principle or soul which exists within the man. Aristotle concludes:

> The real cause why each of them comes into being is that the secretion of the female is potentially such as the animal is naturally, and all the parts are potentially present in it, but none actually. It is also because when the active and the passive come in contact with each other in that way in which the one is active and the other passive ... straight-away the one acts and the other is acted upon. The female, then, provides matter, the male the principle of motion.[25]

This transformation of the relationship between culture and nature to one where the former acts upon and transforms the latter will become central to modern political theory's notion of the individual citizen, as will be discussed. What is critical to note for now is, first, the way in which man, through his capacity for reason, language, arts and sciences, will be applying his knowledge to and acting upon the world around him, thereby creating something new. Second, the extent to which this 'active' faculty is associated with the (male) citizen or head of household should also be noted. In Aristotle's case it is a new life, in John Locke's case it will be property; but the fundamental duality and the relationship between the two is based on the same basic principle of an active rational creature transforming nature to create an entirely new entity.

The duality between culture and nature in defining politics in Ancient Greece is incorporated but transformed in modern thought. From the writings of René Descartes onwards, modern thinking is characterized by two basic features: putting the 'rational *individual*' at the heart of western knowledge and a belief in science as the means to discover universal laws which govern these individuals. Science, in the words of Francis Bacon, is about conquering nature: 'I am come in very truth leading you to Nature with all her children to bind her to your service and make her your slave.'[26] The culture/nature divide is transformed by Descartes into an individual mind or thought which precedes the existence of the body. 'I think therefore I am.' Descartes's thinking mind is the beginning of an abstracted non-corporeal mind who, through deduction, discovers the universal laws which govern the physical, moral and political world around it. The dualism between culture and nature has thus completed its transformation in modern thought from culture and nature to active mind versus matter; and subject versus object.

The belief in an abstract rational mind, which can transcend time and space in order to discover the universal laws of nature and morality, is the foundation for modern thought, or what some have termed the 'Enlightenment project'. The possibility of such a God's eye view perspective abstracted from any relation to the temporal or spatial world around it and the universality of the laws it discovers has been the subject of criticism by both postmodern and feminist critics. Is the perspective truly objective or is it partial? Are the laws discovered universal to all human beings or are they the products of a particular time and place in history? Ultimately, is it even possible to have a 'God's eye view'?

Modern *political* theory is a reflection of the Enlightenment project, beginning with the rational individual and attempting to explain how a political society is formed. Unlike with the Ancient Greeks, a collectivity or *polis* is not assumed but must be explained in terms of the rational choice of individuals. For Thomas Hobbes, John Locke and Jean-Jacques Rousseau, the individual precedes the *polis*; the state in turn only exists when consented to by the people who live within it. The dualism of culture and nature is thus transformed in modern political theory from the Greek split between rational and irrational parts of the soul and state into a distinction drawn between a state of nature and civil society, in order to explain how individuals in their natural, pre-political state would agree to form a *polis* in the first place and why they would choose to live within its constraints. To find the reasons for such a choice, Hobbes and Locke look to universal natural laws and rights (immutable laws built into the very 'nature' of the world) to underpin their political theory. Thus the social contract theorists, like Aristotle, use 'nature' in two different ways; the first, in the case of the state of nature, as a pre-cultural point of origin (nature is that which is untouched by reason or language). This concept of nature is wild, uncontrolled biology and instinct, which will be transformed and transcended by culture (through reason and language). The second concept of nature (as in natural laws and rights) is nature as that which is inherent to human beings and therefore cannot be changed by culture (through reason or language). Nature in this sense of the word demands that political society reflect the basic 'natural laws and rights' which inhere in humanity itself, as will be discussed.

In order to discover the origins of political society, Hobbes applies scientific methodology, more specifically the 'resolutive-compositive' method of Galileo. Through this method, Hobbes believes it is possible to break a society down into all of its constituent parts, examine the laws which govern each of those parts and develop a theory about the compound effects of the forces at work which would eventually generate the need for civil society. Thus the *Leviathan* begins with the composite parts of 'man', leading to man forming, in turn, the many composite parts of the commonwealth.[27] Within his method, one can see many of the assumptions about science: first, that it is possible to take a view of the world as if from nowhere; second, that it is possible to pull things apart without distorting the relations between the composite parts; third, that scientific method will bring an order to the chaotic and untamed natural world, by enabling the discovery of laws which make sense of all these different parts and how they interact with one another; finally, that such laws are universal, or in the words of Hobbes 'natural', meaning they are part of the very constitution of all 'men'.

From the beginning the state of nature is defined as the mirror image of culture. The binary nature of these two concepts or their logical interdependence is articulated by Hobbes, himself, when he defines the state of nature explicitly as an absence of English seventeenth-century culture:

> There is no place for Industry... no Culture of the Earth; no Navigation; nor use of the commodities that may be imported by Sea; no commodious Building; no Instruments of moving ... no Knowledge of the face of the earth; no account of Time; no Arts; no Letters; no Society.[28]

In the state of nature all are free and equal because there is no common authority over them. Natural law governs the state of nature but only to the extent that individual reason recognizes and acts in accordance with these laws. Both Hobbes and Locke ultimately argue that individuals in the state of nature are moved by their appetites, ambitions and emotions rather than reason, and the state of nature degenerates into a state of war. Politics and political authority thus emerge with civil society; with the forming of laws and government to impose a common authority over all the individuals. There are no 'politics' in the state of nature, just brute savagery, violence and instability. For Hobbes, the state of nature is the state of war, one against all. For Locke, the state of nature, while peaceful for a time, will also always lead eventually to the state of war, particularly with the introduction of property. It is insecurity which motivates individuals, who are naturally competitive, self-interested, egoistic and ultimately aggressive, to form civil society and agree to political authority. Natural laws, which exist in the state of nature, become the basis of civil law in civil society. The difference between the two states (nature and society) is civil law, backed up by common authority and sanctions which in turn rest on reasoned consent.

At the heart of this conception of politics is the notion of 'natural rights'. Natural rights represent the liberty each individual is born with in the state of nature and the basis upon which any political society may be formed. For Hobbes, natural rights extend as far as the right to self-preservation, but for Locke, rights extend to the protection and preservation of property, broadly conceived as the life, liberty and estates of the individual. Rights, based on individuals being free and equal in the state of nature, have become, over the past 300 years, a linchpin of western political discourse. From newspapers to scholarly papers to international instruments to political speeches, the protection of individual rights is now the cornerstone of liberal democratic thought. Natural, or laterally human, rights have two key characteristics. The first is that you are born with them; thus each human being is equal to all others by virtue of mere birth. Second, the exercise of these rights within civil society depends on your capacity to be defined as a 'person'. From the beginning, these two claims caused problems for political theorists with regard to gender. For once you have claimed that men and women are equal in the state of nature, and are born with the same natural rights, as Hobbes does explicitly, then you must accord them equal rights on entering civil society. The seeds are sown. The theory of universal rights will provide many subsequent writers (including Mary Wollstonecraft and J. S. Mill) with a foundation to argue for women's rights. The early rights theorists, however, made a distinction between male citizens and their wives, servants and slaves in civil society on two grounds: the public/ private divide, which will be discussed shortly, and their differing capacity to exercise reason. On both of these grounds citizenship will be exclusionary.

The relationship between citizenship (therefore the exercise of certain rights) and reason is clearly demonstrated in Locke's theory of property. For John Locke, the fundamental goal of government, of politics, of civil society is to protect and preserve property. 'The great and *chief end* therefore of Mens uniting into Commonwealths, and putting themselves under Government is *the Preservation of their Property.*'[29] As Locke makes clear when he distinguishes between his three different types of power (paternal, political and despotical), distinctions can be drawn between different types of power based on one's property.[30] Locke's basic thesis in this chapter is that to be a citizen and to exercise power and be part of the *polis* one *must own property*. The question immediately arises: how does one become a property owner?

In his well known theory of property, Locke argues that it is the labour of the individual which first creates the right to exclude others from using either the fruit of the land or the soil itself. Like Aristotle, Locke argues that it is by acting upon an inert and passive nature that man creates something new. It is the application of reason through labour which gives men the right to claim dominion over land, to become property owners, but it is a very specific form of labour. It is agrarian labour or 'tilling, planting, subduing' the land. This type of labour defines property (through the application of reason and industry) and in turn citizenship. Other claims to property (occupancy, hunting grounds, mining, grazing) are not in accordance with 'reason' or God's will and therefore are not legitimate foundations for either owning land or claiming political power. As Locke takes America as his primary example of people living in the state of nature, the implications for aboriginal peoples in America, both men and women, are, needless to say, profound.[31]

Wives and female servants of male citizens were also prevented from owning property and exercising citizenship, in Locke's theory, even if they did engage in agrarian labour, because of where the value of their labour accrues in the patriarchal family. In defining the reasonable and industrious subject, Locke states: 'The Grass my Horse has bit; the Turfs my Servant has cut . . . become my Property . . . The labor that was mine, removing them out of that common state they were in hath fixed my Property in them.'[32] Labour within the family done by servants accrues to the individual head of the household, and the products of their labour become the property of the freeman. Thus, female servants are clearly excluded from being subjects with their own labour. This is equally true of the wives of citizens. As Locke states in the First Treatise, 'Conjugal power . . . [is] the power that every Husband hath to order the things of private Concernment in his Family, *as Proprietor of the Goods and Land there*, and to have his Will take place before that of his wife in all things of their common Concernment.'[33] It is worth noting that in this First Treatise, Locke makes an explicit distinction between the 'Subjection that is due from a Wife to her Husband' and 'that which Subjects owe the Governours of Political

Societies': two kinds of power (conjugal versus political) which Locke himself says are far apart; the political being dependent on the ownership of property.[34]

Thus, wives and servants are extensions of the free man's subjectivity in the creation of property, and simply cannot exercise political power. Locke not only defines these powers in relation to one another explicitly: political power could not exist if parental, conjugal and despotical power were not equally there to deal with those 'relationships' which did not involve free citizens. The entire edifice of politics is built in this way. For wives and female servants, the relationship to all others and political authority is thus mediated through the male citizen's freedom and rights. As such, they are neither subjects in themselves nor property owners, nor citizens.

So far we have discussed conjugal power, exercised by male citizens over their wives; parental power, exercised by both men and women over their children; and the power exercised by masters over their servants. It is necessary also to consider despotical power, one of the three kinds of power Locke mentions in the chapter on the three different types of power. Despotical power, according to Locke, is reserved for those without any property at all, and is only to be exercised over slaves. For Locke, authority over servants and slaves (both male and female) is quite different. In defining slavery at the beginning of the Second Treatise, Locke states that slaves can only be justifiably enslaved when they are conquered in a 'just war'. Thus, he speaks of those living in a 'perfect condition of Slavery . . . between a lawful Conqueror, and a Captive.' A servant, on the other hand, is a person whose labour was sold 'not under an Absolute, Arbitrary, Despotical Power. For the Master could not have power to kill him, at any time, who at a certain time, he was obliged to let go free out of his Service.'[35] Similarly, towards the end of the Second Treatise, Locke describes slaves as 'Captives, taken in a just and lawful War, and such only are subject to a Despotical Power'.[36]

These distinctions between the powers exercised over different groups of people were not simply abstract theorizing for Locke. From his colonial correspondence, it is clear that Locke makes a distinction between African slaves and American 'Indians', for example. In the Fundamental Constitutions of Carolina, penned by Locke, is the provision that every free man 'shall have absolute power and authority over his negro slaves'. Further, the Instructions give to Governor Nicolson of Virginia in 1698 claim that slavery of Africans is justified by their being taken captive in a just war. Locke, himself, held shares in the Royal Africa Company. On the other hand, temporary laws written in Locke's own hand in December 1671 forbade the enslavement of 'Indians'. In simple terms, Locke's hierarchy of freedoms seemed to imply that wives had property in the children and therefore rights within marriage, servants had rights over their own life (the limit of their property) but not their labour, 'Indians' had rights over basic subsistence (fruits and animals of the earth) through labour but not over property in land (for a variety of reasons) and, finally, African slaves had no rights whatsoever (and were therefore the only group who could be rightfully subjected to despotical power).[37] In each category (wife, servant, Amerindian, African slave), while never explicit in Locke's theory, are both men and women.

Women are thus subjected to varying degrees of power and oppression in Locke's theory, depending on their categorization in his scheme and their closeness to culture and reason versus nature and body. For Locke, the extent to which one has property (through the exercise of reason and industry) determines the type of power that may be exercised, within the confines of the patriarchal family. Moreover, unlike the free man and his wife, who had different degrees of power, male and female servants, or male and female slaves, had a similar relationship *vis-à-vis* their masters. As with Aristotle, these distinctions, between wife, servant, slave (and for Locke, European, 'Indian' and African) are critical in understanding the limitations of some feminist analyses of liberal democratic theory in relation to women of colour. For often when analyses are done on Locke's *Two Treatises*, with regard to gender, the analysis begins and ends with the wives of the free man, when clearly there are women who also exist in the categories of servants and slaves. This will be explored in more depth in the chapters on the feminist critique of the public/private divide and contemporary feminism. We will turn now and look at the ways in which Marxism constructed the culture/nature duality.

Karl Marx and Friedrich Engels began their analysis of human history by claiming to turn the culture/nature divide on its head.

> In direct contrast to German philosophy which descends from heaven to earth, here we ascend from earth to heaven . . . We do not set out from what men say, imagine, conceive . . . in order to arrive at men in the flesh. We set out from real active men and . . . we demonstrate the development of . . . morality, religion, metaphysics . . . and their corresponding forms of consciousness.[38]

For Engels and Marx, we must begin with the material world of nature. The production of those things necessary to sustain life is the foundation of human history. Marxism shares with liberalism a belief in the human capacity to exploit nature for life-sustaining purposes. Thus Marx states: 'All production is appropriation of nature by the individual within and through a definite form of society' or 'In production . . . men act upon nature'.[39] Thus culture, in the sense of technology and science, according to both the liberals and Marx, is the force which acts upon nature and is the engine of human history. On the other hand, Marx also argues that it is not cultural ideas, in the form of religion, morality, politics or philosophy, which rule over the material or natural world, as the liberals claim. Rather, these forms of cultural expression are merely a reflection or justification for some deeper set of relations within the production of material goods. In this sense of culture, Marx is, as he himself claimed, turning previous philosophy on its head. But he is not overturning the basic conceptualization of the relationship between matter or nature versus science and technology. Thus both the liberals and Marx claim to be scientists. For Marx, science, in the form of scientific socialism, will help us to understand both the relationship between technology and matter, in the form of production, and how in turn these relations create the ideas, religion, philosophy and politics which have been called 'culture'.

For Marx, politics and the relationship between the state and citizen can only be understood in terms of the ways in which nature is exploited; that is, how economic production in society as a whole is structured. Different classes, as well as men and women, can be described only by the role they play (or do not play) in production. Families, in turn, also serve a specific function in each society in relationship to the nature of material production.

At the heart of production is a division of labour. Marx argues that the first division of labour is a 'natural' one, meaning it is based on biology: 'The division of labour . . . was originally nothing but the division of labour in the sexual act . . . that division of labour which develops spontaneously or "naturally" by virtue of natural predisposition (e.g. physical strength), needs, accidents, etc. etc.'[40] He goes on to argue that this 'natural division of labour' in the family forms the basis for all other divisions of labour and leads to wives and children becoming the 'slave[s] of the husband' because he has 'the power of disposing of [their] labour power'.[41] Marx takes for granted women's work in the home, based on what he sees as the natural roles of men and women. In Capital, Marx asks the question of housewives working outside the home: 'How will [the] internal economy be cared for: who will look after the young children; who will get ready the meals, do the washing and mending?'[42]

Marx, elsewhere, divides the world into two types of labour: the labour of production and reproduction, associated with men and women respectively. Marx spends most of his time discussing the former, leaving it to his colleague Frederich Engels to explore 'reproduction' and 'the family' much later in his book *The Origins of Family, Private Property and the State*. His ideas will be discussed in the next section on the public/private divide. Suffice it to say that for Marx, politics is not about reasoned debate, rational choice or contracts between citizens. Rather, the political sphere is one in which the more fundamental power struggle between classes is waged on the one hand by the bourgeoisie in their national assemblies and city halls, and on the other by the proletariat in strikes and other forms of industrial action in the workplace. Women are in neither of these groups, but tied to reproduction and the private sphere by virtue of the capitalist mode of production and to the natural sphere by virtue of the biological division of labour. The most important point here is that while production and history are fundamentally about the transcendence of culture, through technology, over nature, reproduction is firmly within the natural sphere.

Thus Marx, like all modern thinkers, believes that human culture through technology must and will transcend nature. Production is the engine of this transformation. With collective production under communism, socialized man will finally be free through his common control over the material/natural world: 'Freedom . . . can only consist in socialized man, the associated producers, rationally regulating their interchange with Nature, bringing it under their common control, instead of being ruled by it as by the blind forces of Nature.'[43]

At the time he wrote, Marx believed most human beings, rather than being in control of 'nature', were ruled by it, existing in a near bestial state in capitalist society.[44] However, through the logical working out of the contradictions inherent in the current economic system, this type of existence will necessarily give way to a new society. It is this transformation (to socialized production) and not the one from 'the state of nature' to civil society which will witness the true transcendence of culture over nature. The distance we have travelled down this road from nature to culture can be measured, according to Marx, in terms of the relationship between men and women:

> The immediate natural and necessary relationship of human being to human being is the relationship of man to woman . . . From this relationship the whole cultural level of man can be judged . . . It shows how far the natural behaviour of man has become human or how far the human essence has become his natural essence.[45]

This progression from nature to culture can also be seen in the various levels of development among different peoples in the world. Like their liberal predecessors, Marx and Engels accept the distinctions between African slaves, Amerindian 'barbarians' and industrial capitalism as different stages in human development in history. Engels comments: 'For now slavery has also been invented. To the barbarian of the lower stage a slave was valueless. Hence the treatment of defeated enemies by American Indians was quite different from that of a higher stage.'[46] As with Locke, western industrialized countries were in a higher stage of development, the Indians in a lower stage and the African slaves in an even lower stage according to the laws of scientific socialism. Unlike Locke, however, Marx saw the need to free all men (and implicitly women), and communism was the inevitable means to achieve this end.

Marx viewed himself and his writings as turning previous philosophy 'on its head'. He means by this that he does not begin with the world of culture (reason, language, ideas and philosophy) but with the natural material conditions of human beings. In this sense he shifts the focus of previous thinkers towards the material basis of society. But he continues the trend first enunciated by Hobbes and Locke of attempting to find the 'truth' of history and therefore of current politics in the 'natural laws' which govern our world, through science. Needless to say, the 'laws' they discovered were different, but all these modern theorists were convinced that they had found, through science, the basic structure built into the very nature of the world which could explain human history, the nature of universal progress and the goals for the future. To this extent, the belief in an objective observer, a material natural world to be discovered and a set of universal natural laws continued to demarcate the distinction between culture and nature throughout modern political theory. Second, the notion that man must transcend nature through labour and technology is maintained in Marx. The objective, however, must be to take control of the natural world through a *collective* use of labour, technology and science. Reproduction remains firmly within the natural sphere. Where women fit into either the scientific view of the world or the transcendence of culture by nature will be discussed more fully in the feminist critiques of the culture/nature duality.

Private versus Public

The second great duality which demarcates politics from what is not politics is the public/private distinction. Politics, from its inception, has existed in the public domain. Public only has meaning, however, in relationship to what is not public, namely the private sphere. In Ancient Greece, a distinction was drawn between two schools of inquiry; the first, namely politics, was the study of goodness in the collective life of a community; the second, ethics, was looking into the goodness of an individual. The Greeks also made a distinction between the *polis*, or city-state, on the one hand and the *oikos*, or family, on the other. From Plato and Aristotle's first societies, politics has always been constructed as a public practice, separate from either the individual or the family, which continues to be the way politics is largely defined to this day. It is thus critical, if one is to understand the relationship between politics and gender in western political thought, at its most fundamental level, that the evolving boundary between the public and private spheres be fully analysed. Let us begin with Ancient Greece.

The fundamental distinction between public and private spheres, and in particular the relationship of husband and wife, is succinctly summarized by Meno in the dialogue of the same name: a man's virtue lies in administrating the state; a woman's is to 'order her house and keep what is indoors and obey her husband'.[47] In the *Republic*, Plato understands and accepts this division between public and private. He believes, however, that private interests have only divided citizens and undermined their interest in the well-being of the *polis* as a whole. In essence, Plato's ideal republic will set out to eliminate the private sphere altogether. A by-product of this goal is Plato's claims for equality between the sexes in the guardian class.

In Plato's mind, the key to the ideal republic is the elimination of the internal divisions within a state which pull leaders away from the collective good towards their own private interests. 'The best run state is one in which as many people as possible use the words mine and not mine in the same sense of the same things. What is more, such a state most nearly resembles an individual.'[48] It is private concerns which divide the state, in particular private property. Women fall into the category of property. Thus, in the *Republic*, Plato talks about 'satisfactory arrangements for the possession and treatment of children and women', and later of 'legislating about the possession of wives'.[49] His decision to construct a 'community of women and children' simply transformed women (in the guardian class) from being the private property of individual men into the common property of all men (within the guardian class). Plato explicitly links the common interest of his *Republic* to this transformation. 'Our citizens then are devoted to a common interest which they call *their own* . . . and the element in our constitution to which this is due is the community of women and children in the guardian class.'[50] Plato gives some indication how wives are the source of disunity in his discussion of imperfect societies, particularly in those city-states which are directed towards achievement and honours. Plato writes of the child of a man who is not directed towards making money:

> When he hears his mother complaining that her husband isn't one of the bosses and being slighted by other women because of it; she sees that her husband is not very keen on making money . . . all this annoys her and she says that the boy's father isn't a real man and is far too easy-going, and goes on with all the usual complaints women make in the circumstances.[51]

Plato adds, 'And, as you know . . . servants who seem quite loyal will sometimes repeat the same sort of things to the children behind their master's back.' Thus it is in the private *oikos*, in particular the wives and servants, which is the source of divisions within society.

In order for Plato to eliminate these divisions, it was necessary to abolish the private sphere of the family. In so doing, Plato needs to find a role for the women who had previously filled the roles of either wife or slave in the private sphere. His famous tripartite scheme of guardians, auxiliaries and common people is the framework. Most of his attention is focused on the guardian class. He begins with his extraordinary claim that men and women should be trained equally for the role of ruler. In the fifth book of the *Republic*, Plato addresses the issue of education for the guardian class. Since reason is what is critical to this group, Socrates argues that one cannot make a distinction based on bodily attributes. Therefore, he concludes that men and women are equally qualified to rule. 'The only difference apparent between them is that the female bears and the male begets, we shall not admit that this is a difference relevant for our purposes.'[52] Men and women rule equally, while family life (reproduction and childrearing) is done within the public sphere.

By eliminating the private sphere, Plato creates a specific type of society. The skills which guardians are to be taught are necessarily those of a traditionally masculine variety, namely analytical thought, ambition, pride and military skills. Other skills, such as nurturing, caring and intuition, are to be eliminated. Indeed, one of the most controversial aspects of Plato's utopia is the elimination of a nurturing and emotional relationship between parent and child. Thus, equality may be illusory for women, if in conforming to this world, they are just to become 'men'.

The *Laws* provide evidence of Plato's view that wives should be subject to their husbands in the private sphere. The critical difference between the *Republic* and the *Laws* is the reinstatement of private property, and with it marriage and the inevitable split between private and public spheres. In the *Laws*, men may decide who they marry but women are to be 'given' by male relatives in marriage. Further, in the *Laws*, wives are virtually excluded from the ownership of property. Only unmarried women are allowed to bring an action in court. By the introduction of the private sphere back into the discussion of political life, wives once again become the private property of their husbands. Any of the formal claims for the equality and rationality of women yield even further to the gendered nature of public versus private life.

What is critical to note here in setting the basic foundations for the western definition of politics based on a duality between public and private is the link between wives in the private sphere and their lack of power. Plato gives women two choices: become either *The Laws*' 'private wives' with little power or authority or *The Republic*'s philosopher-kings. Plato is mainly interested in the ruling class. As such, he leaves out from his analysis the majority of women (and men) who would fall into the category of slave, servant or 'common' person. This leads to the second point about the public/ private divide: that for both western political theory and much of the first and second wave feminist analyses which follow, the focus is on the issue of 'wives', ignoring large groups of women in these societies who are excluded from this category, as it is constructed within these theories. There are always servants and or slaves in the private sphere, who have traditionally been ignored and/or implicitly defined as male. Female servants or slaves are thus erased from both political theory and many of the feminist critiques.

Aristotle is the first of many critics to challenge Plato's abolition of the family in the guardian class, believing very strongly in the need for both a public and a private sphere. His account of the development of political society begins with an account of what he calls the 'first societies', namely families. These were formed, according to Aristotle, not by deliberate intention but by a 'natural impulse'. The purpose of the private sphere, the family, was to meet basic biological needs. 'The first form of association naturally instituted for the satisfaction of daily recurrent needs is thus the family.' The public sphere, or *polis*, on the other hand, goes beyond the needs of 'mere life', existing instead for the sake of a 'good life'. Thus the two fundamental dualisms between nature and culture and between private and public life come together in Aristotle. On the one hand is the private sphere, in which the needs of mere nature (food, sex, shelter) are met in a domain inhabited by wives and slaves but ruled over by free men. On the other is the public world of reason and culture, which meets the higher spiritual needs of the good life for free men alone. Thus, along with the fundamental distinction in Greek political thought of *nomos* versus *physis* is the distinction between *oikos* and *polis*.

Aristotle goes on to discuss how both these societies should be governed. Most of the *Politics* is a discussion of how the *polis* should be governed, but he begins with the household. Aristotle argues that men must rule over their wives, being 'naturally fitter to command than the female'.[53] Man is naturally fitter to rule because he possesses moral goodness and reason in a fuller and more perfect form. He then distinguishes between wives and slaves: 'The slave is entirely without the faculty of deliberation; the female indeed possesses it, but in a form which remains inconclusive.'[54] Once again in his discussion of the household, Aristotle seems to erase the possibility of a 'female slave', making a distinction between 'female' and 'slave' as if these two attributes could not exist in any one person.

Aristotle concludes with regard to wives, which will become a common refrain throughout political thought, that men have authority over their wives but it is the rule of the 'statesman over his fellow citizens' rather than of the 'monarch over his subjects'. This limitation on the natural authority of men seems to be based on two reasons: the first is a recognition that wives have some authority over the children produced in any marriage; the second is a belief that wives, unlike children or slaves, have some capacity for rationality, which underpins the right to authority in both Ancient Greek and modern liberal thought. The rule of free men over slaves is like that of the parent over the 'child', rather than despot over subject. Aristotle states: 'We may disagree with those who are in favour of withholding reason (i.e. rational instruction and admonition) from slaves, and who argue that only command should be employed. Admonition ought to be applied to slaves even more than it is to children.'[55] This link that Aristotle draws between slaves and children is common in western political theory. Thus Aristotle creates a private sphere of family, serviced by wives and slaves ruled over by male heads of household, who will allow the *polis* to thrive. Without the biological needs being met in the former sphere, the latter simply could not operate.

In summation, politics for the Ancient Greeks is bounded by the sphere of public life. For Plato, the private sphere must be eliminated (in the guardian class) if the interest of the whole community is not to be divided by the interests of private families. The radical implications of eliminating the family for wives of the guardians is understood by Plato, and hence the need for his elaborate schemes of reproduction and equality between the sexes in training and education. Some have argued, however, that by creating a sphere in which only the public may exist, Plato in effect leaves no choice but for these wives to become 'masculine' in political life, by the very way he defines the virtues of the guardian class. Equality, therefore, may be at the expense of retaining a difference between the genders and in particular those qualities traditionally associated with femininity. Finally, Plato largely ignores the majority of men and women who fall outside of this category of 'guardian' in his analysis, seeing them as providers of the biological needs of the guardian class. Aristotle, on the other hand, has anchored the origin of his political societies on the more primitive household societies. The key difference is that the *polis* is both public and of the cultural rather than natural world. The family, in particular the wives and slaves, on the other hand, supplies the needs of 'mere life'. Rule within the family naturally falls to the man for reasons of morality and capacity for rational thought, but his authority over wives is different from his authority over female slaves: Aristotle claims that the former has some capacity for reason, while the latter has none.

Thus the construction of private and public domains, so critical to our very understanding of politics in Ancient Greece, in essence either excludes women, as wives and slaves, from the public domain (as in Aristotle) or allows them to enter, among the guardian class, but only by making them men (as in Plato). For Plato, the abolition of the private sphere for the guardians leaves the majority of men and women continuing to live in private families, and presumably also to provide the necessary biological requirements for the guardian class. Either way, women, as women, are not within the boundaries of 'the political' in Ancient Greece, either in the practice of the day or in the theories of the philosophers.

Modern thought continues this dichotomy between public and private. While this division is perhaps most critical to political theory, the duality is also central to modern philosophy more generally. In 1784, the famous philosopher Immanuel Kant provided his answer to the question of what is modern philosophy or what is Enlightenment in the form of an article in a leading German periodical. Kant argued that modern philosophy is an escape from an immaturity of reason. Human maturity will only be achieved, according to Kant, when 'reason' is given full reign in our society and we 'dare to know' all there is to know. This is the Enlightenment project. In positing this freedom of reason, Kant makes an important distinction between public and private uses of freedom. 'Reason must be free in its public use and must be submissive in its private use.'[56] Michel Foucault draws the conclusions about the important distinction Kant makes between public and private reason.

> [With private reason], Kant does not ask that people practice a blind and foolish obedience but that they adapt the use they make of their reason to these determined circumstances; and reason must then be subjected to the particular ends in view. Thus there cannot be, here, any free use of reason. On the other hand, when one is reasoning only in order to use one's reason, when one is reasoning as a reasonable being ... when one is reasoning as a member of reasonable humanity, then the use of reason must be free and public.[57]

Reason is thus qualified in modern philosophy by the sphere within which it is used. In the private sphere (which for Kant includes not simply family but the private roles one must play in society – from minister to shoemaker which have particular private ends), the application of reason is directed towards specific ends. In the public sphere, reason is the application of reason for the sake of knowledge, and is thus unfettered by any constraints. Kant makes clear that this free reason and knowledge is not something which women should partake in. The role of reason in women's lives should be limited to the family and in particular their husbands, in keeping with his theory of private reason for specific ends.

Laborious learning or painful pondering, even if a woman should greatly succeed in it, destroys the merits that are proper to her sex . . . The content of women's great science, rather, is humankind, and among humanity, men. Her philosophy is not to reason, but to sense. In the opportunity that one wants to give to women to cultivate their beautiful nature, one must always keep this relation before his eyes.[58]

The distinction between public and private is fundamental to modern *political* philosophy. Curiously, the family becomes central to Hobbes's and Locke's analyses of political authority because of their need to attack the generally held theory of their day, namely patriarchy or paternal right. Its leading exponent, Sir Robert Filmer, argued that as fathers have right over their children, so do kings have authority over their subjects. In both cases, God bequeathed this right to Adam, which by right of father to child had been passed down through the generations to fathers in families and kings in political states. Like Aristotle, Filmer argues that it is the generative power of man which gives him right over both wife and child. Men are 'the principal agents in generation'; as such they create patriarchal right both in the home and in the political world. It is this fundamental theory of patriarchy as the right of political authority that both Hobbes and Locke wish to attack.

Hobbes begins by arguing that the generative power rests in both the man and the woman in the state of nature, attacking Filmer directly. 'There be always two that are equally parents; the dominion therefore over the child should belong equally to both . . . whereas some have attributed the dominion to the man only . . . they misreckon it.'[59] Hobbes goes further to say that, where any question arises as to the paternity of the child, the mother has dominion. 'If there be no Contract, the Dominion is in the Mother.' He concludes that 'Every women that bears children becomes both a mother and a *lord*.'[60] The only reason the man has any right over the child is by virtue of a contract between the parents. Hobbes argues that servants within the family are similarly the result of a covenant made between master and servant. This contract, Hobbes admits, may be to 'avoyd the present stroke of death', and so the contract becomes 'so long as his life, and the liberty of his body is allowed him the Victory shall have the use thereof at his pleasure'.[61]

Hobbes concludes: 'The Master of the Servant, is Master also of all he hath . . . in case the Master, if he refuse, kill him, or cast him into bonds, or otherwise punish him for his disobedience, he is himselfe the author of the same; and cannot accuse him of injury.'[62]

Hobbes thus defends the authority that masters have over servants or slaves in different terms from Aristotle. It is not that slaves are naturally enslaved but that they have by contract agreed to such servitude. While Hobbes wants to argue that the authority is based on consent and agreement, in fact the authority is based on force. As later theorists will argue, a notion of consent cannot be legitimate if it is acquired under threat of death.

Hobbes at the end of his chapter on paternal dominion, in which he defends the rights of mothers in the natural state, concludes by defining family as a patriarchal institution. The 'Family if it be not part of some Common-wealth, is of it self, as to the Rights of Soveraignty, a little Monarchy . . . wherein the Father or Master is the Soveraign'.[63] What is peculiar about this final definition of family is its assertion that the Father is Master, despite the rights of mother described early in the same chapter and the absence of any foundation for such authority. It is clear that, despite Hobbes's claims about right by consent and the rights of mothers within the family, ultimately conjugal society is ruled by men based on *natural* authority. Thus Hobbes says, in the *Dialogue on the Common Law*, that 'the Father of the Family *by the Law of Nature* was absolute Lord of his Wife and Children'.[64] Thus, while rule in the political sphere will be determined by consent and contract, rule in the private sphere over wives will be determined by appeals to natural authority, and rule over servants is acquired by force.

Locke arrives at the same conclusion, but begins by claiming that in fact marriage is a contract formed in the state of nature between husband and wife. '*Conjugal society* is made by a voluntary Compact between Man and Woman.'[65] Locke goes as far as to say that wives have the right to separate from their husbands. Despite this apparent appeal to rational authority (that is, contract) as the basis of conjugal society, Locke does not base the rule of the husband over the wife on rational choice. One might wonder why Locke does not. He could have argued that wives, on recognizing men to be 'the abler and stronger', would rationally agree that authority should rest with their husbands. Instead, Locke appeals to a natural authority: 'But the husband and Wife . . . having different understandings, will unavoidably sometimes have different wills too; it therefore being necessary that the last Determination, i.e. the

Rule, should be placed somewhere, it *naturally* falls to the Man's share, as the abler and the stronger.'[66] How can Locke reconcile this natural subjection of wives with his belief in authority by rational consent?

For both Locke and Hobbes, wives in relationship to their husbands become an exception to the demolishing of Filmer's patriarchal authority, despite the fact that they have been used in the state of nature to help in the demolition. While political authority is based on rational choice, parental authority is limited to children until the age of reason, servants are bound by contracts and slaves through defeat in a just war, wives are to be subject to their husbands, ultimately by natural authority. The place of wives is so inconsistent with Hobbes's and Locke's overall theories that both authors eventually write as if they do not exist at all.

In Hobbes's final definition of family, where he claims the husband to be sovereign, wives do not appear at all: 'whether that Family consist of a man and his children; or of a man and his servants; or of a man, and his children, and servants together . . . the Father or Master is the Sovereign'.[67] Similarly, Locke's chapter entitled 'Paternal, political and despotical power', as has been discussed, distinguishes between the three sources of authority: paternal, or the power of parents over children; political, that which 'every man . . . has given up into the hands of the Society'; and despotical power of master over slave. Despite the fact that every other relation in the family is covered (slave and child), nowhere is the natural authority that husbands have over their wives mentioned. For both writers, it becomes difficult, if not impossible, to reconcile their need to attack patriarchy and thereby give equal rights to mothers/wives in the state of nature with the natural authority of husbands which they both seek to sustain in civil society. Wives simply disappear from the conclusions of both writers about sovereignty, rights and power because they just do not fit in.

The difference for wives between the natural state and civil society is most clearly manifest in the distinction Locke draws between marriage contracts made in the state of nature and those made 'under positive law' in civil society. In the state of nature, Locke states that the conjugal contract can be written in any number of ways:

> Why [can] this *Compact* . . . not be made determinable, either by consent, or at a certain time, or upon certain Conditions, as well as any other voluntary Compacts, there being no necessity in the nature of

the thing, nor to the ends of it, that it should always be for Life; I mean, to such as are under no Restraint of any positive Law, which ordains all such Contracts to be perpetual.[68]

The natural rights in the state of nature, including the right to negotiate any conditions within the marriage contract, are eliminated by civil society with the introduction of a public/private split, the enforcement of the subordination of women as the private property of the husband and the fundamental goal of government to preserve private property, all supported by civil law. So Locke concludes in the First Treatise, 'Any Authority to *Adam* over *Eve*, or to Men over their wives . . . only foretells what should be the Woman's Lot . . . that she should be subject to her husband, as we see that generally the Laws of Mankind and customs of Nations have ordered it so.'[69] Locke decides that it is because so many nations have 'ordered' the subordination of wives to husbands that he concludes there must be 'a Foundation in Nature for it'. Yet there is nothing in his own theory of the natural state, or the marital contracts within it, which points to this 'natural' subordination of wives to husbands. On the contrary, his anti-patriarchal arguments seem to point in the opposite direction. Yet in both the first and the second treatises he simply asserts the natural authority husbands have over wives, and the uniform nature of the marriage contract which must be embraced by civil law.

As the commonwealth is formed, women face double jeopardy in the public and private spheres. They are excluded from the public sphere – that is, political life – altogether, because they are only extensions of their husband/master's property. Wives do not exist as citizens in relation to men and other women; they exist only in relation to their husbands. Within the private sphere, they become subject to the natural authority of their husbands, supported by civil law; their authority extends only as far as the marriage contract, although Locke believes they enjoy some rights within the family, in particular over their children. Other categories of women within Locke's analysis face even greater subordination within the family. Female slaves face the despotic power of their master, as African female slaves did in the colonies overseen by Locke and his patron the Earl of Shaftesbury. Female servants were, like wives, extensions of the male citizen's property, but without any of the rights the wife enjoyed through her marriage contract – over her own children, for example. The only right they have is to leave the service of their master (which distinguishes them from slaves).

Civil society thus has profoundly different implications for male citizens and women, as wives, servants or slaves. The question from the woman's perspective must be: even given the vagaries and insecurities of the state of nature, why would a woman who is equal and free in the state of nature, has dominion over her children, has rights equal to that of men and can act in accordance with her own will consent to a civil society where she loses any right to public life and must conform within the family to the rule of her stronger and more able husband or master? For wives, if this authority of the husband is based on nature, who is to say that such an authority would not be exercised capriciously and arbitrarily – the very thing Hobbes and Locke argued people are trying to escape by creating civil society. In his chapter on paternal power, Locke defines liberty in the following way: 'not to be subject to the arbitrary Will of another, but freely follow his own'.[70] As wives, servants or slaves, civil society and civil law simply represent the enforcement and strength of a subjection to an arbitrary will that is geater than the presumably more insecure one in the state of nature.

Seen from these points of view, the progression from the state of nature into civil society, so eagerly embraced by Locke and Hobbes, is a regressive move for women across all categories within the family: a movement away from freedom and equality for wives, albeit insecure, to a certain life of limited freedom and authority; a movement away from a state of insecure and perhaps escapable servitude for servants and slaves to a civil society whose entire weight is behind the enforcement of such subordination. If, as Locke claims, the purpose of this transformation is to secure one's life, liberty and property against the capricious and arbitrary will of another, then for women the civil state is a singular and quite spectacular failure. Where free men may choose the world of culture or civil society, women might quite rationally choose to stay in the state of nature. The difference between the two states is the nature of the public and private spheres. In civil society the division between public and private cannot be traversed by women. Their relationship is to their husbands/masters, who in turn form a contract with all other free men to create a public or political sphere. This will be considered in further detail in chapter 3, on the feminist critique of the public/private divide. We turn now to look at Marx's views of this duality.

Karl Marx wrote very little on the family or the private sphere of reproduction, as his analysis was focused on production. When he did comment on the family or the private sphere, his views varied over time. In earlier writings he seemed to defend the traditional nuclear family; later writings tended towards an abolition of the private family. Initially, Marx seems to view the 'citizen' of a state as a male head of household, like the liberals:

> Is not the state linked with each of its citizens by a thousand vital nerves . . . the state will regard . . . a living member of the state one in whom its heart's blood flows, a soldier who has to defend his Fatherland . . . a member of the community with *public* duties to perform, *the father of a family, whose existence is sacred*, and, above all, a citizen of the state.[71]

In another early article, Marx defends tough divorce laws, attacking a proposed new law which would make divorce easier. He concludes, in accordance with Hegel, that a family is an ethical relationship wherein members must be 'compelled to obey the laws of marriage'.[72]

In later works, however, Marx, followed more strongly by Engels, attacks the bourgeois family, calling ultimately for the abolition of the family in the *Communist Manifesto*. The Marxist analysis of the family is fully developed by Engels in *The Origin of the Family, Private Property and the State*. He begins by distinguishing between production and reproduction:

> According to the materialistic conception, the determining factor in history is, in the final instance, the production and reproduction of immediate life. This, again, is of a twofold character: on the one side, the production of the means of existence, of food, clothing, and shelter and the tools necessary for that production; on the other side, the production of human beings themselves, the propagation of the species. The social organisation under which the people of a particular historical epoch . . . live is determined by both kinds of production.[73]

Engels argues that there are three historic periods where the nature of the family and the status of women varies in accordance with the mode of production and property relations during those periods.

We thus have three principal forms of marriage, which correspond broadly to the three principal stages of human development: for the period of savagery, group marriage; for barbarism, pairing marriage; for civilization, monogamy supplemented by adultery and prostitution. Between pairing marriage and monogamy intervenes a period in the upper stage of barbarism when men have female slaves at their command and polygamy is practised.[74]

In the second stage, Engels uses many examples of aboriginal peoples in the Americas, arguing that among the Seneca Iroquois, for example, which he considers in the stage of 'barbarism', and in primeval Europe, 'the position of women is not only free, but honorable'.[75] While Engels recognizes the differences among different groups of peoples in terms of gender relations, he nevertheless believes, as Marx did, that they all fit into a universal scientific mode of development, whereby societies must move from lower stages through each successive stage eventually to capitalism. Thus Engels would argue, like Locke, that the Iroquois women must move from their existing state into a 'civilized state' before they eventually evolve towards communism.

For Engels, the creation of the private monogamous family, because of the invention of private property and the need to ensure lineage from a father to his children, was the 'world historic defeat of the female sex'.[76] Monogamy is necessary to ensure an orderly transfer of a father's private property to his own children. Thus for Marxists the family, reproduction, the private sphere and the subordination of women are all ultimately just reflections of the public mode of production. Once you have changed the latter, the inequality of the former will inevitably disappear.

In the quote below, it should be noted that Engels is perhaps the first political theorist to acknowledge and comment on the differing status of women within the household, recognizing not only the difference between wife and slave, but the power that the former had over the latter and equally the extent to which the husband used both for sexual purposes. This is the reason why he says that monogamy in capitalist societies, like in ancient times, often means in reality polygamy of men only, involving either prostitutes or slaves, respectively. Nevertheless, Engels at the end of this commentary, like all that have come before, equates 'woman' with 'wife':

> To her husband she is after all nothing but the mother of his legitimate children and heirs, his chief housekeeper and the supervisor of his female slaves, whom he can and does take as concubines if he so fancies. It is the existence of slavery side by side with monogamy . . . that stamps monogamy from the beginning with its specific character of monogamy *for the woman only*, but not for the man. And that is the character it still has today.[77]

Ultimately, like Plato, Marx and Engels argue that the equality of women will be an important by-product of eliminating the private sphere. Marx and Engels are, over and above the equality of women, explicitly interested in the 'emancipation of women' as well. Thus Engels argues that women must move into the public realm:

> To emancipate woman and make her the equal of the man is and remains an impossibility so long as the woman is shut out from social productive labor and restricted to private domestic labor. The emancipation of woman will only be possible when woman can take part in production on a large, social scale, and domestic work no longer claims anything but an insignificant amount of her time.[78]

The private realm of liberal capitalism is to be abolished. 'The first premise of the emancipation of women is the reintroduction of the entire female sex into public industry... this... demands that the quality possessed by the individual family... be abolished.'[79] The *Communist Manifesto* similarly calls for the abolition of both private property and the family. In this work it is clear that Marx, like Plato, envisions within his ideal society the possible outcome that women under communism move from the private property of individual men to the communal property of all men: 'Bourgeois marriage is in reality a system of wives in common and thus, at the most, what the Communists might possible be reproached with, is that they desire to introduce, in substitution for a hypocritically concealed, an openly legalized, community of women.'[80]

Thus Marxism transforms the public/private split of liberal thought into the division between production and reproduction respectively. Unlike the liberals, who want to protect the apolitical sanctity of private property and the family, Marxists envision a communist society in which, as with Plato, there will be no private property or private families. The key for Marxists is the communist revolution, which will overturn the relations of capitalist production and eventually create a communist state. Changes to the relations of reproduction will inevitably follow, it is argued, since they are determined by the relations of production. Women will thus become 'equal' or 'emancipated' in communist society by becoming fully integrated in public life and devoting only a 'minor degree' of their energies to their previous private life. Ultimately, as feminists argue, what is lacking here is an analysis of the role of gender and patriarchy. Women's role in the private sphere benefits not only capitalism, Marxist feminists argue, but also men. As a result, in simply changing the mode of production you will not necessarily change the relations of reproduction, because even without capitalism, patriarchy will still exist. Finally, in abolishing the private sphere, it will be argued by some feminists, Marx and Engels, like Plato, are devaluing women's qualities and simply turning them into men.

Perhaps the one aspect of this public/private divide which is shared by both the liberal and Marxist theories is the notion of politics as a 'fraternity'. Brothers who are equal and struggling together for a political realm that they can share equally, in contradistinction to either the patriarchy of traditional monarchies for liberal theorists, or the ruling elite of capitalism for the socialists, are the hallmark of a fraternal public sphere. Liberal revolutionary notions of brotherhood are reflected in the French revolutionary slogan of 'Liberty, Equality, Fraternity'. Indeed, as has been discussed, the liberal notion of citizenship is that of men who join together in a contract or bond between equals, relinquishing some of their individual rights in order to unite with the community. While this is seen most clearly in Jean-Jacques Rousseau, all the social contract theorists have at the foundation of their theories this sense of a fraternal joining together. For Marx, the summation of *The Communist Manifesto* expresses this fraternal solidarity in a resounding call to arms: 'Working men of all countries unite'.[81] Socialists up to the present day call each other brothers or comrades and defend the need for a fraternal underpinning if significant change is to occur in society.[82] The public fraternity of either liberal or socialist theorists must be seen in contrast to the individualized lives of women within the private spheres of their families. The private sphere, in other words, divides not only family from family but woman from woman; while the public sphere does not attempt to unite families but rather men, heads of households or brothers. Any notion of a sisterhood or sorority among women is developed only with feminist political theories. This underlying notion of fraternity is explored in more depth in the feminist analysis of the public/private divide in the following chapter.

3

Public versus Private:
the Feminist Critique

The distinction between public and private is central to political theory as a whole, as has been discussed.[1] In some political thought it is explicit and held to be critical to the well functioning society (Aristotle). In other theories it is also explicit, but one sphere is destroyed in order to make way for the full flourishing of the other (Plato, Marx). With modern liberal political thought, the distinction between public and private is as profound but often more implicit. As liberal practice puts the private realm of family and property beyond the gaze and touch of the state, so modern liberal theory has made the private sphere a realm beyond the touch of political thought. Feminist theory in the latter half of the twentieth century began to realize how potent this duality was for the ways in which male and female roles are constructed and the means by which women, from the very understanding of what is 'political', may be excluded or simply made invisible. The feminist understanding of what constitutes public and private and how it has evolved is the subject of this chapter.

In 1974, a collection of essays edited by Michelle Zimbalist Rosaldo and Louise Lamphere, entitled *Woman, Culture and Society*, posited a simple premise:

> In what follows it will be seen that an opposition between 'domestic' and 'public' provides the basis of a structural framework necessary to identify and explore the place of male and female in psychological, cultural, social and economic aspects of human life . . . though this opposition will be more or less salient in different social and ideological systems, it does provide a universal framework for conceptualizing the activities of the sexes.[2]

The impact of this ground-breaking set of essays and its central theme of a bifurcation of the world was enormous on feminists of many disciplines. As anthropologists, Rosaldo, Lamphere and many of the other contributors to this book were searching for universal explanations or causes for why 'women everywhere lack generally recognized and culturally valued authority'; that is, a unicausal explanation for a multicultural phenomenon. This quest for a single 'universal framework' for all human cultures has been challenged by many feminist scholars as fundamentally misguided. Linda Nicholson comments:

> We need to think about gender and female devaluation historically. There has been a tendency among feminist theorists to employ a causal model of analyzing the origins of such devaluation. By translating questions of origins into questions of causes, the tendency has been to search for cross-cultural facts generating a supposedly cross-cultural phenomenon. But as female devaluation is not one fact but many, interlinked with specificities of culture, so also should we abandon the search for one cross-cultural cause.[3]

Rosaldo herself in later works recognized the difficulties with the search for universal meanings in all cultural forms.[4] Instead, the public/private divide was employed in more scaled down, and historically particular, efforts to understand specific disciplines or cultures where such a dualism was relevant. Most relevant is the work of feminist political theorists, who explored the role of the public/private divide in order to explain the development of western political thought and its implications for the practice of politics in western societies.

Feminist political theorists began to understand, in response to Rosaldo and Lamphere's search for a universal cause and explanation, that any true understanding of the relationship between gender and politics could only be understood in terms of the historical context within which any given political theorist wrote. The result was a set of penetrating analyses which concluded that 'politics' needed to be rethought and the distinction between public and private reconstructed. As a recent book on the historical evolution of feminist theory and the public/private divide comments on this critical period in feminist thought:

> The need to understand how the categories had been created and used historically in political theory and social practice became clearer, even as critiques (coming mainly from political theorists and philosophers) illuminated divided allegiances within the feminist camp . . .

[compelling] us to recognize that adding women back into the polity would require a rethink of the basic political categories and perforce, the dissolving of the false barrier between public and private.[5]

The first two critical books of this kind were Susan Moller Okin's *Women in Western Political Thought* and Jean Bethke Elshtain's *Public Man, Private Woman: Women in Social and Political Thought*. In both cases, these feminist theorists uncovered and made explicit the public/private divide in western political thought, and more importantly analysed the implication of this division for the relationship between gender and politics. Many other feminists have built on this foundation, developing a body of work around Ancient Greek, modern liberal and Marxist political theories, which both deconstructs the dualism contained in these theories and reconstructs a feminist conceptualization of politics.

Okin argues that at the heart of political theory are two basic premises that affect women. The first and most important to the current discussion is her conclusion that the private sphere or family is critical to political philosophy's understanding of the role of women.

First, the most important factor influencing the philosophers' conceptions of, and arguments about, women has been the view that each of them held concerning the family. Those who have regarded the family as a natural and necessary institution have defined women by their sexual, procreative and child rearing functions within it. This has led to the prescription of a code of morality and conception of rights for women distinctly different from those that have been prescribed for men.[6]

Beginning with Plato, Okin argues that the conception of the ideal state in *The Republic* is premised on a fundamental distinction between public and private interests. Plato's main concern is to eliminate any source of disunity in the state, particularly for those who are going to be the guardians or rulers. Thus he concludes that for the ruling class the private sphere of both property and nuclear families must be abolished. It is the abolition of the family which causes Plato, according to Okin, to argue for the equality of the wives of the guardians, not the other way around.

In other words, the famous defence of wives as guardians has more to do with the need for cohesion in the public realm than with a belief in the equality of these women. This is why Plato may still speak of 'the right acquisition and use of women and children' and 'the law concerning the possession and rearing of the women and children'. Wives are not equal to their husbands in the guardian class, as much as they are their communal, as opposed to private, possessions. Nevertheless, Okin is clear that Plato's abolition of the family is important in challenging the existing relations between the sexes: 'Plato's abolition of the private sphere of the guardians' lives entailed as a corollary the radical questioning of all the institutionalized differences between the sexes.'[7] Or rather between the sexes in that class.

As Okin argues, when the private sphere and nuclear family are reintroduced in Plato's other great work, the *Laws*, wives are once again excluded from public life based upon their gender and their 'natural' function. There are greater powers bestowed on men: including the right to choose marriage partners, the right to own property, the right to all aspects of military service. While he continues to argue that these women should be involved in some types of public service, the specific ones he mentions are traditional domestic, nurturing jobs (feeding and providing for children), and he excludes women from the actual education of children, since it is 'the most important' of jobs and he explicitly says must be filled by a male citizen. Okin points out that wives are excluded from almost all aspects of military service in *the Laws*, whereas in the *Republic* it was argued that both should participate. Thus, the fundamental distinction between the *Laws* and the *Republic*, as Okin has documented, is the presence of a private sphere with a family and property. For male citizens, this distinction makes minimal difference in their role, but for their wives the roles vary greatly. As Okin has demonstrated, the existence of the private sphere and family creates not only a radically different political system, but a radically different role for wives within it.

Like Okin, Elshtain notes that Plato's use of the possessive towards wives in the guardian class reflects Plato's belief, less in the equality of these women than in moving them from being private possessions of men to being a collective possession. Elshtain states: 'Socrates concludes: "... we'll still suppose that our guardians and *their women* must practice the same things" (emphasis mine [Elshtain's]). (Again the term "their women" is perhaps more suggestive than Plato appears to recognize.)'[8] Elshtain concludes that Plato's *Republic*, far from embracing women's equality by allowing wives in the guardian class to enter the public realm, in fact strips these wives of everything that situates them as 'women' heretofore: a home, social relations and identity within the family.

By definition and in advance, the woman gives up any hope of offering a coherent account of her social experience . . . For her . . . Plato's ultimate reality, is surely an unreality, for it fails to touch the wellsprings of her bio-social, specific identity. In the realm of the ahistorical, eternal, and extra-linguistic Forms there is no place for a finite, historical, language-using self. *The Republic* exemplifies a purely abstract vision of a future condition which bears no relation to humans-in-history, with no coherent connection to some recognizable past and the beings who lived in it . . . What woman would accept parity with a elite group of men on these terms – terms that dictate her homelessness and the stripping away of her psycho-sexual and social identity?[9]

Elshtain's analysis provides an important prelude to some of the deeper questions asked, by postmodern feminists in particular, about the relationship between a public realm of politics which may be abstracted from time and place and the very rooted nature of woman in her own body, her social relations and, most particularly, her family. In essence, would these wives lose their identity if they were to become rulers in Plato's ideal republic?

Diana Coole argues very strongly in the affirmative to that question. For her, this is the most profound problem in Plato's *Republic*. As Coole states, 'While it is true that Plato offers women a formal equality in the *Republic*, the main thrust of the argument is that womanly qualities should be eliminated.'[10] Coole argues that in breaking the bond between mother and child, in subjecting these wives' fertility to a rigorous regulation, in emphasizing the qualities of military virtue over those of nurturing and caring, Plato is in essence 'virtually eliminating gender'.[11] Moreover, in creating laws which control family life, Plato 'drags private life into the full glare of the community'. Given Plato's association of wives with privacy and sedition in other parts of the *Republic*, Coole argues that the elimination of the private sphere is fundamentally about legislating and controlling these women, and specifically their fertility.

Thus the public/private divide in Plato's *Republic* and the *Laws* is critical to our understanding of both politics and the role of gender, in particular as it affects the wives of citizens, as these feminist scholars have pointed out. For Okin, the differences between the *Republic* and the *Laws* demonstrate that while free men continue as citizens regardless of what happens to the private sphere, both the nature of politics and the role of their wives change drastically with the elimination of the private sphere in the former book. Elshtain argues that the *Republic*, like most of the political philosophy which is to follow in its abstract political form, simply denies the 'women's' reality of 'the private sphere', namely the non-abstract historical connections of family, self and social relations. Similarly, Diane Coole concludes that by eliminating the private sphere and all the virtues associated with it (caring and nurturing of family and friends), Plato in essence eliminates, in the case of the wives of the guardians, women as women.

In many ways, Aristotle's conceptualization of politics, *vis-à-vis* the family, is the bedrock of political theory and consequently the subject of much criticism by feminists. Unlike Plato, Aristotle believed fundamentally in the distinction between public and private spheres and the very different purposes for which each functioned. For Okin, at the heart of Aristotle's argument about the importance of the public and private spheres and the respective roles of men and their wives within these two spheres is his belief in 'functionality'. For Aristotle, there were purposes for both spheres, and each functioned in accordance with these ends. As Ernest Barker says in his notes to the *Politics*, 'The elementary association of husband and wife [has] first been attributed to the natural necessities of reproduction and self-preservation . . . the polis, as the third and final form, is now attributed to the satisfaction of still higher and more spiritual needs.'[12]

Thus, for Okin, what Aristotle's argument is really all about is creating a society in which a few elite men can spend their lives in rational activity. As Okin states, 'society is most properly structured when it enables the privileged few to spend their lives in rational activity, and . . . the functions and therefore the nature of all others must be fixed accordingly'.[13] Thus women can only be understood in terms of the function of the private sphere and their role within it. The slave and wife have distinct roles: the former's is to provide the needs of daily subsistence, the latter's is reproduction and domestic service. As Aristotle himself says, when questioning Plato's analogy of men and women to male and female sheepdogs (concluding that both should be able to function as long as they have the capacity to do so), 'animals, unlike women, have no domestic duties'.[14] Thus, because women are within the domestic realm and their function is defined by their roles, Aristotle argues that their level of reason and the nature of their virtue are also circumscribed. 'All the moral standards applied to woman, therefore, are determined by her function as the bearer of new citizens and the guardian of the household.'[15] As Okin concludes, Aristotle is involved in a tautology which begins with the relegating of wives of freemen to the private sphere. Because wives exist for domestic purposes, they have only the reason and virtue required for that role. But he also argues that because they have only limited reason and virtue they are not qualified to be part of politics of the public realm.

> What has happened is that Aristotle arrives at the conclusion that women is inferior to man by a completely circular process of reasoning. Because he perceives woman as an instrument, he has assigned her an entirely separate scale of values . . . Aristotle's view of society as rigidly hierarchical, patriarchal and functional allows him to 'prove' things about its various classes by drawing on assumptions that already presuppose the things he claims to prove.[16]

The same tautological argument would hold true for female slaves: in this case he assumes slaves to be without reason, which is why they do the physical labour; but then to the question as to why are they without reason, the answer is that their function is to be labourers. In the same way as with wives, Aristotle's functionalist framework allows him to build his arguments on assumptions which presuppose what he is trying to prove. Okin does not extend her analysis to slaves, since she defines women as wives, but both groups of women find themselves subject to the same inescapable and faulty logic.

What is perhaps most disturbing in Okin's analysis is her review of contemporary commentators on Aristotle's functional view of the world, most of whom distance themselves from *The Politics* analysis of slavery, while simultaneously endorsing or remaining silent on wives and their function within the domestic sphere, often simply accepting the idea of the husband and wife as given. It is disturbing for two reasons: first, because while the power imbalance between master and slave is seen as morally unacceptable among these commentators, the imbalance between husband and wife is not; but, second, it would appear that the commentators, as much as Okin herself, conceptualize 'slave' as male and circumscribed by racial or ethnic identity only (non-Greek for Aristotle; African for modern commentators), and not along gender lines. In other words, the reality of female slaves is once again eliminated. Ultimately, however, Okin's analysis of 'politics' creates a sphere in which women, as either wives or slaves, will be excluded. Of critical importance to later feminist analysis is Okin's conclusion that the political realm, as conceived by Aristotle (a place wherein free male citizens exist), *cannot exist* without the private realm inhabited by wives and slaves.

Jean Bethke Elshtain arrives at a different conclusion about Aristotle's *Politics*. She begins with a similar attack on Aristotle, arguing, like Okin, that Aristotle's analysis of the distinction between public and private is both teleological and sexist: 'Aristotle absorbs woman completely within the oikos or household, denies woman any possibility of a public voice or role . . . Aristotle constructed this tidy arrangement under the terms of a set of teleological presumptions and an explanatory theory flowing from those presumptions which contain irresistible outcomes of women, men and politics'.[17] Unlike Okin, however, Elshtain believes that there is much in Aristotle's vision of politics which should appeal to feminist thinkers. Elshtain provides a prelude to much of the communitarian and participatory democracy literature in her robust defence of Aristotle's belief in politics as the highest form of human activity. What feminists must reject is the rigid division between *oikos* and *polis* and the gendered implications of that division, while simultaneously adopting the idea of a collective identity and active citizenship.

> Aristotle's version of the production and reproduction of the *oikos* need not serve as structural supports for political activity . . . This leaves the door open for feminist thinkers to turn Aristotle to their own purposes and to take up and insist upon a concept of citizenship as the touchstone of collective and individual public identities. Thus far such a vision is lacking in feminism.[18]

Other feminists have questioned Elshtain's conclusion that one can simply drop Aristotle's *oikos* without, in Elshtain's own words, 'eroding the overall structure of the theory'.[19] Finally, like all the other feminist critiques we have looked at so far, Elshtain equates women with wives.

Thus, the feminist scholarship which began to analyse the public/private divide found it to be at the centre of the foundations of political theory, and our understanding of politics. Politics, in other words, happens in the public realm; the private sphere stands outside of politics in Ancient Greek thought but is essential to its survival. In other words, one can neither exist nor be defined without the other in political thought. The construction of the public and private spheres in Ancient Greek thought also defines the role of men and women, as feminist scholarship has demonstrated. In essence, either women are excluded from the political realm by virtue of their function in the domestic sphere (as in Aristotle) or they are allowed to enter, as 'wives' of the guardians, but only after becoming 'men' in all but name (as in Plato's *Republic*). The great flaw in these critiques has been the equating of women with wives, with very little attention paid to female slaves, who have a different relationship, both to the free man or Greek citizen and to his wife. One can safely conclude, however, that women, whether as wives or as slaves, are excluded from 'politics' in Ancient Greece, in both theory and practice.

Feminist scholarship has also analysed the role of the public/private divide in modern political philosophy. This may be divided into two parts: liberal political philosophy and Marxist political philosophy.

The public/private divide in liberal political theory became an important subject of research in the 1980s.[20] Feminists saw the importance of these questions to their own work. Zillah Eisenstein, in her book *The Radical Future of Liberal Feminism*, describes her project in the following terms:

> The reality that underlies the patriarchal bias of liberalism is that women have been defined by their reproductive capacities ... My concern is to elaborate the historical formulation of motherhood that equates childbearing with childrearing and as a result assigns woman a place outside the public sphere of life. In this study, we shall see woman's exclusion from public life operating on two levels. Woman is relegated to childrearing by biological fiat on an individual level, which is then reformulated through the formation of the state and the institutionalization of public–private domains on a political level.[21]

While the public/private divide has had a continuous history throughout western thought, Eisenstein argues, liberal political philosophy underpinned by a capitalist economy has the most highly developed sense of a division between the public and private spheres, which helps both to strengthen and to obscure patriarchy in liberal democratic states.[22] In challenging the social contract theories of Thomas Hobbes and John Locke, Eisenstein argues that in essence what these precursors to liberal thought have done is to make a division between the public world of government and the private world of family, while simultaneously opening up a world of potential equality and freedom for all. Thus, at the heart of liberalism and social contract theorists' concepts is a contradiction between a world where everyone has equal rights by nature in the state of nature, and a political state which relegates women to a private sphere of the family without political rights and embraces men in the public sphere of politics as citizens with civil rights. 'Liberalism explicitly espouses a commitment to rationality, individualism and property and the inherent freedom involved here, while implicitly it embraces the paternalism and patriarchal values of the family that were a part of the foundation of bourgeois society.'[23]

The role of the family, and in particular the relationship between men and women in liberal theory, is developed by Carole Pateman in 'Feminist critiques of the public private dichotomy' and later in *The Sexual Contract* and *The Disorder of Women*.[24]

> The way in which women and men are differentially located within private life and the public world, is . . . a complex matter, but underlying a complicated reality is the belief that women's natures are such that they are properly subject to men and their proper place is in the private domestic sphere. Men properly inhabit, and rule within, both spheres. The essential feminist argument is that the doctrine of 'separate but equal' and the ostensible individualism and egalitarianism of liberal theory, obscure the patriarchal reality of a social structure of inequality and the domination of women by men.[25]

Pateman argues, like other feminists, that Hobbes and Locke are fundamentally anti-patriarchalist in their arguments concerning the origin of political or public authority (that is, authority must be based on consent of the governed rather than authority of the father, as Sir Robert Filmer has argued). Pateman goes on to argue, however, that they are nevertheless patriarchalists when it comes to authority within the private sphere or the family. Moreover, because the private sphere or family is defined as either prior to or outside of the public or political realm, it has remained obscure or been ignored in political theory. Pateman makes these two points in her discussion of the 'sexual contract'.[26]

Pateman argues that Filmer, Hobbes and Locke ultimately all agree that a wife's subordination in the private sphere to her husband's authority has a 'foundation in Nature', based on him being 'the abler and stronger', not on the consent of the governed (that is, the wife), as is the case in liberal political society.[27] In essence, Pateman argues that the two spheres are founded on two very different contracts. The social contract in the public sphere is distinguished by Pateman from a 'sexual contract' in the private sphere. The social contract of Hobbes, Locke and Rousseau is explicitly a contract between men. It reflects the attempt to found society on a concept of 'fraternity' (contract between equals) rather than patriarchy (authority based on the relationship between father and son). This contract, however, is possible only by virtue of a preceding sexual contract between men, governing access to women and creating the private sphere and the patriarchal authority within families. Thus the social contract which founds civil society in Hobbes and Locke is not a contract between free and equal individuals in the state of nature (that is, all adults) but explicitly it is a contract between male heads of households. The marital couple is both prior to and beyond the realm of politics in liberal political theory. And the authority between the couple is based on the natural patriarchal right of the husband.

Thus Hobbes and Locke provided feminists, like Carole Pateman, with a contradiction. On the one hand they relegated wives to the private sphere without any political authority or rights. On the other hand they laid the foundation, in the state of nature, that all adults were born with equal rights, regardless of their position in civil society. And all of this could be brought together by a fraternal social contract. It should be noted that liberal feminists have used the second claim, namely to equal rights by nature, in order to push for women (largely those who would be classified as 'wives' in western political thought, rather than as servants or slaves, as was clear in the fight for the vote) to enter the public sphere as citizens with the right to vote and participate in politics. Other feminists, however, have argued that taking on the language of 'rights' has meant that women have had to represent themselves not as mothers or family members but as public individuals, free of any tie or relation. As Elshtain comments:

> Women later were to use the language of rights to press claims. Their arguments had to be compressed within the linguistic forms of the liberal tradition. This meant that woman's 'reason' as a public presence couldn't give voice to the private, social bases of female identity, couldn't allow woman's experience to 'speak to' the public realm.[28]

In the nineteenth century, liberal thought again transformed the division between public and private. The private sphere was not so much the realm of natural authority and individual rights, as Locke and Hobbes had described, but a realm of freedom and privacy from the state and public opinion, as articulated by English philosophers Jeremy Bentham and John Stuart Mill. Moreover, by the nineteenth century, liberals, such as Mill, recognized that the exclusion of wives from political life by Hobbes and Locke was simply inconsistent with claims of freedom and equality. However, as liberal feminists have pointed out, even though the liberal logic forced Mill to accept men and their wives' equal participation in the public realm, unlike Plato, he was unwilling to tackle the implications for the family of including these women in the public sphere. Instead Mill assumed, conveniently according to Anne Phillips and Carole Pateman, that while women would have the right to enter the public realm, they would choose to stay in the private. Phillips comments:

> Mill . . . rejected the idea that women's position as wives and mothers should exclude them from participation in public affairs, but he hoped and expected that women would still stay in their sphere. Arguing that legal equality need not prevent women from 'choosing' to be wives and mothers, and conversely that their continuing as wives and mothers need not unfit them for public concerns, nineteenth-century liberals turned a blind eye to the fact that women and men occupied separate spheres.[29]

For Pateman, Mill's premise of wives remaining in the private sphere entirely undermines his own defence of their political right to vote and participate in politics. 'Mill's acceptance of a sexually ascribed division of labor, or the separation of domestic from the public life, cuts the ground from under his argument for enfranchisement . . . A despotic, patriarchal family is no school for democratic citizenship . . . How can wives who have "chosen" private life develop a public spirit?'[30] At the heart of the liberal, particularly social contract, theorists' vision of society, according to Pateman, is a fraternity. 'The contract is made by brothers, or a *fraternity*. It is no accident that fraternity appears historically hand in hand with liberty and equality, nor that it means exactly what it says: brotherhood.'[31] Pateman's argument centres on the notion that while the social contract theorists imagined that they had eschewed 'patriarchy' as the basis for political authority, they had brought in 'brotherhood' or fraternity to replace it. Such a conceptualization of citizenship 'cannot simply be universalized to women', since the fraternal pact has been constructed 'in opposition to women and all that our bodies symbolize'. Thus if we are to create a truly democratic society, it will be necessary to 'deconstruct and reassemble our understanding of the body politic'.[32]

Anne Phillips argues that liberalism of the nineteenth and twentieth centuries developed yet another construction of the public and private divide, beyond that of the family versus political life. The secondary division is between the role of state and the role of the free market. With the utilitarian philosophy of Mill, one is free to maximize private interests in the market, without interference by the state. Phillips comments; ' "Private" in this sense is not about the family; abstracting entirely from the domestic sphere . . . And because the family is now completely out of the picture, liberalism can more plausibly pretend that we are indeed the private and isolated individuals on which its theories rest.'[33] The political debate which ensues from this kind of distinction is in fact that which has most frequently occurred between libertarians, liberals, socialists and communitarians. With the family out of the way, the debate around public versus private in political theory and public policy includes issues such as privatized versus public health care, the privatization of national industries, the relationship between private businesses and public regulation, publicly funded versus private education. This is the very stuff of what we would now call political debate, says Phillips, yet, in creating a private which is attached to the individual rather than the family (which continues in liberal theory to be simply outside of political debate), the public/ private divide so described once again ignores gender. 'In seemingly universal concern over the limits of the state and the freedoms of the individual, liberalism talks in effect of a world occupied by men.'[34]

The final aspect of Mill's public/private divide that should be addressed is the right to privacy; that is, freedom from interference by either the state or public opinion. The right of privacy continues to be a critical issue in liberal-democratic states to this day, and a vexing question for feminist commentators. Feminists often find themselves at one and the same time both arguing for more public involvement in areas traditionally associated with the private sphere (childcare, elderly care, domestic violence and so on) and defending the right to privacy against a state which may interfere more with women's privacy than with men's (in areas such as reproductive freedom, sexual orientation, rape laws and welfare policy enforcement). Liberal feminists maintain both, arguing that the right to privacy must be defended equally for women and men.

Some feminists go further, arguing that it is critical to bring a gendered lens to our understanding of privacy, and therefore to identify privacy needs which are specific to women as women. Anita Allen writes:

The privacy rights of women are multi-dimensional. I maintain that a conceptually adequate theory of privacy and the right to it should account for these dimensions. I also maintain that protecting the privacy interests of women requires more than the recognition of equal rights for men and women under the law. It requires promoting respect for women in those areas of social and family life outside the reach of the law. It also requires the recognition of extensive freedom of choice for women with respect to sexual, marital and reproductive concerns.[35]

Ruth Gavison concurs with Allen that specific privacy rights of women must be addressed, and they comprise secrecy, anonymity and solitude.[36] Allen adds the right of choice. Under each of these general categories, both Gavison and Allen provide specific examples of how women are differentially affected. Women's right of secrecy is violated in several ways: women are often asked to supply information on job applications about their marital or family status; female victims of sexual assault have limited protection of their privacy rights when it comes to counselling notes taken in the aftermath of a sexual assault;[37] information which welfare mothers are required to give with regard to their children or their living arrangements is particularly invasive. The right to anonymity for women is invaded, it is argued, when they face in public places interference by men 'seeking their names, phone numbers, or other personal information . . . one evident effect of continual invasions of anonymity is that women come to believe they are "fair game" if they venture into public places into which men may go to find repose'.[38] The right of solitude for women is constrained both within the family home and outside of it. Women are not only fearful of walking alone in certain circumstances (late at night, in wooded areas and so on) but advised not to do so by the police and other representatives of the state. Within the home, the right to be alone is often under pressure for the woman who takes on more of the work related to children or elderly relatives. Finally, women must have the right, Allen argues, to make a private choice about sex, childbearing and marriage. Laws regarding inheritance, abortion and birth control often interfere with such privacy rights.

Mill's political philosophy of privacy rights was conjoined by the Victorian notions (particularly in the middle and upper classes) of a private sphere of cultivated and civilized life and behaviour. Women, as wives, for Mill in particular, anchored this private civilized world, which must be defended and protected from public intrusions. As Elshtain comments: 'Surely in Mill's work there is a recognition, on some deep and tacit level, that the public world of bourgeois liberalism was dependent upon a particular vision of the private world in which women played the role of softeners and civilizers and the family was the haven in a heartless world.'[39] Thus the right of privacy, or a private sphere of freedom, as articulated by the nineteenth-century philosophers Bentham and Mill, is a double-edged sword for feminists. On the one hand, some feminist scholarship has argued that the rights of privacy, of non-interference from the state in the areas of private secrecy, anonymity, solitude and choice, are critical for women. On the other hand, the defence of an inviolate private sphere may solidify the wife's place in the 'civilized' haven of the home.

Liberal political philosophy of the nineteenth century faced its toughest attack in the writings of German philosopher Karl Marx, as has been discussed. The public/private divide of Marxist thought is reflected in the demarcation by Marx and Engels between production and reproduction. Engels concludes that the relations within the family (or the reproductive realm) are a direct consequence of the modes and relations of production in the economic sphere. As a result, the communist revolution, in bringing about the abolition of private property and overthrowing the capitalist mode of production, will inevitably lead to the abolition of the nuclear family and, Engels argues, the emancipation of women.

Feminist scholars sympathetic to Marxist analysis began their challenge to traditional Marxism by questioning the underlying premise that the relations of reproduction and the realm of ideas are determined or fundamentally circumscribed by the mode of production. Instead, they argue that neither sphere should be subsumed by the other, and develop a 'dual-systems' political theory to explain power relations in modern society. In the public sphere or the realm of production, on the one hand, is the system of capitalism, which creates a class relation of power for the owners of capital over the workers. On the other hand, patriarchy, or the power of men over women, is the system which dominates the relations of reproduction. Both must be given equal weight in our understanding of history if we are to understand the power dynamics at work in our society, between capitalist and worker, and between men and women. As men are defined by economic class, women are defined by family roles. Thus Juliet Mitchell comments:

> Men enter into the class dominated structures of history while women (as women, whatever their work in actual production) remain defined

by the kinship pattern of organization. Differences of class, historical epoch, specific social situation alter the expression of femininity; but in relation to the law of the father, women's position across the board is a comparable one.[40]

Thus Marxist feminists argue that the family and the relations of reproduction cannot simply be understood in terms of capitalism and private property. Women's place in the home, and their unpaid labour, can be understood only in terms of patriarchy; that is, the systemic system of power that men have over women. The source of this patriarchy varies with different feminist approaches. Juliet Mitchell argues that patriarchal relations are rooted in the psychological development of men and women as children. Shulamith Firestone adopts a more materialist analysis, arguing that patriarchy is rooted in the biological needs associated with reproduction.[41]

Other feminists, such as Iris Marion Young, have criticized the dual systems theory of Hartmann, Firestone and Mitchell, on the basis that it fails to take into account the various types of oppression different women may experience due to factors outside of either economics or gender (for example, race or disability). Dual systems theories can thus 'inappropriately dehistoricize and universalize women's oppression'.[42] Second, despite language to the contrary, dual systems theories ultimately analyse women's inequality as a function of materialism, adopting an economic analysis which in essence is blind to gender differences. Young argues that the solution is to bring together an analysis of both gender and economics into one unified theoretical framework. The central category of such a framework, for Young, is the gender division of labour. The split between public and private is analysed by Young on the basis of men's and women's labour in each, and the value attributed to them as a central aspect of both patriarchy and capitalism. Ideologies such as femininity that are used to justify this difference in power are the result:

> Preexistent patriarchal ideology and the traditional location of women's labor near the home initially made possible the marginalization of women's labor, according it secondary status. Bourgeois ideology, however, greatly expanded and romanticized, at the same time that it trivialized, women's association with a domestic sphere and dissociation with work outside the home. The ideology of femininity which defined women as nonworking emerged as a consequence of and justification for the process of marginalization of women that had already begun.[43]

Examining the labour that women do in the private sphere was thus critical. Not only had it been largely overlooked by liberal political theorists and economists as simply not important to political life or market economies respectively, but traditional Marxist analyses which considered labour to be so central to their analysis also ignored non-wage labour, such as unpaid housework in the private sphere.

Over the past twenty years there has been an enormous amount of literature which has developed around the question of housework, care and its relation to capital. Mariarosa Dalla Costa, one of the first feminists to analyse this division of labour, argued that women's labour in the home creates surplus value, as Marx defined it.[44] Dalla Costa concluded that women should demand wages for the work they do in the private sphere, thus taking their work out from under the economic authority of their husbands and making it public. Dalla Costa's book sparked an enormous debate on the relationship between housework and wage labour or capital as a result.[45] By focusing on 'unpaid work', these feminists are dealing mainly with the 'wives' of husbands rather than domestic servants. Consequently, the role of class and race in this type of work was often ignored by feminists as they focused on the 'unpaid labour' of wives. This will be discussed in depth shortly, when we look at the critique made by feminists of colour of both liberal and socialist feminist focus on the public/private divide.

The distinction long drawn in political theory between a public and private sphere is transformed by socialist and Marxist feminists into a question about paid and unpaid labour. In calling for a wage for household labour, many of these feminists had the goal of making housewives themselves aware of the value of their own work in the private sphere and the fact that they were not paid for this labour in the way their husbands were for their labour in the public sphere. Heidi Hartmann comments: 'Demanding wages and having wages would raise [housewives] consciousness of the importance of their work; they would see its *social* significance, as well as its private necessity, a necessary first step toward more comprehensive social change.'[46]

The focus on women's work in the home by socialist feminists has spilled over into other areas of public policy analysis. Marilyn Waring, a former member of parliament in New Zealand, began her analysis by questioning the underlying premise of economics that only goods or services which pass through the market system have value. She concluded that the national accounts of the world's countries have virtually ignored the contribution women have made, in the form of housework or work in the private sphere. In essence, women do not count because they exist outside of the public place of exchange for labour, namely the free market; their labour is contained within the private unpaid world of the family.[47] In international circles, this failure to account for the value of household labour has developed such a high profile that at the recent United Nations Conference of Women in Beijing in September 1995, one of the most significant agreements reached was the commitment by all governments to calculate the value of both paid and unpaid work in their national accounts. As a result, Canada in its 1996 census included, for the first time, a set of questions about unpaid housework.

The general conception of the public/private duality by some feminists, as described above, has been challenged by other feminists who believe the theoretical split, into a public sphere disinterested in and remote from a private sphere of either the self-interested individual or the family, reflects the lives of white, middle-class, heterosexual women rather than those of working-class women, single mothers, women of colour or lesbians. Women as housewives is a focus not only in traditional political theory (on those few occasions when women are addressed) but also, as we have seen, in both the liberal and socialist feminist response. In the former, as a starting point from which to attack patriarchy; in the latter, as a starting point for analysing the division of labour. In both cases, feminists of colour and lesbian feminists have challenged the assumed and underlying perspective of such a model as a particular view rather than one universal to all women.

This is not to say, according to most of these critiques, that feminism should give up on the public/private divide as a tool for feminist analysis. Indeed, this duality is profoundly relevant to women in all societies touched on by 'liberal' or 'Marxist' ideology, in that it is the theoretical underpinning for the political system within which all citizens must work and live, as has been discussed. What is needed is to go beyond those feminist analyses which have cast the public/private divide in such a way as to ignore factors other than gender and class; for example, sexual identities and race. Through a variety of feminist commentaries, it has become clear that the implications of the public/private divide are very different for different groups of women. Let us begin to examine the critique of early second wave feminism, by looking at the critiques of the public/private divide in liberal feminism by feminists of colour.

It has been argued by some political theorists in recent years that one of the single greatest failings of western political philosophy has been the failure to recognize multicultural diversity, despite the fact that most political communities have to some extent been multicultural. Will Kymlicka writes in his *Multicultural Citizenship*:

> The Western political tradition has been surprisingly silent on these issues [of multiculturalism]. Most organized political communities throughout recorded history have been multi-ethnic, a testament to the ubiquity of both conquest and long-distance trade in human affairs. Yet most Western political theorists have operated with an idealized model of the polis in which fellow citizens share a common descent, language, and culture.[48]

The common descent, language and culture, in the modern period, that Kymlicka refers to is of course that of middle-class Europeans (and their colonial offspring). The mainstream[49] of feminist political theory has, until the 1980s, been no exception. The public/private divide as it was conceptualized and recast by white middle-class feminists has been challenged by women of colour; challenged in the first instance by African American women in the United States.[50] bell hooks, in her book *Feminist Theory: from Margin to Center*, describes the problem with much of the feminist theory she had encountered: 'The willingness to explore all possibilities has characterized my perspective ... Much feminist theory emerges from privileged women who live at the center, whose perspectives on reality rarely include knowledge and awareness of the lives of women and men who live in the margin.'[51] In both this work and her previous book, *Ain't I a Woman? Black Women and Feminism*, hooks questions the public/private divide as it has been reconceptualized in liberal feminist thought in particular, and its relevance for African American women. As hooks points out, the history of black and white men and women in America is diverse and complex; their views on and relationships to the public and private spheres of liberal theory differ radically as a result. Over the past twenty years, early second wave feminist conceptions of the public and private have been criticized for assuming certain realities with regard to women of color which simply do not hold. It is necessary, therefore, to consider the particular cultural and historical contexts within which different women develop to understand fully how the public/private divide works in the lives of different groups of women, and not just those of a middle-class white background.

There are four basic ways in which the assumptions made about the public/private divide of both liberal and socialist feminism simply do not fit the historical experience of men and women of colour in western liberal democracies. First is the assumption that 'men' are in the public sphere. Unlike white men, men of colour have often been denied access to many parts of the public sphere, from voting to restaurants to unions. This exclusion of certain groups of men, as well as women, based on their racial identity, has created a relationship between men and women of colour that is different from the theme of female solidarity (against men) of traditional feminist thought. Second, the assumption that women are in the 'private sphere' varies between different groups of women. Women of colour have had a long history of working outside the home, a fact often ignored by liberal and socialist feminist demands to emancipate women 'through work in the public sphere'. Third, poor women of colour have often done the domestic labour inside their own home, like white middle-class women, but they have also done domestic work in their master's home, as slaves or later as servants. Moreover, in the 1990s, as white middle-class feminists find 'emancipation' through work in the public sphere, their vacated domestic sphere is often being filled in by poorer women of colour. Finally, while white women are often connected at a private and intimate level with white men (through marriage and family), women of colour are, demographically, far less likely to have such intimate links with white men. All these differences have enormous impacts on the strategies chosen by different groups of feminists to define their goals and bring about changes.

Taken together, these four aspects of the public/private divide in relationship to race or colour thus pose an enormous challenge to the assumptions made by liberal and socialist feminism about the relationship between gender and this duality, as well as the ends and means of feminism. We shall consider each of these differences in more depth to understand how the public/private divide of liberal thought was experienced in completely different ways, in both historical and contemporary terms, by different groups of women, and the profound implications these differences make for the nature and goals of the feminist movement.

First, we must consider the relationship between men of colour and the public sphere. While liberal and socialist theory assumes that men are in the public working world (of production) and women are at home (in the sphere of reproduction), this conception does not do justice to the reality of many men of colour, who, unlike white men, were often barred from the public or political realm. As Diane Lewis points out, whether it was in trade unions, the job market or voting rights, the 'systematic exclusion of black men from the public sphere suggests that black sex-role relationships cannot be adequately explained by the notion of a structural opposition between the domestic and public spheres or the differential participation of men and women in the public sphere.'[52]

The implication for feminism is that, unlike white middle-class women, who are fighting for inclusion in the public sphere *against* white men, women of colour are often fighting *with* men of colour for the same goal. Consequently, the struggle by black women and more broadly women of colour to enter the public and political spheres was a goal they shared with men of colour. The vote is an example of how the struggle to be part of the public sphere, part of the social contract, to be a citizen in the *polis*, broke down along racial lines. In both the USA and Canada, white men exercised the vote for decades before either white women or men and women of colour exercised the vote.[53] While white women suffragists initially fought for the right of both white women and black men and women to vote, when the vote was eventually granted to black men before white women, leading white suffragists bitterly denounced the decision, in clearly racist terms.

When only Black men received the vote, black and white activists together decried the exclusion of women's rights, but their protests took different forms. Black suffragists did not abandon Black men; white suffragists quickly abandoned Black women. White women's rights advocates like Elizabeth Cady Stanton who had never before argued women suffrage on a racially imperialistic platform in 1869 stated her outrage at the enfranchisement of Black men: 'If Saxon men have legislated thus for their own mothers, wives and daughters, what can we hope for at the hands of Chinese Indians, and Africans? . . . I protest against the enfranchisement of another man of any race or clime until the daughters of Jefferson, Hancock, and Adams are crowned with their rights.[54]

Similarly, in Canada, the leading suffragist Flora MacDonald stated in a lecture:

No matter what line of reform, women are labouring to obtain, they are handicapped by not having the power to vote. Today we are welcoming to our shores thousands of immigrants, most of which are ignorant, illiterate and often the scum of the earth and in a few years they will be empowered to vote and make laws for the women of our land. This is the time to combine and obtain suffrage.[55]

It is worth noting that once again, in the way this is written, 'women' and 'immigrants' are two different categories, meaning that 'women' are non-immigrants and immigrants are only men. Moreover, 'immigrant' has taken on pejorative meaning (with undertones of both class and race). Defined in this way, immigrant (particularly poorer non-European) women, as so often happens in western politics, quite literally disappear from the political radar screen. The feminist movement, and its relationship or openness to men, thus differs, according to bell hooks, depending not just on gender but on race and history. Calls by white feminists for an exclusive solidarity between women ignore the racism of the feminist movement, as expressed in the quotes above, and the shared exclusion of women and men of colour from the public sphere:

> As with other issues, the insistence on a 'woman only' feminist movement and a virulent anti-male stance reflected the race and class background of participants . . . [Black women's] life experiences had shown them that they have more in common with men of their race and or class group than bourgeois white women. They know the sufferings and hardships women face in their communities; they also know the suffering and hardships men face and they have compassion for them . . . There is a special tie binding people together who struggle collectively for liberation.[56]

Aboriginal women, who have experienced, with their male counterparts a shared historical reality due to colonialism and its aftermath, express similar sentiments towards mainstream feminism:

> I do not have the luxury of focusing on my oppression as a woman. We, as Aboriginal women, work with our men as best we can to ensure that our liberation encompasses the liberation of all of us. The reclamation of Aboriginal women's autonomy cannot come separately, it is part of the whole struggle for liberation. Can feminists understand that?[57]

Thus, to understand the role of the public/private split in liberal feminist theory, it is critical to note that men of colour have historically been denied access to the public sphere, and when they did make gains, found that some of their most outspoken critics were white feminists. This has created a historical common sense of purpose between men and women of colour which makes difficult the mainstream feminist's emphasis on solidarity between women, *in opposition to* men, where 'empowerment would necessarily be at the expense of men'.[58]

The second point to be considered with regard to race, feminism and the public/private divide is that women of colour have from the beginning often worked outside their domestic home in large numbers; a fact which has gone largely unrecognized in liberal or socialist feminism. In her famous speech before the 1851 Women's Rights Convention, former slave Sojourner Truth asked the rhetorical question whether or not she was a woman, given her work outside the home: 'And ain't I a woman? Look at me! Look at my arm!... I have ploughed and planted, and gathered into barns, and no man could head me! And ain't I a woman?'[59]

Initially, hooks argues, when African women came to America, they saw nothing unusual or inconsistent with being a woman and working in the fields and outside of their home. It was only when they accepted the values of a white patriarchal society divided into two spheres that they began to view being a 'woman' as requiring a 'domestic' role:

> Originally displaced African women attached no stigma to female labor in the fields but as they assimilated white American values they accepted the notion that it was debasing and degrading for women to work in the fields. As a farm laborer, the black male slave performed as a free person, but black women were well aware that it was not deemed ladylike or respectable for women ... By completely accepting the female role as defined by patriarchy, enslaved black women embraced and upheld an oppressive sexist social order and became (along with their white sisters) both accomplices in the crimes perpetrated against women and the victims of those crimes.[60]

African-American women have, since the days of slavery and until today, always been much more likely to work outside the private sphere than white middle-class women. Thus, as liberal feminism began to take shape from the 1960s onwards, many white middle-class women were in the role of 'housewife', while many black women worked outside the home, often in low-wage, dead-end jobs. Each group's perspective on the public and private sphere varied, according to hooks, depending on where they felt themselves most oppressed:

> Historically, black women have identified work in the context of family as humanizing labor, work that affirms their identity as women, as human beings showing love and care, the very gestures

of humanity white supremacist ideology claimed black people were incapable of expressing. In contrast to labor done in a caring environment inside the home, labor outside the home was most often seen as stressful, degrading, and dehumanizing.[61]

This recognition has a profound effect on how we view early second wave feminism, for the demands by feminists from Simone de Beauvoir to Betty Friedan to Shulamith Firestone for women to move from the private sphere of work to the public sphere, in order to be emancipated, ignored the reality of many black women in the same time period, who were already working outside the home, in jobs that not only were dehumanizing but did not make them any more independent or 'emancipated'.

> Middle class women shaping feminist thought assumed that the most pressing problem for women was the need to get outside the home and work – to cease being 'just' housewives . . . They were so blinded by their own experiences that they ignored the fact that a vast majority of women were . . . already working outside the home, working in jobs that neither liberated them from dependence on men nor made them economically self-sufficient.[62]

Because of the differences in their experience with regard to work outside and within the home, the goals of white women and women of colour could thus be opposed, as hooks concludes with regard to black and white women in the United States, and their views on the public/private split: 'Many black women were saying "we want to have more time to share with family, we want to leave the world of alienated work". Many white women's liberationist were saying "we are tired of the isolation of the home . . . we want to be liberated to enter the world of work".'[63] This conclusion is linked to the third point made above about poorer women of colour and the public/private divide, namely the extent to which women of colour have laboured in the domestic sphere of homes other than their own. There are two aspects to this division of labour as it applies to both gender and race: first, it is women of colour rather than men of colour who do this type of work; second, it is in the homes of richer, often white, families that this labour was and is done. What has often gone unrecognized in most feminist analyses of the 'private sphere' is the imbalance between white middle-class women and poorer women of colour with regard to domestic labour.

The relationship between domestic labour and women of colour has a long history, dating back to the days of slavery for African American women, as hooks notes: 'Black men were not forced to assume a role colonial American society regarded as "feminine" . . . few if any black men labored as domestics alongside black women in the white household (with the possible exception of butlers, whose status was still higher than that of a maid)."[64] The role of women of colour in domestic service has enormous implications for current feminist goals with regard to the public/private divide. Today, it has become clear that the imbalance described above has increased, as some women (those, as hooks describes them, at the centre) vacate the private sphere and move into the public world of work, in keeping with both liberal and socialist philosophy. As a result, the work which they had previously done in the private sphere is now being done by other groups of women, a phenomenon which one scholar has entitled 'the racialization of women's household work'.[65] This relationship between women in the public sphere, domestic labour and immigrant women is the subject of a growing body of literature.[66]

> The growing interest in paid domestic labor reflects a recognition among some feminists that the employment of domestic workers in private households is a crucial means through which asymmetrical race and class relations among women are structured . . . The low status of paid domestic work, and the structural inequities and systemic racism that drive immigrant and visible minority women to accept such work, color-codes, as it were, the market of the industry.[67]

Childcare in Canada provides a good case study of how the public/private division, economic status and race intersect to create the type of arrangements we see now increasingly in many middle-class homes. As dual earner middle-class families struggle to work outside the home and raise children, the crisis of childrearing in the private sphere becomes overwhelming. While public childcare, given that it is available, could be one solution, many men and women who grow up with the liberal sanctity of the public/private divide often still hold fast to the notion of a 'private' family sphere to raise their children in, especially infants. One of the great tensions within liberal feminist philosophy plays itself out nearly every day in many homes where women are entering the public sphere of work in ever greater numbers, while simultaneously trying to hold on to a traditional notion of a domestic sphere or family.

One alternative solution to public childcare, which allows men and women who can afford it to maintain the illusion of a 'private' family sphere, is foreign domestic workers or 'nannies'. The child is still raised within the 'private sphere', but by a surrogate 'wife/ mother', who does the traditional work of childcare, cleaning and cooking. In Canada, women of colour, from Southeast Asia and the Caribbean in particular, have immigrated under programmes like the Canadian Live-in Caregiver Program to take on such roles. In essence, the public/private spheres are maintained intact, but the public/private gender and race division of labour is transformed. The implications for feminism are profound. While certain groups of women are 'emancipated' in the terms of de Beauvoir and Betty Friedan from the drudgery of domestic work, other groups of women (often, but not exclusively, of colour) coming from poorer parts of the world take over these tasks.[68] Because they work within a private home, they often do not enjoy the same rights as others in Canada. Bakan and Stasiulis conclude that even under the most basic test for liberal feminists, that of equal citizenship, domestic labourers do not enjoy the same rights as their employers.

> While migrant domestic workers lack many basic citizenship rights (including the choice of employer and domicile), their employers in contrast generally enjoy full citizenship rights. The increasing demand for in-home child care in developed capitalist states and the similarly increasing but highly regulated supply of Third World migrant women together work to structure and mediate citizenship rights across and within national boundaries.[69]

Thus the gender division of labour has some very different implications for women of colour and middle-class white women. From the days of slavery, black women, rather than black men, have taken on domestic labour in the homes of their masters. In other words, the public/private division and the values attached to it continue to exist through the construction of political theory and practice to this day, but it is the most marginalized in society – that is, women of colour – who take on these tasks of little value, in greater numbers than their white counterparts.

Critical to this public/private divide is the premise that domestic work is of less value; a premise which scholars like Kate Rogers argue is Eurocentric. In her analysis of Algonquin and Iroquois women, Rogers concludes that while a division of labour occurs between men and women in these societies – the primary responsibility of men was 'the protection of the tribe'; of women, 'the maintenance of the household'[70] – women's roles are not devalued as they are in western political thought. Instead, they are of equal standing:

Although the gendered, social roles of Aboriginal women resembled those of women from the colonizing societies, the status, autonomy and freedoms attached to these roles differed greatly. This difference occurs for several reasons. One reason is that low-technology subsistence-based economies, such as traditional Aboriginal societies, interpret women's reproductive, nurturing capabilities in a different fashion than capitalist societies.[71]

Rogers concludes that it was only with the meeting of cultures between aboriginal and European peoples that the domestic sphere became devalued. Thus, for both aboriginal women, with regard to their value in the domestic sphere, and African American women, with regard to working in the fields during slavery, it was colonialism, and the power of one cultural group exercised over another, rather than that exercised by men over women, which imposed western political concepts of gender roles in the public and private spheres.

The reaction by some aboriginal women has been to embrace the 'private sphere' rather than to 'escape' it, as recommended by many liberal feminists. It should be noted that this view of the private sphere is not without its adherents in the mainstream feminist community. Jean Bethke Elshtain, for example, concludes that Iroquois women provide liberal feminism with a model by which maternity and nurturance can be valued and maintained and women not be forced to abandon all the activities and values traditionally associated with the private sphere.[72]

Finally, many women of colour have pointed out the very distinct relationship that white women have to white men because of the family or the private sphere. 'As wives, secretaries or assistants to white men, white women are physically integrated around centers of power.'[73] Audre Lorde makes the point that such closeness to power is an illusion:

> White women face the pitfall of being seduced into joining the oppressor under the pretense of sharing power. This possibility does not exist in the same way for women of colour. The tokenism that is sometimes extended to us is not an invitation to join power: our racial 'otherness' is a visible reality that makes it quite clear. For white women there is a wider range of pretended choices and rewards for identifying with patriarchal power and its tools.[74]

Nancy Henley argues that such intimate relations mean that white men must have 'frequent interaction – verbal and nonverbal – with women', leading to a socialization of white women towards passivity and allegiance to white men.[75] White women as a result experience a highly private, individualized sense of control. Hurtado and Henley argue that this intimate relationship to power is why white feminists have developed a closeness to psychoanalytic theories (or individualistic psychological frameworks) to answer social problems, in a way that women of colour have not. Hurtado concludes: 'As a result the white feminist movement is the only political movement to develop its own clinical approach – feminist therapy – to overcoming oppression at the interpersonal level.'[76] For women of colour on the other hand, who do not have, demographically, the same daily intimate interactions with white men, goals and strategies differ. Feminists of colour may resist the notion, for example, that psychoanalysis is the solution to their problem; such an approach would 'depoliticize and individualize their concerns'.[77] Similarly, society treats these groups differently. As Hurtado succinctly puts it, when white women rebel they are thrown in mental institutions, when black women rebel they are thrown in prisons: 'this difference in treatment is related to the distance of each group from the centre of power'.[78]

As many feminists have questioned the relevance of the white middle-class liberal feminist conclusions regarding the nature of the public and private divide to other groups of women, there are specific questions also raised about the Marxist or socialist analysis of the productive/reproductive divide. In particular, the dual systems theories of Hartmann and Mitchell, which analyse both production and reproduction in terms of patriarchy (gender relations) and capitalism (class relations), ignore any other explanatory factor. Race, in other words, or the reality of women who face obstacles other than class or gender, is simply not addressed. Gloria Joseph comments: 'The categories of Marxism are sex-blind *and* race-blind . . . Both Marxist and feminist analysis thus do a gross injustice to Black women whose historical experiences of slavery have left them with a most peculiar legacy of scars.'[79]

A Marxist analysis of the public/private spheres during the period of slavery, for example, would find that black men and women, because they both worked outside the home, had a strange kind of 'equality'. Angela Davis comments:

> To extract the greatest possible surplus from the labor of the slaves –
> the Black woman had to be released from the chains of the myth of
> femininity . . . In order to function as slave, the black woman had to
> be annulled as woman . . . The sheer force of things rendered her
> equal to her man.[80]

This is the same point hooks makes in her critique of liberal feminism, but she added that while African American men and women were often equal in terms of the labour they did outside of the house, women were still more responsible for domestic labour, whether it be in their own families, their master's household as slaves or other people's households, as noted above.

Moreover, the call by socialist feminists for the abolition of a 'private sphere', or at least greater involvement of the public sphere in the private lives of women and families, raises, it is argued, enormous questions for women marginalized on the basis of their race, sexuality or class. Such women are likely to experience too much interference in the 'private sphere' from the public realm or the state. Whether it is the case of the single mother on social assistance confronted by an overly zealous welfare bureaucracy, or the immigrant women who faces questioning and probing about her domestic affairs, or African American woman challenged on the street by the police for no reason, there are many examples of the issue of privacy and the need for civil rights to protect that private sphere posing different sets of challenges for different groups of women. In fact, the concern for many marginalized groups of women is to find a private space in which they may be free to act without interference, rather than a greater role for the public sphere, as some liberal and socialist feminists argue. Hurtado concludes that women of colour have a very different view on the private sphere:

> The American state has intervened constantly in the private lives and domestic arrangements of the working class. Women of Color have not had the benefit of the economic conditions that underlie the public/private distinction . . . There is no such things as a private sphere for people of Color except that which they manage to create and protect in an otherwise hostile environment.[81]

If second wave feminist theory excluded or ignored women of color in its critique of the public/private divide in political theory and practice, lesbian feminists, and more recently queer theorists, have made similar challenges to mainstream feminism on the basis of assumptions about sexual identity. Beginning with Mary Daly, Adrienne Rich and Audre Lorde, lesbian feminists have charged that while second wave feminism challenged the underlying patriarchal assumptions about gender in political theory, it failed to address the heterosexual assumptions of the private sphere in the same body of thought.[82] In particular, the nature of the family and the importance of one's identity to the public/private divide is critical, as we shall see, for lesbian feminist scholarship.

Ancient Greek political thought, in particular Plato's dialogues, is replete with references to homosexuality, but predominantly male homosexuality. Several of the dialogues speak explicitly about the nature of love in both heterosexual and homosexual unions, most particularly the *Symposium*. Nevertheless, Ancient Greek philosophy, like modern political philosophy, assumed at the heart of its theories a distinction between a public world of male citizens, which included an important homosexual component, and a private world of heterosexual unions, the family or household. This private sphere, as defined in political theory, leaves no room for unions other than heterosexual ones. It is this historical and long-standing exclusion of non-heterosexuals from the notion of 'family' which is challenged by lesbian feminists. 'In challenging their exclusion from the institutions of marriage, child-bearing and rearing, as well as their own families of birth, lesbians and gays transform the norms defining kinship and biological reproduction, suggesting a redefinition of what love consists in.'[83]

Feminists have long recognized the importance of the family to the development of both gender and political identity. Jean Bethke Elshtain published an edited book of articles on the family in the history of political thought, in which she concluded that the family is important, not only for looking after the needs of its members in everyday life as political thinkers have claimed, but also as 'a mechanism for the internalization and reproduction of authority structures'.[84] Despite the recognition that the family exists to internalize and reproduce 'authority structures', by and large liberal feminists have not analysed the degree to which this authority is heterosexual in nature.

Many Marxist and radical feminists have not fared much better on their analysis of the family. In particular, when feminists like Eli Zaretsky and Nancy Chodorow have concluded that the heterosexual family is the one area which stands in opposition to the dehumanizing nature of capitalism and the public world, they undermine the examination of the 'personal' or private lives of families and the inherent political nature of power within that unit; in particular, for lesbians, the degree to which the family represents not a refuge from power, authority and politics but often the site of one's most difficult conflicts. As Bat-Ami Bar On comments on the work of Zaretsky and Chodorow:

Neither Zaretsky's nor Chodorow's work includes an examination of the family as a social institution that legitimizes specific sexual relations . . . Both Zaretsky and Chodorow concede that the family is male-dominated, yet they believe that the family is redeemable and affirm its value . . . Zaretsky's and Chodorow's treatment and affirmation of the family tends to make the family immune to a lesbian-feminist critique. Thus, they have contributed to the more than a decade-long reprivatizing and depoliticizing of personal life.[85]

Thus, the role of the family has posed problems for lesbian feminists, both in political theory generally and in the way it has been appropriated by feminists without reference to its heterosexual underpinnings.

As the gay and lesbian communities became more radical and public, mainstream liberalism and feminism have begun to adapt their theories to this challenge. Rather than continuing to say that one is without identity, liberals, including some mainstream feminists, began to use the language of rights within liberal theory to defend one's right to a particular, private, identity. Thus, for example, liberal feminists defended the right to one's 'sexual orientation' or 'lifestyle', distinguishing between the private sexuality of the individual on the one hand and the public identity of the individual as 'citizen', without any specific identity, on the other. In essence, sex is private and what one does in the privacy of the bedrooms is one's own business. In the famous words of Canadian Prime Minster Pierre Elliot Trudeau: 'The state has no place in the bedrooms of the nation.' Lesbianism is thus subsumed within the discourse of civil rights: every individual having the right, as a private individual, to any given sexual orientation, or more specifically the right to engage in sexual practices within the privacy of the bedroom. This distinction between a public 'citizen' and private being (including one's sexuality) which characterizes modern liberal theories of rights (including feminist versions) is highly suspect to many lesbian feminists.

For some lesbians feminists, such a distinction was problematic for two reasons. First, lesbianism is reduced to sexuality and sexual behaviour, when lesbian feminism is claiming to be so much more: 'As long as straight women see lesbianism as a bedroom issue, they hold back the development of politics and strategies that would put an end to male supremacy.'[86] Second, it allows women to be lesbians only in the private sphere, within the confines of specific personal relationships, while publicly they take on a non-identity which is, in reality, a very specific, heterosexual, identity. This dual reality where one has different public and private identities is, for lesbian feminists, living 'in the closet'. One scholar writes of this experience in academia:

> Caught between silence on one side and fear on the other, the typical closeted gay academic spends his or her professional life in a state of constant duplicity, internally and externally divided . . . To live in the closet, in this void, is to be constantly aware of what one is *not* saying, is *not* doing, is *not* experiencing or receiving, because you are afraid to be fully, publicly yourself.[87]

The response to these divisions between private sexuality and public non-identity by feminists such as Adrienne Rich, Mary Daly and Audre Lorde has been to create a unified public and private identity in the notion of 'women-identified women'.[88] If one is to challenge the assumed heterosexuality of political theory and other texts, what Rich calls the 'compulsory heterosexuality' of western thought, then lesbianism, it is argued, must unleash 'women identification [as] a source of energy, a potential springhead of female power'.[89] Lesbianism is thus not simply about sexuality, but a form of resistance to patriarchy and the privatization of women, through a community of women who publicly identify with other women, what Rich terms the 'lesbian continuum'.

The implications for the public/private divide are once again profound. Lesbianism is not a personal private matter relegated to the bedroom, but a public identity which in bringing together a community of women-identified women undermines the privatization of women within heterosexual marriage, as assumed by liberal political thought. 'The personal', in that motto of the women's movement, does indeed become 'the political'. Anne Koedt comments: 'The original genius of the phrase "the personal is political" was that it opened up the area of women's private lives to political analysis. Before that the isolation of women from each other has been accomplished by labeling a woman's experience "personal".'[90]

For Koedt the opening up of women's experience to political analysis must not entail a collapsing of the private sphere, in particular of privacy. 'While it is true that there are political implications in everything a woman qua women experiences, it is not therefore true that a woman's life is the political property of the women's movement.'[91] In the United States in 1970, the question of privacy was an issue over which lesbian and non-lesbian feminists, in the forum of the National Organization of Women (NOW), found themselves in conflict. At the national board meeting of that year in Chicago, presided over by Betty Friedan, a group of lesbian women proposed an amendment to the NOW Bill of Rights to guarantee the right to 'sexual privacy'. According to Abbot and Love, they were forced to withdraw the motion because 'the Board did not want to be on record as voting against it'.[92]

For lesbians, the whole question of privacy and the private sphere has been an area of deep and emotional divide. On the one hand, in order to create this public identity and community of lesbians, some lesbian feminists argue that the private sphere must be collapsed entirely and women 'in the closet' forced out. Others argue that, of all groups in society, lesbians should be the ones to defend an ongoing right to privacy against the state, groups or other individuals. This question of public/private in terms of individual privacy, and its implications for lesbians and gays, has been the subject of enormous debate within that community. From 'outing' public figures who wish to keep their sexual orientation 'private', to holding parades celebrating 'gay pride', to fighting for public spaces for gays and lesbians, the divide between public and private is constantly at issue.

Thus, lesbian feminists begin their critique of liberal feminism by challenging their assumption, along with most other political theorists, of a heterosexual family within the private sphere. Marxist feminists have either challenged the family on the basis of its economic relations, without questioning the assumed heterosexuality of either private or communal marriages, or taken on the family as the one oasis of human values in the sea of capitalism. More profoundly, several lesbian feminists and queer theorists have challenged the role of identity in political theory. From the notion that the observer can view the world from an unidentified 'nowhere', to the idea that science is an objective process by which the world can be understood, to the premise that a division can and should be made between private sexuality and public citizenry, lesbian feminists have challenged the assumptions of mainstream liberal feminism and western political theory. In their critique, the public/private divide faces new questions about its implications for those who do not fit within its self-defined family.

The construction of a public and private realm by political theory has thus been attacked by feminists on all sides as a means by which women have been excluded from political life, while simultaneously being subjected to its power. The response to this exclusion can perhaps best be summarized in the phrase adopted as the motto of the women's movement in the 1960s and 1970s: 'the personal is political'. This claim opens up both the public and the private spheres for political analysis, for an understanding of how power works in all aspects of both men's and women's lives. Its interpretation, as we have seen, varies enormously in accordance with different feminists' views. Liberal feminists have tended towards trying to include women in the public sphere, while maintaining the family and the private sphere (supplemented by state intervention in the form of childcare, elderly care – in other words, as women enter the public sphere, the public realm must take greater responsibility for the needs in the private sphere). At the same time, they have argued that issues which have been seen traditionally as 'private' must be subject to public laws: for example, sexual assault, domestic violence or child abuse. Other feminists, like Elshtain, have argued that the liberal feminist response continues to devalue the private sphere and its values. Rather, feminists should find ways to bring the private language and values of the family to the public sphere. In a general way, Elshtain represents one voice among many feminists who embrace women, and the values they express in nurturing and caring in the family as 'different'. Some radical and socialist feminists have argued that the only way forward for women is to abolish the private sphere. Others claim the family is the one oasis of human values in a world otherwise dominated by capitalist modes and relations of production. In general, the liberal, socialist and radical feminist response to the public/private divide has been challenged by both women of colour and lesbian feminists who argue that the 'universal claims' about the public and private sphere made by these groups of feminists continue to exclude their reality.

4

Culture versus Nature: the Feminist Critique

The distinction between culture and nature is, as has been described, the second dualism critical to the construction of western political theory and, by extension, politics. The cultural sphere is the rational human realm, namely everything in this world that is created through reason and language (for example, civil society). 'Nature' has two distinct meanings and correspondingly two very different relationships with the cultural realm. The first definition of 'nature' is all that is wild, uncontrolled, *left untouched* by culture, reason or language (for example, the state of nature). Nature in this sense is seen as our origin, our bodies, our biology; a sphere which exists prior to culture, but can be (and often it is argued should be) controlled, shaped, even transcended by the cultural realm. A secondary meaning of nature is that which is innate, part of the order of things, and therefore *cannot be changed* by culture, reason or language (for example, natural laws, or a natural division of labour and so on). This definition of nature is a *matter of the innate essence or function*; what is 'the nature' of something? The extent to which culture can or should shape, overcome or transcend nature is a constant tension in western philosophy generally, but more particularly modern political theory.

Like the public/private divide, feminists have challenged this dualism, which serves as a foundation to western thought, for its role in constructing gender and politics in a particular way, so as to distort or exclude women. Beginning with the Ancient Greeks, politics has always been associated with the resolution of conflict through reason and language rather than violence or war. It is reason which must attempt to control the more 'natural' instincts of pride and passion, in both the *polis* and individual in Plato's *Republic*. Aristotle similarly grounds his political philosophy in the rule of the rational over the irrational. At the same time, Aristotle argued that there is a 'natural' difference between men and women, based on their biology, which necessitates different roles in society. Feminists have analysed the extent to which these basic building blocks of ancient politics excluded women from not only the 'public' realm but also the 'rational' or 'cultural' realm of politics.

The tension between the two definitions of 'nature' becomes particularly apparent in modern political philosophy. Modern philosophy begins with a distinction between mind/body, while retaining the idea that the former must overcome or transcend the latter. Modern *political* philosophy transforms this duality between nature and culture into the divide between the state of nature and civil society, where contract ends the former in order to begin the latter. In this sense, culture must transcend nature. At the same time, modern political philosophy also distinguishes between what is natural, and therefore cannot be changed (for example, natural authority or laws), and what is created by humans and therefore mutable (education, laws, contracts). Civil laws must therefore reflect the natural rights and laws which are inherent to humanity. At the age of reason, adults enter into contracts in order to secure their natural rights against a world which is, by and large, perpetually teetering towards lapsing back into a state of nature, and, by extension, a state of war. So while human culture must under these circumstances overcome or transcend nature through reason and industry, it can only do so within the parameters set by natural right and law.

Marxist political thought has adopted many of the modern views with regard to science, technology and the need for culture to transcend nature. At the same time, Marx and Engels both argue that the most basic 'natural' division of labour is the sexual division of labour based on reproduction. These basic underpinnings of liberal and Marxist thought, where men are the active rational men associated with culture and science and women are more closely linked to nature, or 'natural authority' is applied to one gender whereas 'rational' or cultural authority is applied to another, were challenged by feminist scholarship. In ever deepening critiques, feminists have ultimately sought to deconstruct the duality itself, inherent in western political thought, between nature and culture.

As with the public/private divide, the question of culture versus nature was made explicit in the classic text *Women, Culture, and Society*. Sherry Ortner put the question: 'Is Female to Male as Nature is to Culture?'[1] Like Rosaldo and Lamphere's attempt to find the universal solution to the 'women problem' in the public/private divide, Ortner concludes that universally men are more closely associated with culture and women with nature and this explains women's universal subordination.

> What could there be in the generalized structure and conditions of existence, common to every culture, that would lead every culture to place a lower value upon women? Specifically, my thesis is that woman is being identified with . . . something that every culture devalues . . . Now it seems that there is only one thing that would fit that description, and that is 'nature' in the most generalized sense. Every culture, or, generically 'culture', is engaged in the process of generating and sustaining systems of meaningful forms . . . by means of which humanity transcends the givens of natural existence, bends them to its purposes, controls them in its interests.[2]

Ortner's thesis, like Lamphere and Rosaldo's, has both had an enormous impact on feminist studies far beyond anthropology, and been criticized for applying a western duality between culture and nature universally to all cultures.[3] Like Rosaldo, Ortner acknowledges in subsequent work that the search for a unicausal explanation of women's subordination is misguided.[4] Beyond that, she also acknowledges that the terms 'nature' and 'culture' have a multitude of meanings. Despite their differences, Ortner and her critics do agree that the fundamental duality between culture and nature is central to western thought and practice.

Ortner's distinction between men and women in relation to culture and nature, as she herself acknowledges, is a reiteration of a central thesis in Simone de Beauvoir's *Second Sex*, but applied to cultural anthropology. de Beauvoir's thesis, which has generated an enormous debate among feminists about the relationship between women, their bodies and nature, is that women are far more constrained by their bodies and their reproductive functions than men. Moreover, this relationship to biology and reproduction prevents women from fully participating in the rational or cultural sphere and transcending mere natural life:

> Here we have the key to the whole mystery. On the biological level a species is maintained only by creating itself anew; but this creation

results only in repeating the same Life in more individuals. But man assures the repetition of Life while transcending Life through Existence . . . by this transcendence he creates values that deprive pure repetition of all value. In the animal, the freedom and variety of male activities are vain because no project is involved. Except of this service to the species, what he does is immaterial. Whereas in serving the species, the human male also remodels the face of the earth, he creates new instruments, he invents, he shapes the future.[5]

For de Beauvoir, and some feminists who follow, not only are women perceived to be more closely linked than men to nature, but this is seen as a very negative side to women's existence, that women will never become fully autonomous or free until they have the same degree of control over their biology and body that men do. Her solution is to attempt to move women away from their own 'biology' and towards the cultural realm of men, from the repetition of life through reproduction, to the transcendence of life through reason and industry. While her solution may be new, de Beauvoir's association of the male with culture and female with nature is simply a twentieth-century example in the history of western philosophy of this gendered dualism, as has been discussed. The feminist critique of this duality in western political thought provides us, along with the public/private divide, with a second important means to understand how women have been excluded and subordinated by this tradition.

Beginning with the Ancient Greeks, the distinction between culture and nature, or *nomos* and *physis*, has been central to the feminist critique of political thought. Most feminist scholars recognize that Plato's scheme is important to the history of feminist thought for two key reasons related to culture and nature. The first is that Plato denies that there is any great 'natural' distinction between men and women: most of the differences are due to differences in socialization and education. A whole school of feminists, including liberal feminists, who could be more accurately described as 'feminists of sameness', have followed Plato in this basic principle that men and women are fundamentally the same by nature but culture creates differences.[6] Consequently, through the right set of policies and legislation which basically treats men and women exactly the same but allows for equal opportunity for both, women and men will enjoy equality in the political world. A second important contribution of Plato that feminist scholarship has recognized is the explicit incorporation of biology, reproduction and childcare into his scheme of politics. As Susan Okin comments:

The real significance of the treatment of the subject of women in Book V of the *Republic* is that it is one of the very few instances in the history of thought when the biological implications of femaleness have been clearly separated out from all the conventional, institutional, and emotional baggage that has usually been identified with them.[7]

In other words, unlike other political philosophies, which discuss the activity of public and rational discourse of politics as separate from the private and natural activity of reproduction, Plato deals with these issues head on and simply makes them part of the questions that need to be answered within an ideal republic as he has constructed it.

There is much in Plato's *Republic*, however, which has been challenged by feminists as either exclusionary or oppressive to women. Part of this can be explained in Plato's construction of the public/private divide, as has been discussed. But the culture/nature divide has equally profound implications for the relationship between politics and gender in Plato's ideal state, and the political theory which follows on its heels.

First, feminists have pointed out that for all Plato's claims of equality between men and women, he still links women to the world of biology, nature and bodily appetites. And, most importantly, this is a basis upon which women, despite the formal recognition of the potential of equality, will in fact be excluded from politics.

While there is no logical reason for excluding women from the guardian class . . . it is unlikely given his remarks about the nature of their souls elsewhere, that Plato believes many would attain such a status . . . Indeed when the discussion later turns to the selection of the highest class, that of the philosopher kings who are the most truly rational, Plato opens with the claim that he has 'now disposed of the women and children' and must begin again with the training of rulers (by implication, all male) . . . For Plato has already identified the philosophical nature with a love of wisdom that suppresses bodily desires – precisely the 'natural talent' in which he found women especially inferior.[8]

Like the public/private divide, the distinction between culture and nature not only excludes women from Plato's *Republic* but creates a basis for power or authority over women, in particular their bodies and reproductive capacities. The belief in reason, culture, order over the disorder of nature is taken to an extreme and collective end in Plato's *Republic*. The implications for women are profound, as Coole concludes:

> Plato . . . subordinates irrational and exclusive passions . . . to the rational controls of the state . . . this is of special significance in the case of women. We have seen that an aura of mystery and a supposed affinity with dark forces accrued to the female by virtue of her reproductive abilities . . . Plato's solution for reproduction goes further in virtually eliminating gender but it is the functions and qualities associated with women, rather than men, which are to disappear [mother–child bond, women's fertility, lactation] . . . the natural world of fertility is to be brought firmly within the ambit of reason, and women's power is consequently demystified, rationalized.[9]

Thus some feminists have concluded that Plato, despite his claims for equality between the sexes, has created an ideal state which through the relationship between culture and nature and the links to gender ultimately both excludes women from the political sphere and subjects their bodies and biologies to the rational authority of the larger political order. Feminists to this day continue to be concerned about any claims for state control over women's bodies.

Like Plato, Aristotle associates the sphere of culture, rationality and reason with politics, and likewise concludes that the best ordered state is one in which the rational rule over the irrational. Unlike Plato, however, Aristotle argues that only men are truly rational and therefore fit to rule. The exclusion of women from political life by Aristotle begins with his association of women with the natural world of reproduction, biology and bodily functions, and the association of men with rationality, culture and the mind. Both men and women are made up of body and soul, but as Coole points out, men, for Aristotle, 'are born with a natural capacity for reason', while women 'have a higher quotient of the irrational, material component'.[10] Aristotle states explicitly that men are to rule and women to be ruled on the basis of this natural distinction. Critical to this concept of natural differences is that any amount of education or culture is not going to change these 'natural' distinctions.

This is a fundamental difference between Plato and Aristotle on the relationship between culture and nature. For Plato, education and training can shape both men and women into guardians or rulers, but for Aristotle, there are natural functions to which we are innately born, and no amount of culture is going to change these natural distinctions. Society, therefore, must accept these innate differences as given, and reflect them in who exercises power over whom. These two approaches – one which tends to support the idea that reason can reshape nature, and the other which tends to argue that cultural institutions must respect the natural order of things or fail – has been central to western philosophy up to the present day. Often both views are found within the same philosopher's work. The implications for women of these two approaches, as feminist scholars have made clear, are profound.

> Plato's approach is a rationalist one: he believes in the power of reason to devise and order an ideal political organization. Aristotle, on the other hand, adopts a naturalist approach . . . While the Platonic method favours radical change, its Aristotelian successor offers a conservative argument predicated upon naturalist and functionalist premises. The former, with its stress on the educability and (in principle) equality of souls, would strike a greater resonance in the liberal and socialist approaches of the modern world. But as we will see, it was the structure of the Aristotelian claim of natural sexual distinction that would dominate well into the eighteenth century. To this extent it would be correct to see Plato as a progenitor of radical sexual politics and Aristotle as the harbinger of women's oppression.[11]

What ultimately distinguishes Aristotle from Plato, according to feminist scholarship, is not simply his acceptance of 'natural differences' but the tying of this to defending his present day status quo; that is, the existing functions of each of the parts of Greek society. Nature is defined not simply as a sphere untouched by culture, but also as that which is innate to a given thing, a functional notion of its 'nature'. It is the functionalist model coupled with the belief in an innate and immutable character which is at the heart of feminist critiques of Aristotle's thought. It is not only conservative by definition but circular. Okin comments:

> Aristotle's view of society as rigidly hierarchical, patriarchal and functional allows him to 'prove' things about his various classes by drawing on assumptions that already presuppose the things he claims to prove. If it were not for his initial assumption that the free and leisured male is the highest of mortal beings, there would be no grounds from which to argue that all other members of the human race are naturally defined by their functions in relation to him.[12]

Thus, Aristotle's functionalist philosophy begins with the needs of free male citizens. From this base point, all other 'natural' functions and roles are deduced. Women exist for biological needs within the household; men for the higher purpose of political life within the state. Thus Coole states: 'the household's natural function is therefore to fulfill the preconditions making such a [political] life possible. Women and slave exist for the sake of rational male citizens ... a prerequisite of the good life rather than participants in it.'[13] Or, as Okin comments, 'It is only if we accept the premises that society is most properly structured when it enables the privileged few to spend their lives in rational activity, and that the functions and therefore the nature of all others must be fixed accordingly, that we can accept ... Aristotle's conclusions about the nature and the natural position of women.'[14]

The second important change that Aristotle makes to western philosophy's understanding of nature is found in his writings on biology, and is critical to western philosophy's evolving understanding of the relationship between culture and nature. Aristotle is the first philosopher to associate culture with an 'active' principle of form and nature with a 'passive' principle of matter; the former to act upon the latter. As many feminists have pointed out, Aristotle seems intent on dislodging women from the central function of giving birth. It is man, according to Aristotle, who gives form to the human embryo; women simply provide a vessel and the biological support for the new life. Many feminists have questioned Aristotle's assumptions about the active part of reproduction being attached to the man and the passive role attached to the woman. de Beauvoir, for example, writes: 'Nor does Aristotle explain this division, for if matter and form must co-operate in all action, there is no necessity for the active and passive principles to be separated in two different categories of individuals.'[15]

This definition of nature creates a very different relationship with the cultural sphere. Where, as we discussed earlier, Aristotle defines nature as something innate to the function and purpose of a given thing, it cannot be changed by reason or language. Instead, cultural institutions must embrace and reflect such natural distinctions. This second concept of culture as active and nature as inert transforms the relationship between culture and nature into a battle, where the former must dominate, impose itself on the inert passive latter. As Aristotle argues, it is the active principle of men which gives life to the passive form or matter within women in the reproductive process. This dualistic kernel, of an active mind versus passive nature, will develop and flourish in modern philosophy according to feminist scholarship, particularly as an underpinning to science and scientific method. The notion of an active male principle which must give form to or shape passive inert nature is also at the heart of the radical feminist and ecofeminist critique of western philosophy. In essence, ecofeminists agree with Aristotle that women are closer to nature, but argue that far from giving life, men tend to be destructive of life and nature. Aristotle's version of reproduction is a misguided and distorted attempt to put men at the centre of the life-giving process. Women, as life-givers, have a special connection with nature and the desire to protect life.

Susan Griffin writes: 'Women have long been associated with nature. And if this association has been the rationalisation of our oppression by a society which fears both women and nature, it has also meant that those of us born female are often less severely alienated from nature than most men.'[16] Aristotle is often seen, by ecofeminists, as the root of western philosophy's view that culture must dominate nature. Carolyn Merchant comments:

> The objectification of nature is rooted in Aristotle's locus of reality in the objects of the natural world . . . the dualism between activity and passivity hypothesizes an active subject – man – who receives, interprets and reacts to sense data supplied by a passive object – nature . . . Nature . . . is composed of dead passive matter set in motion by efficient or final causes . . . Stemming from the same Aristotelian roots as the ideology of objectivity is the association of passivity with femaleness and activity with maleness . . . The Aristotelian identification of the female principle with passivity and the further association of passivity with object and the natural world have furnished the basic philosophical framework of Western culture . . . Feminism challenges these linkages.[17]

It should be noted that some feminists, while accepting many of the critiques of Aristotle outlined above, argue that Aristotle also provides a model for an active and participatory *polis*, if feminists transform it to their purposes.

> Aristotle's participatory vision stands out as a towering contribution to our understanding of . . . politics as a human activity . . . The key is to assay what one can drop without so eroding the overall struc-ture of the theory . . . This leaves the door open for feminist thinkers to turn Aristotle to their own purposes and to take up and insist upon a concept of citizenship as the touchstone of collective and individual public identities.[18]

Thus the duality between culture and nature in Ancient Greek thought is at the heart of the feminist critique of both Plato and Aristotle's claims about gender and politics. First and foremost, for both thinkers men are associated with the *polis*, the realm of *nomos*; order, light, culture, freedom and reason. Women are associated with the realm of *physis*; disorder, darkness, nature, necessity and passion. This distinction not only defines what is and is not within the *polis*, or political sphere, it also excludes women from that sphere. Moreover, women become subjugated under the authority of men as the cultural world overcomes or acts upon the natural world; transforming it through reason, industry and order. Plato uses the rational world of his ideal republic to impose order on the chaos of reproduction and biology, and by definition upon women. For Aristotle, it is women's lack of rationality and their connection to a passive world of biological and natural needs which creates the natural authority of men. In conclusion, the feminist analysis of the role of culture and nature in Ancient Greek thought underlines the exclusion and subjugation of women which lies at the foundation of western political theory.

Feminist critiques of modern philosophy often begin with the distinction drawn in René Descartes's philosophy between mind and body or mind and matter. At the heart of modern philosophy is a belief in 'science'. Science, as Francis Bacon stated, is 'the chaste and lawful marriage between Mind and Nature'.[19] The marriage metaphor, according to feminist analyses of modern scientific thought, is apt, since 'the complement of the scientific mind is, of course, Nature – viewed so ubiquitously as female.'[20] Science, as it developed from the sixteenth century through to the twentieth century, has been critical to the feminist analysis of how the relationship between gender, culture and nature has been constructed. Lynda Birke comments:

> Nature vs. culture [is] a distinction which has become central to Western ideas . . . 'Nature' is often regarded as somehow disorderly, chaotic and intractable; by contrast, our concept of 'culture' has come to include the capacity for human mastery over nature. Science, too, is implicitly part of that distinction for it is science that has long promised to give up mastery over our environment, to force nature to yield up 'her' secrets . . . the nature/culture dichotomy has historically been associated with gender in the sense that nature is usually thought of as female, while 'culture' is considered to be much more of a masculine domain.[21]

The modern belief in science underlies political philosophy as much as any other discipline within philosophy. As will be discussed, Thomas Hobbes and John Locke underpin their political analysis with this basic understanding of scientific inquiry. We begin first with the feminist critique of Cartesian dualism, in which a rational scientific mind exists prior to and dominates the material world which surrounds it. We will then turn to the feminist critique of the Enlightenment and the increasing tendency in western thought to find a materialistic or 'natural' basis for our understanding of the world, in particular of political society.

Cartesian dualism, according to feminist scholars like Evelyn Fox Keller, Sandra Harding and Nancy Chodorow, begins with a separation or abstraction between the self and the world which surrounds its. Quoting Bacon's reference to science as a marriage between mind and nature, Keller comments:

> Having divided the world into two parts – the knower (mind) and the knowable (nature) scientific ideology goes on to prescribe a very specific relation between the two . . . Not only are mind and nature assigned gender, but in characterizing scientific and objective thought as masculine, the very activity by which the knower can acquire knowledge is also genderized. The relation specified between knower and known is one of distance and separation. It is that between a subject and object radically divided . . . Simply put, nature is objectified . . . Concurrent with the division of the world into subject and object is, accordingly, a division of the forms of knowledge into 'objective and 'subjective'. The scientific mind is set apart from what is to be known, i.e., from nature and its autonomy is guaranteed . . . In this process, the characterization of both the scientific mind and its modes of access to knowledge as masculine is indeed significant. Masculine here connotes, as it so often does, autonomy, separation, and distance. It connotes a radical rejection of any commingling of subject and object, which are, it now appears, quite consistently identified as male and female.[22]

The separation and autonomy of masculinity, as represented by the 'scientist', can be traced, according to some feminists, to early childhood development. Nancy Chodorow's psychoanalytical analysis of mothering concludes that the single distinguishing feature between men and women is their sense of distance from the world outside of them. 'Boys come to define themselves as more separate and distinct, with a greater sense of rigid ego boundaries and differentiation. The basic feminine sense of self is connected to the world, the basic masculine sense of self is separate.'[23] Nancy Hartsock argues:

> Because the problem for the boy is to distinguish himself from the mother and to protect himself against the real threat she poses for his identity, his conflictual and oppositional efforts lead to the formation

of rigid ego boundaries . . . The female construction of self in relation to others leads in an opposite direction – toward . . . valuation of everyday life, sense of a variety of connectednesses and continuities both with other persons and with the natural world.[24]

Thus it is argued that the 'marriage' between mind and nature is one which makes the very nature of science masculine, in the sense of an active subjective mind which needs to work itself out autonomously and from some distance against a passive objective world. As with Ancient Greek political thought, the very construction of rationality against an irrational world is, according to the feminist critique of science, inherently gendered.

Subject and object create another problem for women, which Simone de Beauvoir makes a central theme in her *Second Sex*, and that is 'otherness'. If one groups sets itself up as the active subjective mind, it becomes the reference point through which the object of analysis or 'other' is defined. As we have discussed, 'otherness' in some ways is inherent in the dualities underlying western philosophy, as not 'x' is always defined in relation to 'x', the point of reference. However, with the distinction between subject and object of modern philosophy, women are caught in a world in which they feel themselves to be subjects but simultaneously recognize they have been cast in the role of 'objects'. How to reconcile these two aspects of women's reality is de Beauvoir's purpose in writing the *Second Sex*:

> What peculiarly signalizes the situation of woman is that she – a free and autonomous being like all human creatures – nevertheless finds herself living in a world where men compel her to assume the status of the Other . . . The drama of woman lies in this conflict between the fundamental aspirations of every subject . . . who always regards the self as the essential – and the compulsions of a situation in which she is the inessential.[25]

Separation, distance and otherness is one aspect of Cartesian dualism; a secondary and perhaps more important aspect of the relationship between culture and nature is the notion that the former must not only be separate from and in opposition to nature but it must also subdue or conquer 'her'. Going back to the marriage analogy of science, Bacon concludes: 'I am leading you to Nature with all her children to bind her to your service and make her your slave'.[26]

As with the duality between public and private, one must transcend the other. Jane Flax writes of Cartesian philosophy:

There is deep irony in Descartes' philosophy. The self which is created and constituted by an act of thought is driven to master nature, because ultimately the self cannot deny its material qualities ... The desire to know is inextricably intermeshed with the desire to dominate. Nature is posited as pure otherness which must be conquered to be possessed and transformed into useful objects.[27]

Ecofeminists argue that this disjunction between culture and nature, and the belief that man must overcome and force nature into submission, must be resisted: 'An ecofeminist perspective propounds the need for a new cosmology and a new anthropology... this involves rejecting the notion that Man's freedom and happiness depend *on an ongoing process of emancipation from nature*, or independence from, and dominance over natural processes by the power of reason and rationality.'[28] Moreover, given the powerful force science is in the modern world, many ecofeminists conclude that they must take direct political action:

To cultural ecofeminists the way out of this dilemma is to elevate and liberate women and nature through direct political action... Often stemming from an anti-science, anti-technology standpoint, cultural ecofeminism celebrates the relationship between women and nature through the revival of ancient rituals centered on goddess worship, the moon, animals, and the female reproduction system. A vision in which nature is held in esteem as mother and goddess is a source of inspiration and empowerment.[29]

Ecological activism, it is argued, is a natural fit for feminists. The motivation for much ecofeminism comes from the relationship between women's 'reproductive biology (nature) and male-designed technology (culture)'.[30] Some feminists argue that male technology and science has not only neglected the natural world, but been destructive through the creation of pollution, nuclear weapons, even carcinogens. Science, far from being an objective tool, is potentially a highly destructive force against the natural world.

While the environment or natural world is seen as one battleground over which feminists must fight the assumption of domination by culture or science, another site for battle is the body. Sherry Ortner comments: 'Gender difference, along with nature/culture, is a powerful question. And the gender relationship is always at least in part situated on a nature/culture border – the body.'[31] The female body and its reproductive capacities lay at the heart of many analyses of second wave feminism. Beginning in 1970, Shulamith Firestone argued that it was women's biology, their reproductive capacity, in short their body, which was at the root of their subordination.[32] Susan Brownmiller, Susan Griffin and Andrea Dworkin all argue that underlying patriarchy is the exploitation of women's bodies.[33] Griffin in particular argues that western thought and practice can be understood only in terms of a profound hatred of, and antagonism towards, nature in general and women's bodies specifically.

The theory spilt over into practice. Consequently, the body has been a focus for many feminist political campaigns. Whether it is the right to birth control, defining sexual assault, free choice on abortion, breast cancer or reproductive technologies, the female body has been the site of continuing battles of science, technology and the state versus nature. Robin Morgan writes:

> To many feminist theorists, the patriarchal control of women's bodies as the means of reproduction is the crux of the dilemma . . . we are reared primarily as reproductive beings rather than full human beings, we are viewed in a (male-defined) sexual context, with the consequent epidemic of rape, sexual harassment, forced prostitution and sexual traffic in women, with transacted marriage, institutionalized family structures, and the denial of individual women's own sexual expression.[34]

Susan Griffin argues that the western 'Christian traditions share a profound contempt for, and fear of, women – specifically a fear of women's bodies'.[35] This fear arises from men's disconnection from nature and belief in the rational, while simultaneously desiring women's bodies and thereby being reminded of their own bodies and natural instincts:

> He says that woman speaks with nature . . . He says he is not part of this world, that he was set on this world as a stranger. He sets himself apart from woman and nature . . . Now we are beginning to know why a woman's body is so hated and feared. And why this body must be humiliated. For a woman's body, by inspiring desire in a man, must recall him to his own body. When he wants a woman, his body and his natural existence begin to take control of his mind. The pornographer protests that he is compelled by desire. That he cannot control himself. And this lack of control must recall him to all that is in nature and in his own nature that he has chosen to forget.[36]

Andrea Dworkin comments: 'Male domination of the female body is the basic material reality of women's lives; and all struggle for dignity and self-determination is rooted in the struggle for actual control of one's own body.'[37]

Moira Gatens argues that the role of 'bodies' is particularly important to political thought, since many theorists, particularly in ancient and early modern political philosophy, write of the political state as if it were a body. Her arguments will be considered in more depth when we consider Thomas Hobbes: 'Discourses on the body and discourses on the body politic each borrow terms from the other. This mutual cross-referencing appears in their shared vocabularies, for example, "constitution", "regime" and "diet". A philosophically common metaphor for the appropriate relation, where one (the mind) should dominate, subjugate or govern the other (the body).'[38] The critiques of the way women's bodies are depicted in modern philosophy are jumping off points for feminists in thinking about new ways to include women's bodies, and more specifically reproduction, in political theory. The reproductive capacity of the body is politicized by feminist theory, in ways never dreamed of in mainstream political philosophy: first as a social construct and second as a source of joy and power to women.

Kate Millet's *Sexual Politics* is the starting point for the former: 'Kate Millet's choice of the two terms "sexual/politics" for the title of her pioneering book powerfully identified sexuality, not as some simple, "natural" experience of women and men, but as being socially constructed with political consequences and as being politically constructed with social consequences.'[39] In other words, for Millet, unlike Firestone, we are not determined by our biology, but by the social construction of femininity. Judith Butler critiques both Millet and Firestone for accepting the distinction between sex and gender as given, thus incorporating into feminism the very culture/nature duality which feminism has critiqued within western political thought. Sex and one's body, she concludes, is as culturally constructed as gender:

> On some accounts, the notion that gender is constructed suggests a certain determinism of gender meanings inscribed on anatomically differentiated bodies, whereas those bodies are understood as passive recipients of an inexorable law. When the relevant 'culture' that 'constructs' gender is understood in terms of such a law or set of laws, then it seems that gender is as determined and fixed as it was under the biology-is-destiny formulation. In such a case, not biology but culture becomes destiny.[40]

Understanding the way in which the body is socially constructed and reconstructing it from the point of view of women is critical to their empowerment. As Adrienne Rich concludes, 'the repossession by women of our bodies will bring far more essential change to human society than the seizing of the means of production by workers'.[41]

The 'body', as a source of joy, is critical to the French postmodern school of thought, specifically the works of Julia Kristeva, Luce Irigaray and Helen Cixous. The body for French postmodern feminism is not simply a biological entity. A word that Irigaray uses is 'morophology', meaning 'the body is not considered an anatomical biological . . . body . . . rather . . . the body as it is lived, the body which is marked, inscribed, made meaningful both in social and familial and idiosyncratic terms.'[42] Cixous argues that, in response to masculine language and suppression of the female body throughout western thought, women must begin to write in a completely different way and language, celebrating women's differences and most particularly women's bodies:

> Woman must write her self: must write about women and bring women to writing, from which they have been driven away as violently as from their bodies; for the same reason, by the same law, with the same fatal goal . . . Woman should break out of the snare of silence . . . Her flesh speaks true. She lays herself bare. In fact, she physically materializes what she's thinking; she signifies it with her body.[43]

Feminist analysis must thus create a new language, a new way of writing, if it is to counter the mainstream modern scientific discourse that is seen to be so decidedly masculine.

> In opposition to this prevailing conception of knowledge as a neutrally expressed body of information produced by a sexually indifferent subject for an unspecifiable perspective, Irigaray attempts to clear a space within language for another voice, body, pleasure . . . [she wishes] to create discourses and representations of women and femininity that may positively inscribe the female body as an autonomous concrete materiality.[44]

Other feminists, on the other hand, believe women must overcome or transcend their bodies. Simone de Beauvoir, Mary O'Brien and Shulamith Firestone are three of the strongest proponents of this point of view, concluding that women will only be truly autonomous when they are able to overcome their biology. de Beauvoir is pessimistic about whether this is possible. She explicitly rejects the French postmodern view that the female body should be the basis for a new philosophy: 'one should not believe that the female body gives one a new vision of the world. That would be ridiculous and absurd.'[45] O'Brien states succinctly: 'The consolidation of rational control over the reproductive processes is the precondition of liberation, and it is urgent.'[46] Firestone argues that autonomy will only be achieved when women control the 'means of *reproduction*':

> To assure the elimination of sexual classes requires the revolt of the underclass (women) and the seizure of control of reproduction: not only the full restoration to women of ownership of their own bodies, but also their (temporary) seizure of control of human fertility . . . The reproduction of the species by one sex for the benefit of both would be replaced by (at least the option of) artificial reproduction.[47]

All these feminists have been criticized by other feminist thinkers for having adopted the very negative attitudes of mainstream philosophy about women's bodies.[48]

The distinction between mind and body, introduced by René Descartes, transforms the culture/nature duality in western philosophy while simultaneously providing an important area of attack for feminists. First, in abstracting a subjective mind from the objective natural world around him, Descartes introduces the notion of separation and abstraction which Keller, Chodorow and Hartsock see as fundamentally masculine in nature, rooted in the male need to separate from and be in opposition to his mother in early childhood. This separation between mind and matter, subject and object, culture and nature takes on a decidedly aggressive tone in the works of Francis Bacon and others. The mind must not simply separate itself out from the rest of the natural world and become something other than 'matter', it must seek to dominate and conquer the world around it. Science and technology, feminists argue, is rooted in this masculine notion of domination over the natural world.

Two specific feminist responses have been to defend, celebrate and embrace the two areas where the battle against 'nature' is being waged most fiercely: the environment and women's bodies. The ecofeminists, such as Carolyn Merchant, Ynestra King and Karen Warren, argue that, beginning with John Locke, the notion that civilization, property and politics as the transcendence of an inert nature by an active transcendent mind and culture must be seen not as an objective science, as claimed, but as an ideology, born of Christian mythology and Enlightenment philosophy. Women and nature are inextricably linked and equally subordinated and dominated. Ecofeminists argue, therefore, that the link between environmental activism and feminist theory is a natural fit. The second site of domination by the mind over matter and nature is, for some feminists, the female body. From French postmodern writers to pro-choice activists, many feminists argue that the place of resistance and emancipation for feminists must be the body. Feminist activists have long fought for women's right to protect the autonomy and integrity of their bodies against any attempt to legislate over or interfere with them. From female genital mutilation, to abortion, to birth control, to reproductive technologies, it is an article of faith among many feminists that women must exercise control over their own bodies. French postmodern thinkers take this a step further to argue that if women are truly to take on the monolithic Enlightenment masculine point of view, they must write from and of their morphological bodies.

Let us turn from Cartesian duality to the Enlightenment itself. While Descartes roots his philosophy in the free-floating mind, the Enlightenment will become increasingly enamoured of a materialist or natural metaphysics. In contrast to the medieval and Christian notions that one learns about the world through revelation and reflection, the empirical science of seventeenth-century England demanded material proof of any hypothesis. As Linda Nicholson comments, 'European-based societies from the seventeenth through the nineteenth centuries increasingly came to think about people as matter in motion . . . The growing dominance of a materialist metaphysics also meant an increasing tendency to understand the 'nature' of things in terms of the specific configurations of matter they embodied.'[49] In political philosophy this is reflected in the need to anchor any theory about government in natural laws, natural rights, a state of nature. As Nicholson points out, this reliance on 'nature', on matter rather than mind, created two very distinct sets of arguments, reflecting the two definitions of nature described above. On the one hand, Hobbes, Locke and Rousseau will argue that some things exist by nature, are innate to a given person or object and therefore cannot be altered; on the other hand, natural instincts or proclivities can be shaped, even changed, by certain external influences, such as education, training or an overarching civil authority. Nicholson writes of Locke:

> *Nature* for natural law theorists such as Locke did not mean just the body in distinction from other kinds of phenomena. It could also refer to the external influences provided by vision or education. Thus, while Locke might point to differences in women's and men's bodies to make a point, he could also in his writings on education view the minds of girls and boys as malleable in relation to the

specific external influences they were subject to. In short, *materialism* at this point in history combines the seeds of what were later to become two very different and opposing traditions.[50]

The two definitions of nature are fuelled by two distinct paradigms in modern political philosophy. The search for material, natural explanations of the world is the scientific impetus of modern philosophy. The belief in a capacity to change what is given by nature, through reason, industry and education, is the liberal impetus in modern philosophy. These two views create a paradox or tension between culture and nature in modern thought. Whereas, with science, nature defines culture (and thereby underpins civil society), in liberalism culture must shape, even transcend, nature. Both these views of the nature/culture duality must be taken into consideration in examining the feminist critique of modern political theorists' construction of both politics and gender.

Thomas Hobbes and John Locke root their theory of government in a state of nature which is governed by a set of natural laws and natural rights. Any political institution, any government which is formed, must be founded on the principles of natural law and right or it will flounder. Similarly, individuals existing in the state of nature are born with certain natural rights. For Hobbes it is fundamentally the right of self preservation; for Locke it is the right to life, liberty and property. The state of nature concept has provided feminists with much room for analysis and criticism. First, feminists have argued that both thinkers' understanding of 'nature', the natural state and human nature is fundamentally masculine, and excludes women as women. Second, the notion of natural rights provided early feminists with a tool to push their own claims, for if rational human beings are born with rights then surely it must be accepted that women have rights too. For Hobbes and Locke, the exercise of natural rights will exclude women, particularly in the crucial area of property. Finally, the transformation of the state of nature to civil society has provided feminists with the most critical evidence that while women remain in the 'natural world', their male counterparts emerge into the political and rational world of civil society. As men are transformed into citizens, freely consenting to rational authority, women will continue to be subject to the natural authority of their husbands.

Let us begin with the state of nature. Hobbes claims that his 'natural man' is in fact universal. Feminists have argued that his state of nature is populated by men only:

The case might be taken further to suggest that although Hobbes' ascription of a nature common to both sexes was progressive, what he accredited them with was an identity that modernity would recognize as specifically masculine: aggressive, competitive and egoistic. It is not then surprising that the family relations he will describe have no room for the caring and compassionate characteristics that later thinkers would define as specifically feminine.[51]

Feminist international relations theory often posits Hobbes's state of nature as a foundational bias which skews understanding of relations between individuals and states towards a masculine conception. Rebecca Grant comments:

> Parables of man in the state of nature claim to be universal models. They aim to define what constitutes the social being, what tendencies he will follow in relations with others. However, the abstract formulation of man in the state of nature has used a male archetype of the individual . . . Women are invisible in the state of nature. They have no role in the formation of laws in the society that replaces the warlike state of nature . . . Not surprisingly, analogies drawn from Hobbes do not lend themselves easily to questions about gender roles and their effect on political behavior. When women are absent from the foundation theories, a source of gender bias is created that extends into international relations theory.[52]

Many feminists have also pointed out that thinkers like Hobbes seem to ignore the very 'natural' aspect of early infancy, where mother and child, far from atomistic and competitive, are symbiotic and nurturing. In a section of her article entitled 'Do women and children exist in the state of nature?', Jane Flax comments: 'Modern political philosophy also conceals a denial of early infantile experience . . . Especially important is the denial of the primary relatedness to and dependence upon the caretaker present in infancy and the consequences of this denial for conceptions of human nature.'[53] It is not simply that masculine characteristics are taken to be human characteristics, but for many feminists the denial of early childhood experience must lead to profoundly misguided assumptions about human nature. It is for this reason that many feminists combine psychoanalytic theory with political philosophy in developing their own analysis of human society.

Second, the state of nature is populated by people who exercise natural rights. The notion that everyone is born with the right to life, and, in the case of Locke, liberty and property provides an opening for early liberal feminist writers, like Mary Wollstonecraft and J. S. Mill, to argue that rights, belonging to human beings innately, must be exercised by both men and women. Hobbes seems to agree with this view, and argues in fact that women have prior right over their children in the state of nature, since her parentage is certain. Locke similarly argues that both men and women have rights over their children. Both writers are using these maternal rights to counter the patriarchal arguments of Sir Robert Filmer in defence of the patriarchal right of absolute monarchy. Some feminists have argued that Locke, in particular, can be seen as an early feminist for his clear and cogent arguments against patriarchy.[54]

Largely, however, feminists have pointed out that women are denied the right to exercise their natural rights. First, they are subject to the natural authority of their husbands within both the state of nature and civil society, because ultimately they are less rational than their husbands. Second, women are not perceived to be the free rational subjects which populate the natural state, but 'wives' of those free men. In essence, the only real 'people' who exist in the state of nature are men. Coole comments of Hobbes's list in the natural state of what might begin war: 'these include other men's persons, wives, children and cattle – a strange selection for any woman to covet'.[55]

Locke's right of property, some feminists argue, incorporates a more profound exclusion of women. In chapter 3 we discussed the importance of women's role in the family (the public/private duality) in preventing women from exercising their right to gain and own property in their own right. Ecofeminists have also argued that Locke's theory of property is based on the modern belief that culture (reason and industry) must dominate nature, couched in Protestant Christian metaphors. Within this view, women are associated with the latter sphere. In the case of Locke, property begins with the application of arts and science, industry and rationality to the wasted land of inert nature. Without property there would be no need for politics, as Locke makes clear. Ecofeminists argue that Locke's political philosophy is, in essence, an attack on both nature and women, through the mythology of a paradisical Garden of Eden, otherwise known as the state of nature. Nature is thus unspoilt but wild, to be harnessed by man:

> Beginning in the seventeenth century . . . the long-term goal . . . has been to turn the earth itself into a vast cultivated garden . . . John Locke's political theory rested on the improvement of undeveloped nature by mixing human labor with the soil and subduing the earth through human dominion . . . Crucial to the structure of the recovery

narrative is the role of gender encoded into the story. In the Christian
religious story, the original oneness is male, and the Fall is caused by
a female, Eve ... while fallen Adam becomes the inventor of the tools
and technologies that will restore the garden, fallen Eve becomes the
Nature that must be tamed into submission. In the Western tradition, fallen Nature is opposed by male science and technology...
Nature, in the Edenic recovery story, appears in three forms. As
original Eve, nature is virgin, pure and light ... As fallen Eve, nature
is disorderly and chaotic, a wilderness, wasteland, or desert requiring improvement ... As mother Eve, nature is an improved garden;
a nurturing earth bearing fruit ... These meanings of nature as female
and agency as male are encoded as symbols and myths into American
lands as having the potential for development, but needing the male
hero, Adam.[56]

In other words, Locke's view of nature in the Second Treatise is
completely in keeping with the general Christian mythology and
Enlightenment philosophy of transforming wilderness into cultivated garden. The three forms described above are very similar to
Locke's notions of a state of nature which begins in bliss (para-
dise), but ultimately degenerates into a state of war (the fall), eventually to be replaced by civil society. Property similarly goes through
the stages of communal ownership, beginnings of private property
and strife followed by government and civil laws which protect
and preserve property. Implicit within this mythology, as Merchant
argues above, is the control and submission of women, through the
rational authority of men.[57]

It is with the transformation from the state of nature to civil
society that the relationship between nature and culture shifts.
While in the state of nature, men are anchored in natural laws
and natural rights, the social contract implies that human beings
must transcend their own human nature through reason, consent
and government. Thus, the need to dominate nature underpins
political theory as much as it does the science of the early modern
period. For both Thomas Hobbes and John Locke, politics begins
when nature yields to the authority of civil society and government. It is in this transformation from mere nature to civil society
that men and women take on particular roles. In chapter 3 we
examined how the feminist analysis of civil society demonstrates
that women are excluded from the public sphere and are constrained
within the private sphere at this point. Similarly, feminists have
also discovered that the move from nature to civilization will likewise exclude them from the cultural realm, and therefore politics.

Women remain in the natural sphere, as civil society is formed, in two interrelated ways. First, they remain reproductive bodies always in relation to men – their purpose in both Hobbes's and Locke's civil societies remains primarily the reproduction of biological life.

> Woman in fact never makes the transition from the mythical 'state of nature' to the body politic. She *becomes* nature. She is necessary to the functioning of cultural life, she is the very ground which makes cultural life possible, yet she is not part of it. This division between nature and culture, the divisions between the reproduction of mere biological life as against the production and regulation of social life . . . are conceptually and historically sexualized, with women remaining mere nature, mere body, reproducing in the private familial sphere.[58]

Second, women, unlike men, are neither subject to their own rational authority nor ultimately allowed to consent to any other authority. Women continue, despite the transformation into civil society and the references to marital 'contracts', to be subject to natural authority, as discussed in chapter 3. For feminist scholars like Diana Coole, the failure to allow women to engage fully in rational consent is inconsistent with the fundamental and underlying claim in the new political theory of both Hobbes and Locke that individuals with natural rights must consent to any authority which is exercised over them.

> Natural versus rational authority . . . became the focus of debate between patriarchalists and contract theorists . . . the substitution of rational for natural authority flounders when it comes to sexual relationships. To this extent the framework of abstract individuals who consent to authority on the basis of rational self-interest, is adulterated, its universalism undermined by discrimination on prerational grounds. It was such inconsistency that would allow early feminists both to criticize liberalism and to use its own radical premises to do so.[59]

A final aspect of nature versus culture in modern philosophy is the debate which emerges within liberal political philosophy around nature versus nurture, or, as one feminist puts it, 'If it's natural, we can't change it.'[60] The debate, which dates back to the times of Aristotle, but is renewed and transformed by scientific inquiry, concerns whether there is a biological basis to the roles, character and behaviours that human beings inhabit, or whether we are blank slates which can be shaped by education, training and society.

As we have discussed above, modern western philosophy, in adopting a device like 'the state of nature', implies a certain biologically determined 'human nature', which feminists point out is actually very masculine in nature. Moreover, there is a natural basis in many of the political philosophies we have discussed for both the different roles and the levels of authority of men and women in society. To this extent there is a thread in western philosophy which seems to imply that, as individuals and societies, we are determined by our biology or nature; cultural institutions including government can only hope to constrain or diffuse our natural instincts. On the other hand, John Locke also argues in the *Essay Concerning Human Understanding*, in a very famous phrase, that we are fundamentally a *tabula rasa* or clean slate at birth, to be written upon depending on the context or environment within which we develop. In other words, we are not biologically determined but are wholly shaped by our culture. The tension between these two points of view, sometimes summarized as the 'nature versus nurture' debate, has been a defining feature of western political philosophy.

Feminists have responded in a variety of ways to this debate. Initially, the second wave of feminism rejected biologically determined arguments and favoured Locke's *tabula rasa*, arguing that the basis of men and women's differences is not biological but cultural or social in construction. In the famous phrase of Simone de Beauvoir, 'One is not born, but one becomes a woman.' Thus feminists believed that if only we were to change society and its institutions it would be possible completely to rewrite the roles men and women inhabit. These beliefs were the basis for the introduction of 'gender' into the feminist lexicon. Gayle Rubin introduced the term 'the sex/gender system' in 1975, defining it as 'the set of arrangements upon which a society transforms biological sexuality into products of human activity'; that is, nature or sex into culture or gender.[61] Feminists were challenging the idea, inherent in much of philosophy since the time of Aristotle, that men and women had different roles based in nature which could not be changed.

For some feminists, this line of argument, that there are no biological differences between the sexes, has led to the conclusion that men and women are fundamentally the same. de Beauvoir provides the first articulation of this view in the *Second Sex*.

The main source of women's oppression is that they have been treated as if they were different from men ... In pre-history, the obvious biological differences between men and women may have had some social and political significance, but in the modern world they need not determine what women are or what they do.[62]

de Beauvoir's famous phrase, 'one is not born a woman, one becomes a woman', speaks to the notion that biologically there is very little difference between men and women, it is society which creates these differences. Susan Okin takes this argument one step further, concluding that the ideal society would be one in which 'gender' as such did not exist: 'A just future would be one without gender. In its social structure and practises, one's sex would have no more relevance than one's eye colour or the length of one's toes. No assumptions would be made about "male" and "female" roles.'[63] de Beauvoir, at least, argues that in any future society women should become more like men. Any differences which have been created between men and women as a result of socialization must allow 'masculine values' to flourish: '[The] modern woman . . . accepts masculine values: she prides herself on thinking, taking action, working, creating, on the same terms as men; instead of seeking to disparage them, she declares herself their equal.'[64] Equality and sameness are thus linked in much of the early second wave feminist thinking. The feminist quest in politics, therefore, is to find equality between men and women by opening up opportunities for women to take on the same roles as men. In terms of the dualities discussed above, de Beauvoir would like to move the 'independent' or 'modern' woman away from the sphere of nature and the private family and into the world of culture and public affairs.

Other feminists, particularly later second wave feminists, have argued, in response to these early second wave feminists, that rather than striving for equality and sameness between men and women, feminists should recognize and value the differences between men and women. This has come to be known as the difference versus equality debate. For difference theorists, the problem with western thought and practice is not that it distinguished between men and women on the basis of biological differences, but that it gave more value to masculine over feminine roles.

The differences of opinion among feminists on the role and value of 'reproduction' or motherhood clearly demonstrate the gap between feminism of 'sameness' and feminism of 'difference'. It has become one of the most important areas of debate within contemporary feminist thought.

de Beauvoir, in an interview, describes motherhood in the following terms: 'I think that motherhood is the most dangerous snare for all those women who want to be free and independent, for those who want to earn their living, for those who want to think for themselves, and for those women who want to have a life of their own.'[65] On the other hand, Dorothy Dinnerstein is one of several feminists who have written about motherhood and reproduction as a central biological difference between men and women. Dinnerstein argues that women have natural maternal instincts like other animals; a fact misunderstood and distorted by western philosophy.[66] Reproduction or 'motherhood' has become a central focus of second wave feminism. As Mary O'Brien comments: 'Where does feminist theory start? I answer: within the process of women's reproduction.'[67] Adrienne Rich's *Of Woman Born: Motherhood as Experience and Institution* draws a distinction between the social institution of motherhood, which controls women's reproductive capacities, and experiential mothering, in which is rooted women's greatest joy and power. 'Throughout this book I try to distinguish between two meanings of motherhood, one superimposed on the other: the potential relationship of any woman to her powers of reproduction and to children; and the institution which aims at ensuring that the potential and all women shall remain under male control.'[68]

In other words, Dinnerstein and others do not wish necessarily to collapse the 'natural' or 'private' spheres and simply move women from these undervalued roles to those that are valued in society. Rather, they would like to understand why reproduction (in terms of both the natural sphere of biology and the private sphere of family) has been so undervalued and how to create a world in which such differences are respected. The distinction which these feminists make between the biology of mothering and the 'institution' of mothering will be challenged by Judith Butler and others as a continuation of the duality between nature and culture.

The relationship between contemporary feminism and the dualities inherent in western philosophy, including the issues of reproduction and motherhood, are discussed at length in the chapters on feminist thought. Suffice it to say here that the 'nature versus nurture' debate within feminist thought has developed over time in the reaction to changes in western political theory and through the evolution of second wave feminism.

Marxist political philosophy also adopts the distinction between nature and culture. The materialism which marked 'Enlightenment' thought – that is, the attempt to find the material or natural basis for individual human beings and their societies – is taken to its logical end by Karl Marx. While Marx himself believed that he was turning western philosophy on its head by looking to the history of material production rather than the history of ideas (philosophy, religion or politics) to understand the state of the world, in many ways he adopts the same idea that other modern thinkers did: that scientific inquiry from an abstract and universalizing distance may uncover the natural laws which underpin modern capitalist society. The notion of universal natural laws, an abstract and distanced point of view and above all the belief in the need for technology to overcome and dominate nature is as much a part of Marx's thought as of Locke's or Mill's. Feminists have argued that this underlying paradigm has important implications for both gender and politics.

Dialectical materialism as the tool of analysis to understand the historical division of labour and the overcoming of nature by technology is fundamentally flawed, according to feminists, for two reasons. First, it is premised on a scientific distance between subjective mind and an objective natural world around it: what is required, therefore, is to make women the subjects and objects of analysis; that is, collapse the distance between observer and observed. 'Consciousness raising' and 'feminist standpoint theory' are two alternatives suggested by feminists to dialectical materialism.

Catharine MacKinnon believes feminists must give up dialectical materialism as a method in favour of 'consciousness raising':

> As Marxist method is dialectical materialism, feminist method is consciousness raising: the collective reconstitution of the meaning of women's social experience, as women live through it . . . To the extent that materialism is scientific it posits and refers to a reality outside thought which it considers to have an objective [content] . . . Consciousness raising, by contrast, inquires into an intrinsically social situation, into that mixture of thought and materiality which is women's sexuality in the most generic sense.[69]

Nancy Hartsock has argued that what is needed is a 'feminist standpoint', or what she and Iris Young call a 'specifically feminist historical materialism'.

> An analysis which begins from the sexual division of labor – understood not as taboo, but as the real, material activity of concrete human beings – could form the basis for an analysis of the real structures of women's oppression, an analysis which would not require that

one sever biology from society, nature from culture . . . Feminist theorists must demand that feminist theorizing be grounded in women's
material activity and must as well be a part of the political struggle
necessary to develop areas of social life modeled on this activity.[70]

The idea of a 'feminist standpoint' is an open repudiation of ever
achieving an 'objective viewpoint' as science claims; rather, it is a
claim that the feminist viewpoint would not be falsely universalistic
but preferable to a 'male' perspective which claims to be universal
and thereby excludes other perspectives.

The gender-specific and differentiated perspective of women is
advanced as a *preferable* grounding for inquiry – preferable because
the experience and perspective of women as the excluded and exploited other is judged to be more inclusive and critically coherent
than that of the masculine group.[71]

Some feminists have critiqued the 'standpoint theory' on the
basis of its 'essentializing' women's perspective; that is, there is a
unitary view or standpoint associated with women (which tends to
exclude other perspectives: women of colour, lesbian women). Second, postmodern feminists argue that the standpoint theorists, for
all their claims to have escaped from Marxist or other Enlightenment theorists' notions of science, still assume that people act rationally in a 'real world' which can be discovered through reason.
This debate is discussed in more depth in chapter 5.

In both cases, with either the feminist standpoint or conscious
raising method, feminists are questioning the capacity of Marxism
to distance the scientist from the natural world around 'him'. Rather,
women must be 'embodied' within the world they are studying
and the theory they are articulating.

The second set of critiques that feminists have raised around
Marx's belief in the necessity of technology to overcome nature has
been articulated by the ecofeminists. Carolyn Merchant counterposes
'Karl Marx and Friedrich Engels' optimism that the control of nature
would lead to advancement' to 'environmentalism' and 'cultural
feminism', which

> reverses the plot of the recovery narrative, seeing history as a slow
> decline, not a progressive movement . . . Over the millennia from the
> Paleolithic to the present Nature has been the victim of both human
> hubris and social changes that overcome 'the necessities of nature'
> through domestication, cultivation and commodification of every
> aspect of an original evolved, prehuman garden. So-called advances
> in science, technology and economy actually accelerate the decline.[72]

Ecofeminists argue that the scientific notion of progress in early modern thought is married to Hegelian ideas of an unfolding history in Marx's thought, which makes the narrative of 'progress' in Marxism a deeply held tenet.

Dialectical materialism is not only flawed in methodology but, many Marxist feminists argue, the subject matter is limited by Marx and to a lesser extent Engels to the question of 'production'. Women's relationship to nature, however, must also be understood in relation to 'reproduction'. Hartsock argues that reproduction has two aspects: contribution to subsistence and contribution to childbearing and childrearing. Juliet Mitchell, Sheila Rowbotham and Michele Barrett have been instrumental in expanding the notion of reproduction beyond Marxist categories and exploring these in greater depth in relation to capitalism: 'By widening the Marxist concept of reproduction to include household labour and childcare, feminists made a major contribution to our understanding of the interaction of gender and the economy. Classic Marxist theory ignores many kinds of activities traditionally undertaken by women, for example housework and child rearing.'[73] At the heart of women's role in Marxist philosophy, as Mitchell makes clear, is her biological status in capitalist society. 'Her biological status underpins both her weakness as a producer, in work relations and her importance as a possession in reproductive terms.'[74] In order to understand the historical development of the economy and women's role in it, it is necessary to look at 'production, reproduction, sex and socialisation of children.'[75] Mitchell concludes with a standard modern claim of culture overcoming nature as the basis of female liberation, with the exception that she broadens culture beyond 'rationality' to mean 'humanity': 'The liberation of women under socialism will not be "rational" but a human achievement, in the long passage from Nature to Culture which is the definition of history and society.'[76]

Finally, nature is also used by Marx in what he does write about reproduction in the sense of a 'natural role'. In particular, Marx, as was discussed in chapter 2, argues that the first division of labour is the 'natural' sexual division of labour. This division of labour, based on physiological differences between men, women and children, creates the foundation upon which all other divisions of labour are built. The first feminist question raised, therefore, is whether capitalism is simply an outgrowth of patriarchy and not the other way around, as Marx and Engels have argued: '[Marx's] claim that the mental/manual division of labour is based on the 'natural' division of labour in the family – would seem to support the legitimacy of my attention to the sexual division of labour and even add weight to the radical feminist argument that capitalism is an outgrowth of male dominance, rather than vice versa.'[77] Other Marxist feminists challenge Marx's claim that there is something 'natural' or physiological in this division. Heidi Hartmann, Iris Young and others argue that in order to understand the sexual division of labour it is necessary to introduce the concept of patriarchy into the analysis; that is, the specific socially constructed subordination of women's labour by men. Michele Barrett argues that Marx's assumptions about the 'natural family' must be challenged as ideology:

> It is only through an analysis of ideology that we can grasp the oppressive myth of an idealized natural 'family' to which all women must conform . . . To argue this is not to suggest that needs for intimacy, sexual relations, emotional fulfillment, parenthood and so on are in themselves oppressive. What is oppressive is the assumption that the present form of such needs is the only possible form.[78]

It is Marx's attempt to turn what is ideology or socially constructed familial relations into a 'natural division of labour', which is therefore universal and unchangeable, that lies at the heart of Barrett's critique. Marxist feminism's approach to the nature/culture divide has been largely to embrace the notion of culture overcoming nature, but to argue that this underlying notion must not be limited to analysis of 'production' but must also be applied to 'reproduction', creating initially a dual systems theory (capitalism in production; patriarchy in reproduction). As the cultural forces of technology and the oppressed classes make themselves felt, liberation will come as they fully overcome the material, natural world, and women overcome patriarchy.

The distinctions drawn between nature and culture, and the second wave feminist response as described above, have been challenged in recent years by the expanding analysis of lesbian feminists and women of colour.

Lesbian feminists have challenged the assumption made in western political philosophy and feminist critiques that heterosexuality is innate, a given in nature, whereas homosexuality must be explained, and the repurcussions for our understanding of 'gender'. Birke comments:

> There are, then, a number of assumptions about the innateness of sexuality. Women's innate sexuality is held to be passive, receptive;

men's to be active, penetrating. The assumed innateness, somehow rooted in biological forces, ensures that sexuality remains that way, on the grounds that what is biological is assumed to be determining and immutable. Moreover, people who deviate from the norm of conventional heterosexuality are assumed also to deviate in the active/passive dimension. Lesbians are thus assumed to be sexually active and non-receptive.[79]

Quoting from some 'psychological studies' of homosexuality, Birke points out the degree to which passivity is connected to femininity, and then these two concepts are linked with male homosexuals.[80] Aristotle's division between the active male form and the passive female matter seems to have been sustained for many centuries.

Some lesbian feminists have also pointed out that throughout modern political philosophy and practice, the assumption is also made that if heterosexuality is 'natural', homosexuality must be a 'deviation'. Two consequences of this assumption are, first, to impose heterosexuality on people, and, second, to turn homosexuality into a 'pathology' which is unnatural and needs to be corrected. In her classic article, 'Compulsory heterosexuality', a response in large part to the work of Chodorow and Dinnerstein, among other feminist thinkers who assume heterosexuality, Adrienne Rich comments:

> The assumption that 'most women are innately heterosexual' stands as a theoretical and political stumbling block for many women. It remains as a tenable assumption, partly because lesbian existence has been written out of history or catalogued under disease, partly because it has been treated as exceptional rather than intrinsic, partly because to acknowledge that for women heterosexuality may not be a 'preference' at all but something that has had to be imposed, managed, organized, propagandized and maintained by force, is an immense step to take if you consider yourself freely and 'innately' heterosexual.[81]

Heterosexuality, despite most of the textbooks in politics and psychology, is not natural according to Rich, but a political construct intimately related to patriarchy. 'The enforcement of heterosexuality for women [is] a means of assuring male rights of physical, economical and emotional access.'[82] Rich argues that women from their earliest experiences are directed towards other women. Perhaps, therefore, it is homosexuality, in the sense of women identified women, which is natural, and the change to heterosexuality which needs to be explained by societal forces. This, by and large, feminism has not done:

If women are the earliest sources of emotional caring and physical nurture for both female and male children, it would seem logical from a feminist's perspective at least, to pose the following questions: . . . *why in fact women would ever redirect that search [for love]* . . . why such violent strictures should be found necessary to enforce women's total emotional, erotic loyalty and subservience to men. I doubt that enough feminist scholars and theorists have taken the pains to acknowledge the societal forces that wrench women's emotional and erotic energies away from themselves and other women.[83]

The second consequence of heterosexuality as a 'natural' or innate state is the implication that those who are not heterosexual are somehow 'unnatural' or deviant. At the heart of much of the lesbian critique of both traditional political theory and feminist thought is a debate over the idea and function of 'nature'.

We can see in the discussion of lesbianism over the past century or so several theoretical strategies and counterstrategies, all of which hinge on the ambiguity of 'nature' and its various transmutations such as 'God' and 'psyche' . . . While lesbian/gay studies scholars have debated the question of nature versus social construction with an awareness of the strategic role of such arguments, it is clear that full social acknowledgment of the claim to 'naturalness' as a strategy would subvert the strategy itself.[84]

Thus, in order to counter those who claim heterosexuality is natural, gays and lesbians have made a similar claim on their own behalf. At the turn of the century, Havelock Ellis argued that homosexuality was innate or natural, and therefore the individual should not be blamed but accepted into society. This notion of a natural base for homosexuality has had profound implications for gays and lesbians:

The assumption that homosexuality is biologically determined has continued into the medical literature of the twentieth century resulting in a number of attempts to change lesbians and homosexual men into heterosexuals, using techniques ranging from hormone therapy to surgery. That these techniques do not normally work does little to alter that assumed biological determinism.[85]

This attempt at assimilation of the lesbian identity into heterosexual culture has been done in two related disciplines, according to Shane Phelan: medicine and politics.

In modernity, politics and medicine are the two primary sites of social control of the body. Politics appeals to the dignity of humans and the needs of the society, while medicine argues about the needs of the body and the means of its control. Politics speaks . . . of sovereignty and obligation, rights and duties; it deals straightforwardly with issues of order and control. Medicine, on the other hand, is the vehicle for a subtler, more insidious power, the power of health and of reproduction . . . Both politics and medicine justify themselves in terms of social concern; it is the 'nature' of these fields to concern themselves with others, with diseases of the body or the body politic.[86]

Thus lesbian and gay scholars have looked to science and medicine as much as to politics in attempting to explain the power which is exerted over them in modern society. Michel Foucault's celebrated history of medicine is directed at uncovering the politics, the power, inherent in the labelling and classification of people, deviance and disease.[87] In many ways, Foucault unleashed a new approach to 'politics', one which looked at the way power was used by science in particular to marginalize, distort or coerce people. 'Resistance' became the key – resisting language and practise which assumed 'deviance' and 'unnatural behaviour'. Gays and lesbians took up both the notion of resistance and the broader definition of politics. 'The history of the gay liberation and lesbian feminist movements begins precisely with the rejection of the medical paradigm and its participants.'[88]

Thus science is seen not as an objective school of thought so much as another forum for politics, within which people's identities are defined. Lesbian feminists challenge, in particular, the notion in Enlightenment thought that a single universal and objective view, a mind outside of matter, is possible. Recognition of our 'identity' is to make explicit where we exist, historically, culturally, geographically. It is this search for 'identity' – that is, public identity as opposed to 'private sexuality' – which characterizes the most recent lesbian feminist challenge to mainstream political and feminist theory. Claudia Card comments in a recent collection of essays: 'Generally recognized lesbian *social identities* are a relatively recent phenomenon, even though lesbian behaviour, relationships and orientations may be as old as humanity and same sex bonding.'[89]

On the question of liberalism's claims to objectivity, Shane Phelan writes:

In its search for facts that are not tainted by subjectivity, positivism must deny that language shapes perception, that theory forms observation. This inability to acknowledge one's own position has left the positivist researcher, reporter, clinician open to the charge of willful blindness and participation in the status quo . . . It is precisely this gap that leads to the rejection of liberalism by gays and lesbians.[90]

As lesbian feminists engage in a 'resistance' struggle (to science and politics), the 'body' is transformed into a battleground or site of resistance. For many recent lesbian feminists, the decision by early gay and lesbian writers to accept their sexuality as 'natural', to reduce themselves to their bodies, their sexual orientation, was a great mistake. Rather, lesbianism is an identity which is socially constructed, and which must resist the notions of 'nature' and natural to be found in mainstream philosophy. Monique Wittig comments:

> We have been compelled in our bodies and in our minds to correspond, feature by feature, with the *idea* of nature that has been established for us. Distorted to such an extent that our deformed body is what they call 'natural', is what is supposed to exist as such before oppression . . . The refusal to become heterosexual always meant to refuse to become a man or a woman . . . Thus a lesbian *has* to be something else, not-woman, not-man, a product of society not a product of 'nature', for there is no 'nature' in society.[91]

For some lesbians, political theory and many feminist critiques have simply not addressed the question of the social construction of the body, sexuality and biology in their treatises. They simply assume that there are two sexes, defined by biological features, who are by nature heterosexual, and from that point culture, politics and medicine help to keep them free from disease, pathology, violence or conflict. Mainstream feminist thinkers, particularly those who accept the notion of a body as the 'natural' distinction between the sexes, are misguided. Judith Butler comments: 'Any effort to ascertain the 'natural' body before its entrance into culture is definitionally impossible, not only because the observer who seeks this phenomenon is him/herself entrenched in a specific cultural language, but because the body is as well. The body is, in effect never a natural phenomenon.'[92]

Thus the lesbian feminist challenge to both traditional political theory and mainstream feminist critiques of the nature/culture divide have centred on questioning the adoption of many aspects of the nature/culture dualism by feminists into their own analyses. First, the assumption that nature divides us into two sexes which are naturally and fundamentally connected through reproduction assumes heterosexuality as an innate norm. Second, if feminism is to take this 'compulsory heterosexuality' seriously, we must broaden our understanding of politics to include all those aspects of modern science and technology which have created the idea of certain people as 'deviants' or 'unnatural'. Finally, at the heart of political analysis must be the notion of 'identity': the embodiment of the observer as well as the observed in the historical, cultural and geographical context within which they developed.

The duality between nature and culture, from the thought of Aristotle until the present day, has had profound implications for women and men of colour. From Aristotle's definition of slavery and his notion that some groups of people are more closely associated with animals, nature and physicality, and others with culture, reason and the mind, the association of culture with Europeans (or in Aristotle's day with Greeks) and nature with non-Europeans (or non-Greeks) has infused western thought. As has been discussed, feminism has failed to recognize the ways in which the distinctions made between groups of people (both men and women) on the basis of a culture/nature gradient have had different implications for different groups of women.

Colette Guillaumin argues, in a recent series of articles, that western theory and practice has mistakenly assumed 'race' to be a natural or biological category. It is, she argues, a cultural construct, created over time by a series of European thinkers. She turns the relationship between nature and culture on its head with regard to a supposedly natural concept such as 'race' and a cultural product such as 'racism', concluding: 'Racism [is] an ideology which produces the notion of "race" and not "races" which produce racism.'[93] Nature, she argues, is the tool used by seventeenth- and eighteenth-century thinkers to define 'race' in the colonial period. Both definitions of 'natural' as described above – that is, function and biology – are adopted in this modern idea of 'race'. Aristotle's concept of function is combined with eighteenth-century notions of biology, what she calls 'endogenous determinism' (natural instincts, genes, chemistry within a given group of people, which biologically determine their character and role in society). This second definition of nature is a product of 'science', as discussed above. Thus Aristotle's defence of slavery based on purpose or function was reinforced by the modern idea of natural groups acting in accordance with not only their purpose but their biology or instincts:

> Aristotle ... talked about the nature of slaves, but it was not with the meaning that we give today to this word ... In order for the modern meanings of the word to come into being there had to be another element, a factor internal to the object. Endogenous determinism, which ushers in scientific development, will come, by attaching itself to the 'purpose', to form this new idea of the 'natural

group'. For beginning with the eighteenth century, rather than appealing to God to explain material phenomena, people turned to analysing mechanical causes in the study of phenomena.[94]

In the creation of these 'natural groups', the spectre of domination and appropriation is immediately apparent. 'The invention of the idea of nature cannot be separated from domination and the appropriation of human beings. It unfolded within this precise type of relationship.'[95] Or as Danielle Juteau-Lee comments, 'The ideology of nature is secreted in the context of social relations involving dependency, exploitation and more specifically, appropriation be it of land, of humans, of their bodies and of their labour, as well as of the products of their bodies and of their labour.'[96] From Aristotle through Locke to Mill, the distinction between different 'biologically determined' groups (women, non-Europeans/Greeks) has underpinned both the natural authority accorded to the male head of household to rule over and appropriate the labour of his wife, servants or slaves, and the right of despotic rule (either by governments or individuals) over 'uncivilized' barbarians or brutes.

In distinguishing 'natural' differences between individuals, and the authority which may be exercised over them, these theorists make distinctions between, first, the wives of free men and slaves or servants in the household, and, second, civilized peoples and 'barbarians'. Aristotle, Locke and Mill all argue that distinctions in the rule of authority can be made on the basis of the level of rationality of the ruled. The authority over Aristotle's slaves, Locke's servants and Mill's barbarians is despotic. The authority over wives, on the other hand, is 'constitutional or civil' in the case of Aristotle and Locke, and a marriage of equals in the case of Mill, in recognition of their different levels of reason or rationality. This distinction was critical during the period of European colonization and slavery, and has subsequently created an important legacy in political thought and practice. Unlike 'white' women, who, it was admitted, had a modicum of reason and therefore some link to the cultural sphere, black women in particular (and others who fall into this colonial definition of the 'other' race) are seen almost entirely as 'natural beings' or animals, without reason or rationality.

The implications for feminist theory and practice are enormous. When feminists analyse the state of nature, the social contract and civil society in modern liberal thought, or Greek distinctions between rationality and irrationality, it is critical to recognize that while some women would be categorized as, and identify themselves as, 'wives' in these texts, many others would fall within the category of 'slave' or servant. Feminism has tended to focus on the former, without recognizing the very different political circumstances for the latter.

At the heart of the distinction between 'wife' and 'servant', both theoretically and historically, is the relationship of different groups of women to the cultural realm, and by extension to white men. Donna Haraway comments:

> Black women were constituted simultaneously racially and sexually – as marked female (animal, sexualized, and without rights), but not as woman (human, potential wife, conduit for the name of the father) – in a specific institution, slavery, that excluded them from 'culture' defined as the circulation of signs through the system of marriage . . . In racist patriarchy, white men's 'need' for racially 'pure' offspring positioned free and unfree women in incompatible, asymmetrical symbolic and social spaces.[97]

Or as Aida Hurtado puts it in the context of the suffragist movement, white women were *married* to white men, black women were *owned* by white men.[98] This distinction in 'authority', as has been noted, can be traced back to Aristotle, but is given full expression in Locke's theory of property. Thus Locke, as was discussed, concludes that while wives have some property in their persons and their children and therefore can exercise some authority (parental authority in particular), slaves or those who have no property whatsoever are subject to despotic power. It should be noted that in relationship to Locke particularly, he also argues that Amerindians have limited right of property based on their limited use of reason and industry.[99]

These differences between different groups of women in relation to 'property', both theoretically and historically, have had profound implications for feminist goals and strategies. For example, the 'body' as a site of political resistance has different meaning for women of colour and white women, owing to the differing authority exercised over 'wives' and 'slaves', and the latter's role as 'property'. Haraway comments:

> To give birth (unfreely) to the heirs of property is not the same thing as to give birth (unfreely) to property. This little difference is part of the reason that 'reproductive rights' for women of color in the United States prominently hinge on comprehensive control of children – for example, their freedom from destruction through lynching, imprisonment, infant mortality, forced pregnancy, coercive sterilization,

inadequate housing, racist education, drug addiction, drug wars and military wars. For American white women the concept of property in the self, the ownership of one's own body, in relation to reproductive freedom has more readily focused on the field of events around conception, pregnancy, abortion, and birth because the system of white patriarchy turned on the control of legitimate children and the consequent constitution of white females as women.[100]

The implication for feminism is threefold: first, in breaking down the nature/culture divide, feminism must recognize the cultural sphere's need to create a biological basis for racial as well as sexual differentiation. Second, feminist analysis, if it is to include all women in its analysis of politics, must incorporate the very different positions of different groups of women in relation to both these spheres, and not just analyse the 'wife' without simultaneously analysing the 'slave'. Finally, because men and women of colour have been categorized together in the 'natural sphere', under the 'despotic power' of white men, in both modern political theory and historical practice, a feeling of commonality between women and men of colour has developed. It is necessary, feminists of colour argue, for many white feminists to recognize this basic reality. bell hooks critiques feminism, particularly separatist feminism, at length about its tendency to 'identify men as the enemy' by lumping 'all groups of men in one category, thereby suggesting that they share equally in all forms of male privilege'.[101]

While both black men and black women have been categorized as close to nature and outside the cultural realm, the latter's closeness to nature is often defined in ways specific to their gender, based on what are defined as 'natural' or biological traits. For example, black women in the USA have historically been depicted at different times in accordance with different stereotypes: a highly sexualized, almost animalistic creature; an asexual passive caretaker or mamma; or a 'she-devil'. Each of these stereotypes is constructed in distinction to the assigned 'natures' of black men as well as white women. Each will be considered in more depth.

Gerda Lerner argues that the myth of black women's closeness to nature as a sexual animal, animalistic in her instincts and capacities, allowed for all kinds of distinctions to be made between black and white women:

> One of these was the myth of the 'bad' black woman . . . A myth was created that all black women were eager for sexual exploits, voluntarily 'loose' in their morals and, therefore, deserved none of the

consideration and respect granted white women . . . A wide range of practises reinforced this myth: the laws against intermarriage; the denial of the title of 'Miss' or 'Mrs' to any black woman; the taboos against respectable social mixing of the races; the refusal to let black women customers try on clothing in stores before making a purchase; the assigning of single toilet facilities to both sexes of Blacks.[102]

Feminists have analysed the use of this mythology during the period of slavery as the justification for the sexual abuse of female slaves by their owners.[103] bell hooks has criticized Susan Brownmiller for failing to see beyond slavery to present day visions of black women, which continue to be of highly sexualized beings:

> Like Susan Brownmiller, most people tend to see devaluation of black womanhood as occurring only in the context of slavery . . . One only has to look at American television twenty-four hours a day for an entire week to learn the way in which black women are perceived in American society – the predominant image is that of the 'fallen' woman, the whore, the slut, the prostitute.[104]

Thus, African American women have been forced to take on the mantle of Eve, the woman, fallen from close communion with God, because of her affinity to nature.

A second myth that has developed around black women has been that of 'matriarch', or black women as mother nature. Angela Davis remarks: 'The designation of the black woman as a matriarch is a cruel misnomer because it ignores the profound traumas the black woman must have experienced when she had to surrender her child-bearing to alien and predatory economic interest.'[105] hooks criticizes sociological theory, which incorporated this matriarchal theory, as racist and misguided:

> Like their slaveowning ancestors, racist scholars acted as if black women fulfilling their role as mothers and economic providers were performing a unique action that needed a new definition even though it was not uncommon for many poor and widowed white women to perform this dual role. Yet they labeled black women matriarchs – a title that in no way accurately described the social status of black women in America. No matriarchy has ever existed in the United States.[106]

The image of matriarch in black households was combined with the stereotype of the black 'mammy', a passive maternal figure, likened by hooks to a 'cow', who provided the basic subsistence needs of the white family:

She was first and foremost asexual and consequently she had to be fat (preferably obese); she also had to give the impression of not being clean so she was the wearer of a greasy dirty head rag; her too tight shoes from which emerged her large feet were further confirmation of her bestial cow-like quality . . . The mammy image was portrayed . . . as passive nurturer, a mother figure who gave all without expectation of return.[107]

The other stereotype of black women was the opposite of 'mammies'. 'The counterpart to the Aunt Jemima images are the Sapphire images [popularized in the *Amos 'n' Andy Show*]. As Sapphires, black women were depicted as evil, treacherous, bitchy, stubborn and hateful, in short all that the mammy figure was not.'[108] Bakan and Stasilus, in their study of domestic servants in Canada, argue that these stereotypes, based on what are deemed 'natural characteristics', continue to have an impact in contemporary domestic service placements.

Out of these historical conditions of slavery and colonialism and of an increasingly international labour market, various racialized and gendered images of domestic workers and caregivers have persisted in the nineteenth and twentieth centuries. One purpose of such ideological stereotyping has been to portray a fictive, universal nonwhite, female, noncitizen Other whose *biological* and ostensibly *natural* makeup ascribes her as inherently appropriate for private domestic service.[109]

In particular, they found in their study of the attitudes of clients towards Caribbean women in domestic service agencies that the two stereotypes of black women identified by hooks (mammies versus Sapphires) are still largely in place. The 'mammy' image has given way recently to the 'Sapphire' image, the shift being in direct correlation to the extent to which Caribbean women have organized themselves:

Regarding the image of the [Caribbean woman], the passive and loving mammy has been replaced by an apparently widely accepted image that is variously aggressive, incompetent, and cunningly criminal. Though shifts such as these are difficult to measure, this one seems to have taken place in inverse proportion to a rise in organized resistance among live-in domestics to abusive conditions in Canadian employment and immigration practices.[110]

The other largest group of women who provide foreign domestic service placements in Canada are also the victims of racial stereotyping. Filipino women are often depicted by both agencies advertising and families hiring domestic servants as naturally 'passive', particularly in relation to children. In both cases, it is critical to feminism to understand the racial and sexual distinctions which are made, in order to see how women of different groups are excluded from the cultural or political realm, based on 'natural' characteristics:

> Viewing citizenship globally, and as a phenomenon that draws on racial/ethnic, gender and class distinctions, further addresses a growing concern within contemporary feminist literature – with the politics of difference and the issue of unequal, oppressive and interdependent relations between and among women. To date, little theoretical attention has been devoted to explaining the historical and structural specificity of various forms and types of difference and how they are constructed or transformed ... These socially constructed differences facilitate structural inequities between predominantly *white female citizens* and predominantly *noncitizen women of colour*.[111]

Avtar Brah criticizes recent feminist critiques of the culture/nature duality for failing to include racism in their analysis. Specifically, she describes Butler's theory of the cultural construction of 'sex' as blind to 'race':

> For Butler, gender is not merely a cultural inscription of meaning on a pre-given sex but is also the very means by which the sexes themselves are established as ... prior to culture, as a politically neutral surface on which culture adds ... Butler's account is silent on issues of racism and class.[112]

Kate Rogers also critiques those feminist theories which focus on biological differences between men and women as ethnocentric *vis-à-vis* aboriginal women. 'Aboriginal women do not focus on the biological differences between men and women in the same terms as western feminists. Although they do not dismiss the importance of one's physiological make-up, they also concentrate on the spiritual content of one's being.'[113]

Finally, Marxist feminism's critique of the culture/nature divide has come under attack for its ethnocentrism. The two methods discussed above, conscious raising and standpoint feminism (seen as feminist methodologies to replace the 'scientific' dialectical materialism), are challenged by other feminists who argue that both reflect the needs of white middle-class women more than women of colour. They do not necessarily need to be jettisoned as much as reconfigured to meet the needs of different women. bell hooks, for example, argues that conscious raising has been too individualized and personalized; it has not tackled the larger social issues which are of greater importance to women of colour.[114] Standpoint theory has similarly been critiqued by Patricia Hill Collins, among others, for failing to deal with the multiplicity of views and experiences in constructing 'standpoints'. While black women may at times share a standpoint with either black men or white women, it is also the case that black women may 'stand apart from both groups'. Moreover, as Collins cautions, within the 'black feminist standpoint' there is a multiplicity of views. The dilemma comes down to this: the need to have a coherent position from which to resist the 'masculinist' claims to knowledge, while simultaneously recognizing a diversity between and within the groups who have been marginalized by these claims to knowledge. This very dilemma has been the subject of great debate among the feminist movement.[115] These debates are discussed more fully in chapter 7.

Thus some feminists have challenged the traditional feminist critique of the nature/culture duality in western thought as being colourblind. First, mainstream feminists have failed to analyse philosophy's need to find the biological or natural basis of racial differences, in the same way that they have analysed sexual differences. As a result, their analysis has focused on the 'wives' of western political theory, from Aristotle to Mill, rather than the 'slaves' or 'servants' or barbarians. As a result, western feminism has failed to see the different notions of power and authority exerted over women of colour as opposed to white women in these theories, and the profound commonality shared by men and women of colour vis-à-vis white men and women. Second, mainstream feminism has also failed to recognize and fully to analyse the specific ways in which women of colour's 'natures' have been constructed in texts, based on supposed 'biological traits'. From passive mother natures to Sapphires to sexual provocateurs, women of colour face categorization based on both their 'race' and their gender. In this chapter, it was shown how women of colour are also defined on the basis of 'natural' capacities, as possessing alternatively qualities of maternal care and passivity, or, as they organize collectively, qualities of aggression and incompetence. The critical point here is that 'biological' traits of race are constructed for cultural or ideological reasons, and shift around as the political sphere shifts. Feminism has simply not addressed this relationship between culture and nature vis-à-vis race in the same way that it has addressed sex.

The construction of gender-based cultural and natural realms in western political thought has thus been challenged by feminists. The duality has been seen as a means by which women have been either excluded from cultural and political life or distorted by the mirrored and interlinked images of both nature and women. Early second wave feminists, like Simone de Beauvoir and Shulamith Firestone, adopted the notion that culture must overcome nature; and women must somehow transcend their own biology and bodies in order to enter the cultural and political spheres. Other feminists challenged this assumption. Beginning with Plato, political philosophy is critiqued by Coole and others for imposing 'rational order' on what is seen to be the 'chaos' of reproduction, biology, nature and therefore, by definition, women. Aristotle's formulation of this relationship as the active rational principle of males giving form or shape to a passive and inert nature is challenged, in particular, by ecofeminists who see in Aristotle a paradigm, central to western philosophy as a whole, that is destructive of both nature and women. This paradigm, it has been argued, underpins modern science. Science as the conquest of nature by reason has since its inception claimed an objective distance between the rational subject and the inert, observable chaotic natural world. Through scientific method and technology, some order can be brought to bear, through the discovery of natural laws. Many feminists have resisted this notion of 'order', using both the environment and women's bodies as sites of resistance. From Hobbes's natural laws to Locke's theory of property to Marx's dialectical materialism, feminists have recognized that women remain attached to the natural sphere, through natural authority in the former two or their relationship to reproduction in all three. One of the key questions in modern political theory has been about the relationship between nature and nurture. While some feminists have adopted the liberal view that all is nurture, women and men are basically the same and gender differences are the result of socialization, others argue that men and women are different, based on their role in reproduction and motherhood, and such differences should be recognized and embraced. Finally, these second wave feminist critiques have been challenged by others who argue that the differences between groups of women have never been fully recognized. In particular, assumptions about identity and politics and the heterosexual nature of human beings, and the lack of analysis of the different ways in which 'nature' has been used to delineate people on the basis of both 'race' and gender, have undermined feminist critiques of the culture/nature divide in western political thought.

Having analysed the ways in which politics has been demarcated by the boundaries between public/private and culture/nature, and the feminist critiques of these boundaries, we will turn to look at three specific and current ideological frameworks in the next chapter and the ways in which the specific tenets of these ideologies reflect the underlying problems outlined in the first four chapters of this book.

5

Politics and Feminism: Deconstructing the Theoretical Frameworks

The study of western politics has created several theoretical frameworks. The three basic frameworks that we will examine in this chapter are liberalism (classical and welfare), socialism (and Marxism) and communitarianism. In each case, we will explore how 'politics' is defined, the basic tenets to which each subscribes, the ways in which the two sets of dualities described in the previous chapters inform or shape these frameworks and the feminist critique of each framework at the level of its basic tenets. This chapter aims to bridge the history of ideas of the previous three chapters with current paradigms of western political analysis, ideology and practice.

Liberalism

Liberalism is the most widely adopted theoretical framework in current western political thought. Its origins can be traced back to the seventeenth century, when thinkers such as Thomas Hobbes and John Locke challenged the heretofore dominant institutions of church and state by founding their political theories on individuals who, they claimed, had rights at birth and governments whose authority was based solely on the consent of those they governed. From its inception, liberal theory began with notions of a rational self-interested individual who theoretically consented to the rules and laws of government, and a government limited by the rights of individuals within a private sphere. Such theories of political right were reinforced by writers such as Adam Smith in the eighteenth century, who defended the economic rights of free markets and the constraints placed on government action by such rights.

Thus when John Stuart Mill came to write his famous essay, *On Liberty*, in the mid-nineteenth century, he constructed his theory of individual freedom on the economic and political foundations of Hobbes, Locke and Smith. Mill's main concern, however, was freedom. Liberalism had evolved from a theory which explained the origins of government, to one that defended the liberty of individuals and their private lives from the encroachment of government or society. Thus, classical liberalism is a political philosophy which limits the public sphere and political intervention in any individual's life to one single justification 'to prevent harm to others'.[1] Within this broad framework, liberal thought developed.

The first and most important tenet of liberal thought is the free and rational individual. Beginning with Descartes, modern philosophy as a whole has begun with the individual as the basic unit of analysis. This individual, in Cartesian thought, is, in the first instance, a rational mind, free from any external factors or prejudices. Through reason, this mind is able to discover general principles about the world which surrounds it, and make choices in its own self-interest. This basic premise of modern thought has application to political philosophy, particularly for liberal theorists. Liberals argue that civil society is, first, nothing more than the sum of its parts, namely all the individuals living within it, and, second, a place where individual interest will inevitably conflict. Government's basic role, therefore, is to preserve and protect the interests of the individuals that live within any given society by resolving conflict between them.

At the heart of this individualistic view of politics is a central belief in the capacity for reason in humans. Reason, since the time of Locke, is a prerequisite for citizenship. It is what distinguishes human beings from animals. The inevitable conflict in nature over scarce resources is resolved by animals through violence and aggression. Thus while animals may be social, they cannot be political. For human beings, politics replaces war or violence as the basis of resolving conflicts. It is because we have the capacity to reason that civil society is created. Without reason there can be no consent, no contract and thus no government.

Reason is also, for Mill and subsequent liberal thinkers, a prerequisite to happiness. Even within his utilitarian calculus of individual happiness, Mill distinguishes between higher pleasures which engage the intellect or reason and lower pleasures which do not. Finally, liberals from the time of Rousseau also argue that rationality is necessary to the exercise of true freedom, for choice without reason may be licence, in the same way that animals choose between one pleasure or another, but liberty for human beings consists in their capacity to make rational decisions. Thus reason is the basis of citizenship, happiness and freedom in liberal political theory. Liberals are aware, however, that people do not always act rationally and act instead in accordance with more natural instincts and emotions. As a consequence, free individuals, if they are to enjoy the maximum amount of happiness, must create the rule of law within which all free individuals must live and consent to an authority to enforce those laws, namely government.

The second tenet of liberalism, therefore, is the consent of the governed as the basis for political authority. If people are by nature free, the only basis upon which government may even be formed and in turn obeyed is if the citizens of that state agree, even if tacitly, to yield to this authority. This is the social contract theory of government. At the heart of this theory is the distinction drawn between a pre-political state of nature, wherein everyone is free to act according to his or her own particular will, and civil society, where they consent to act within a given set of collective laws. The contractarian view of government, from Hobbes and Locke to John Rawls, is based upon a belief that human beings can be stripped of every social, historical and geographical relationship and still be human beings. It is the political philosopher's version of Descartes's completely 'objective' mind. The pre-political state of nature asserts just such a universally atomistic, non-corporeal view of human beings.

The social contract establishes authority in government and the relations between the citizens who sign the contract. Given that the chief end of this contract is the protection and preservation of the individual to exercise his private right to life, liberty and property, authority within the family is, explicitly and by definition, outside the purview of the social contract. The scope of the contract is limited to the public sphere. Thus, the split between public and private life fully emerges, and the atomistic individual of the state of nature becomes the head of a private household, namely the sphere of property, children and wife where he exercises his own natural authority.

The third tenet of liberalism is the rule of law. What emerges simultaneously from this social contract is a set of rules which transcend not only the citizens of the state, but more importantly the rulers. Contemporary liberal theorists often point to regimes in the world today whose lack of a system of abstract, objective laws is a fundamental obstacle to their becoming 'democratic'. Arbitrary power, or individual rulers who can govern by virtue of their own caprice, is the very antithesis of a liberal political system. The liberal commitment to a rule of law is rooted in the principle that every individual, regardless of status or relationship with any other person in the state, should be governed and judged exactly the same as all others. The application of law should be done in strict accordance with abstract objective criteria and not in reference to any particular context of a given individual.

Liberal democratic states are often founded upon a fundamental constitution which lays out the limitations of any government in that state with regard to its citizens. From this higher form of law are derived the other laws which in turn ensure individuals do not transgress against each other. Like the original social contract, liberal constitutions are fundamentally concerned with not interfering in the private sphere of the individual and, as we shall see, the family. Thus, liberal laws from their inception were designed to govern the interaction of people in the public rather than the private world. The private world, in the liberal theorist's mind, was to continue to be governed by the laws of nature, the private morality of the individuals involved or religious tradition, but certainly not by government, laws or public opinion.

The fourth tenet of liberal thought is the belief in universal human rights, initially called 'natural rights'. Early liberal thinkers argued that human beings were born with certain rights. Beginning with Locke's right to life, liberty and property, the theory of natural rights was eventually transformed into a theory of 'human rights'. The list of rights to which liberals now subscribe is very long. The United Nations Declaration of Human Rights includes the freedom of expression, religion, movement, freedom from torture, arbitrary arrest and the right to social security, rest and education, among others. These rights are often broken down into two categories of rights: political or legal rights and social or cultural rights. Indeed, the United Nations has two covenants reflecting the two schools of thought on 'human rights'. Putting aside the political realities of the former Soviet and American superpowers in shaping these documents, the two sets of rights also reflect a division in liberal thought which emerged after the Second World War and will be considered in more depth in the next section.

Finally, and closely related to both rights and freedom of the individual, there is a belief in the equality of individuals. A notion of equality was first introduced into modern political thought by Hobbes's and Locke's natural rights theories. In the pre-political state of nature, all human beings were equal and free. As families formed, private property was created, civil society was established and eventually inequalities arose between people. These inequalities were explained and defended in various ways by liberal thinkers over the past 300 years. From Locke onward, it was largely argued that inequality between people rested on differences in the application of reason and industry. Nevertheless, a commitment to some form of 'equality of opportunity' remained; hence the strong emphasis by many liberal thinkers, beginning with Mill, on the importance of education in society. If people are taught how to exercise their reason and industry, the basic foundation of equal opportunity is established. The extent to which society or government are responsible for ensuring equality of opportunity in social and economic terms versus simply removing legal or political obstacles for any individual to pursue his or her own particular goal is the subject of great debate among the different schools of liberal thought which have emerged in the twentieth century.

Classical versus welfare liberalism

The first school of thinkers were the classical liberals, who believed in a limited government, freedom of the market and the political and legal liberties of religion, expression, conscience and the judicial system. In contrast to them a new form of liberalism, with roots back to the late nineteenth-century reform liberals, emerged in full force after the Depression and Second World War. Sometimes referred to as social welfare liberalism, this school of thought put more emphasis on equality of opportunity, the social or cultural rights to shelter, education, social security and collective bargaining, coupled with a concern for the least well off in society. As a result, this latter school believed in a much larger role of government to provide citizens with housing, schools, healthcare, welfare systems and union-friendly labour laws. Classical liberal thinkers include Frederick Hayek, Robert Nozick and Milton Friedman. Welfare liberalism was articulated by thinkers such as John Maynard Keynes and John Rawls. The basic premises of liberal thought – that is, the rational individual, freedom, rule of law and equality of opportunity – would be subscribed to by all these thinkers. The heart of the debate, which occurred at both a theoretical and a practical level in industrialized countries between 1950 and 1990, was over the role of government in achieving the ends to which they all aspired, and the extent to which society as a whole should concern itself with those who are the least well off.

For the classical liberal, freedom of the individual means the removal of any obstacles or barriers to the free expression of his or her reason or industry (given, by the rules of internal consistency, that these actions do not harm others' free expression). Beginning with Mill, the state's role is simply to ensure that none of the individuals within society suffers harm from others, from either within the society or outside of it. More recent theorists such as Nozick argue that the state must be kept to a minimum, and limited to the singular purpose of protecting individuals from harm and enforcing contracts.

> Our main conclusions about the state are that a minimal state, limited to the narrow functions of protection against force, theft, fraud, enforcement of contracts and so on, is justified; that any more extensive state will violate persons' rights not to be forced to do certain things and is unjustified.[2]

Classical liberalism has over the past twenty years also grown to include a robust defence of economic liberalism, or the free market. Economists such as Milton Friedman have argued that the role of the state in contemporary markets should be minimal, and allow for the free flow of goods and services. Monetarism, which placed a great emphasis on the shrinking of government in all fields, particularly those areas of greatest expenditure, namely the social envelopes of welfare, education and health, was embraced and implemented in many industrialized countries in the 1980s.

Welfare liberalism, on the other hand, argues that the state must concern itself with not only the freedom but the well-being of all its citizens, particularly those who are worse off. Equality of opportunity, therefore, is not simply the removal of legal obstacles to one's free expression, but ensuring that every individual has his or her basic needs met for shelter, food, clothing and education. Neither equality nor liberty means much if these basic rights are left unfulfilled according to welfare liberalism. Economists such as Keynes and Galbraith would argue that the state has an active role to play in the welfare of its country, to serve as both a catalyst for economic growth and a safety net for the marginalized. Perhaps the most highly developed theory defending welfare liberalism is John Rawls's *Theory of Justice*.

Rawls begins with what he calls the 'original position', conceived as rational individuals who exist outside of history and geography, who will create the principles upon which a state should be founded without reference to a particular social, economic or political status. Rawls concludes that if people were to form a political society without knowing where they might end up, they would ensure that the social contract would include provision for the least well off, and defend the freedom of all. Society or the state must therefore be involved in some form of redistributive justice.

Politics, as defined by liberal theory, and therefore underpinning most industrialized countries today, is fundamentally conceived as an implicit contract between the individual and the state. The individual is characterized by two qualities: the first is the capacity for reason, without which politics would be impossible; the second is natural authority or rights over the private sphere, without which politics would be unnecessary. To put it another way, the liberal state becomes necessary only when the individual needs to protect and preserve his private sphere from injury by others, and possible only if individuals are capable, through reason, to consent to government. As we examine each of the tenets of liberal thought in terms of its implicit, and often explicit, gendered nature, it is important to keep in mind these two fundamental dualities which anchor the very understanding of liberal politics: the public and private; and reason and irrationality.

Feminism and the liberal framework

Feminism has had with liberalism, like all the other theoretical frameworks, a multifaceted and complex relationship. On the one hand, many liberal feminists have used liberalism as a basic starting point for pushing towards their goal, namely the equality of women. Liberal feminists, by and large, accept the basic tenets of liberalism as laid out above, but suggest that women have simply been excluded from the liberal framework. Thus liberal feminists believe that women are as rational as men, but that historically they have not enjoyed the same rights as men, have not been subjected to the same rule of law, have therefore not been party to the contract of government and as a result to this day do not enjoy equality with men in any real sense of the word. In other words, liberal feminists do not challenge the fundamental tenets or premises of liberalism as wrong, simply that they must include women as well as men.

On the other hand, more radical feminists would argue that the basic tools of liberalism, the fundamental tenets, are essentially flawed and are constructed in such a way as to exclude women. Beginning with reason, postmodern feminists in particular question the liberal's claim that 'reason' and the unencumbered individual are truly gender free. Second, for different reasons, feminists have questioned the ideas of rule of law, abstract rights and contractual theories of government as fundamentally reflective of a male perspective on political theory and by their very definition exclusive of, or even hostile to, women. Finally, the goal of equality is seen by many radical feminists as misguided, in that it creates a project whereby women are forced to accept a male defined world, where equality becomes sameness and women give up what makes them different in order to become clones of men.

As we go through the critique of the liberal tenets listed above, we will consider the critiques of both liberal and radical feminists. What emerges is a rather complex picture of the various threads of feminist response to the liberal tradition.

The first tenet of liberalism is the 'rational individual'. Feminists who critique the concept of 'reason' or rationalism in modern political thought may be grouped into three broad categories. The first, who may be called 'rationalist feminists', fall largely within a liberal feminist framework and therefore do not challenge reason *per se*, or its centrality in the underlying structure of western philosophy. Rather, they argue that women have reason in the same way men do, but they have to be socialized and educated to use or exercise it. The second school of feminists, who may be called antirationalists, argue that 'reason' and 'rationality' are inherently masculine and some defend what they see as distinctively 'feminine' ways of thinking and knowing. It is not the distinction between reason and non-reason along gendered lines which is problematic, but the tendency of philosophy to undervalue that which does not emanate from rational thought and discourse.[3] The third school of thought is composed of the 'postrationalists' or postmodern feminists, who, in the words of Christine Di Stefano, 'refuse the linguistic and conceptual currency of rationalism altogether... postrationalism attempts to transcend the discourse of rationalism and to offer new decentered, and admittedly partial or fractured, narrative of opposition'.[4] This third group will be considered in more depth when we look at contemporary feminism. Let us consider the first two critiques of reason in more depth now; that is, the 'rational' feminist and anti-rationalist feminist.

Liberal thinkers such as Wollstonecraft, Mill and some contemporary liberal feminists defend the twin notions of reason and universal knowledge as the bedrock for scholarship, feminist or otherwise. For first wave feminists, it was critical that women receive the same education as men if they were to exercise their reason fully. Later liberal, and to a certain extent socialist, feminists have found themselves defending the notion of reason and knowledge against feminist scholarship, particularly postmodern critiques which find 'rationalism' fundamentally masculine. Liberal feminists have recently argued that the challenge made to 'reason' in anti-rationalist feminist critiques has been overplayed. To give up on any notion of a mind which can see from a universal and rational perspective is to give up on being able to see the polity from another, different, perspective. As Anne Phillips comments:

> Some of the contemporary feminist theory *does* overplay its hand, presenting the orthodoxy as more straightforwardly abstract and universal than is in fact the case . . . We do have to detach ourselves (however imperfectly and temporarily) from the crucial facts of our sex, our religion, our nationality, our class, our beliefs, so as to enter imaginatively into experiences that can seem so different from our own.[5]

Or as Nancy Hartsock comments, 'We must do our work on an epistemological base that indicates that knowledge is possible . . . if we are to construct a new society we need to be assured that some systematic knowledge about our world and ourselves is possible.'[6]

Liberal 'rationality', however, has been challenged by other 'rationalist' feminists, based on the conceptualization of 'reason' in much of liberal political philosophy. At the heart of the rationalist feminist critique of 'reason' are two basic challenges. The first is that liberal philosophy has created a notion of 'reason' which is not the objective capacity of the mind, free of any particular content that is claimed, but a concept with very specific content. Second, in conceptualizing reason in certain ways, philosophy has included and excluded certain ways of thinking or being. Beginning with Locke in his *Essay Concerning Human Understanding*, the capacity of reason is associated with certain traits and therefore certain groups of people:

The general reception of [God's] name . . . [proves] that they, who made the Discovery, had made a right use of their Reason, thought maturely of the Causes of things, and traced them to the original . . . The truest and best Notions Men had of God, [are] acquired by a right use of their Faculties: since the wise and considerate Men of the World, by a right and careful employment of the Thoughts and Reason, attained true Notions in this, as well as other things; whilst the lazy and inconsiderate part of Men, making the far greater number, took up their Notions by chance, from common Tradition and vulgar Conceptions, without much beating their Heads about them.[7]

Locke's conception of reason – that is, the specific content of the 'rational mind' – includes as its primary principle a unitary Christian God, and by extension excludes certain groups of 'lazy and inconsiderate men' who do not subscribe to the conclusions to which 'natural reason' leads them. Locke specifically includes among this number the indigenous peoples of the Americas. In other words, reason is to be distinguished from non-rational ways of thinking, 'tradition, vulgar conceptions'; it will lead to specific conclusions (i.e. God as the origin of everything) and ultimately reason will transcend these other ways of thinking. Thus within the conceptualization of 'reason' is the power to include and exclude. In Locke's political philosophy, as has been discussed in chapter 2, reason is also the basis of ownership in property and, by extension, political power: 'God, who hath given the World to Men in common, hath also given them reason to make use of it . . . He gave it to the use of the Industrious and *Rational*.'[8] Thus reason is the foundation of property, and property the basis of citizenship, the social contract and political power. '*Political* [power is] where Men have Property in their own disposal'.[9] Reason, or the failure to exercise it, is thus the basis upon which people may be excluded from having property, and therefore citizenship.

The problem with 'reason' in western political philosophy is not reason itself, according to rationalist feminists, but the way it has been conceived in specific texts and the conclusions which have inevitably been drawn as a result. The exclusion of either aboriginal people or non-aboriginal women from the realm of 'rational thought' is an ideological mistake of thinkers like Locke, who conceive of reason in such a way that it can be exercised by only a minority of people, namely property-owning European males.

Such arguments are fraught with problems according to one of the key anti-rationalist theorists, Genevieve Lloyd:

To affirm women's equal possession of rational traits, and their right of access to the public spaces within which they are cultivated and manifested is politically important. But it does not get to the heart of the conceptual complexities of gender difference . . . For it seems implicitly to accept the downgrading of the excluded character traits traditionally associated with femininity, and to endorse the assumption that the only human excellences and virtues which deserve to be taken seriously are those exemplified in the range of activities and concerns that have been associated with maleness.[10]

Seyla Benhabib argues that some of the earlier groundwork for the deconstruction of the 'rational individual' was laid by two key theorists: Karl Marx and Sigmund Freud.[11] Marx challenged the possibility of conceiving an individual outside of his or her social relations; that is, of a person in a pre-political 'state of nature'. Human beings are by nature, according to Marx, only explicable in the context of their multitude of historical and social relations. Marx also challenges the view that human beings can be split into mind or rationality and matter, and then use the products of the former (ideas) to be the stuff of history. Human beings and their history are rooted in the material world. For René Descartes or Francis Bacon to conceive of the possibility of a mind thinking before a body exists is not only ridiculous but the origin for much of western philosophy's wrong headed conclusions, according to Marx. Thus individuals can only be understood in terms of their relationship to other people and the things in the world around them. Class relations and labour thus become the foundations of Marx's political theory.

Freud challenges the notion of a rational individual from a psychological vantage point. Reason or rationality, far from transcending basic instincts and appetites in human beings, is actually a faculty which channels these stronger subconscious feelings into socially appropriate behaviour. As Benhabib points out, these two important schools of thought serve to break down the Cartesian notion of a rational subject which has been the underpinning of philosophy for several centuries:

The Hegelian and Marxist tradition also shows that the Cartesian ego is not a self-transparent entity and that the epistemic self cannot reach full autonomy as long as the historical origin and social constitution of the clear and distinct ideas it contemplates remain a mystery. This critique joins hands with the Freudian one which likewise shows that the self is not transparent to itself, for it is not 'master is its own house'. It is controlled by desires, needs, and forces whose effects upon it shape both the contents of its clear and distinct ideas, as well as its capacity to organize them.[12]

Postmodern thinkers have provided further critiques of the rational self, arguing that reason cannot be understood as 'objective' but must be understood as a social and historical construct, particularly in relation to power in any given society.[13]

Radical feminist scholarship in the twentieth century has thus been attracted to the work of Freud, Marx and postmodern critiques in their challenges to both an individualized conception of the world and the notion of a universal rational mind which exerts its will over one's own individual body and over 'matter' more generally. Feminists have gone beyond these critiques, however, to consider the role of gender in the conceptualization of 'the individual' and of reason over passion or mind over matter. Thus many anti-rationalist and postmodern feminist scholars have challenged the concept of the 'rational individual' based on the gendered nature of both 'reason' in philosophy and the 'individual' in political thought.

For some feminists, the construction of reason in political philosophy has particular significance in its capacity to exclude or hold power over women. Lloyd, in *The Man of Reason*, concludes that in western philosophy 'rationality has been conceived as transcendence of the feminine'.[14] From Descartes to Hegel, Lloyd analyses how reason is repeatedly distinguished from emotion, intuition and bodily instincts and desires throughout the canon of western philosophy. This distinction between reason and non-reason is simultaneously linked to masculine and feminine traits and personalities respectively. Finally, and most importantly, masculine reason is affirmed not only as having a greater value than all those things it is set against, but in transcending the feminine body, emotions and instincts.

Feminists have also questioned the notion of an abstract 'individual' mind, free from any historical or geographical context. Central to this 'universal' individual is the separation of mind and body in Cartesian logic. From Descartes to John Rawls, there is a belief in the capacity of reason or mind to transcend any particular geographical or historical context in order to discover universalizable 'truths' free of prejudice: in Thomas Nagel's phrase, 'the view from nowhere'. Feminists, such as Susan Bordo, argue that from the time of Descartes, rational thought is taken to be thinking which can completely detach itself from any associations, attachments, emotions or other extraneous factors, other than the mind itself. Deductive reasoning is thus purifying: 'A new theory of knowledge, thus, is born, one which regards all sense-experience as illusory and insists that the object can only be truly known by the perceiver who is willing to purge the mind of all obscurity, all irrelevancy, all free imaginative associations, and all passionate attachments.'[15] In this sense, the mind must transcend its own cultural and historical context; that is, it must transcend 'the body' in the pursuit of knowledge. Such a view of reason, for feminist postmodern thinkers such as Bordo, is misguided and masculinized.

> For Cartesian epistemology, the body – conceptualized as the site of epistemological limitation, as that which fixes the knower in time and space and therefore situates and relativizes perception and thought – requires transcendence if one is to achieve the view from nowhere, God's eye-view... For [the postmodern thinker] ... there is no escape from human perspective, from the process of human making and remaking of the world. The body, accordingly, is reconceived. No longer an obstacle to knowledge ... the body is seen instead as the vehicle of the human making and remaking of the world, constantly shifting location, capable of revealing endlessly new 'points of view' on things.[16]

The duality between mind and body and the implications for gender play an important role in current feminist debates and will be considered in more depth when we discuss contemporary feminism.

The second tenet of liberal political thought is that any legitimate government can be founded only on an implicit contract to which rational individuals consent. From John Locke onwards, liberal political theory divided the world into the public and private realms, and politics fundamentally into a relationship between the individual citizen and the state. Foremost among the critiques of this aspect of liberal theory is Carole Pateman's *The Sexual Contract*. Pateman argues that the social contract of early liberal theorists, whereby citizens agree to form a government, cannot exist without a sexual contract, whereby the authority within the family, between husband and wife, is also agreed to. This second contract is often overlooked in liberal political theory, but is critical to an understanding of the different implications these two contracts, social and sexual, have for citizens and their wives.

In essence, the social contract is the creation of political authority in the state by free men agreeing to obey the government based on their rational consent. The sexual 'contract', on the other hand, is the creation of conjugal authority in the family, through wives agreeing to obey the 'natural authority' of their husbands. In other words, while patriarchy was being attacked vociferously in the public sphere, it was being reinvented in the private sphere. The free and equal individuals of the natural state, Pateman argues, become either heads of private households (if they are male) or subject to the natural authority of their spouse (if they are female).[17]

By virtue of these two contracts, husbands represent their families in the public sphere. Civil society, therefore, was ultimately a fraternity of male-headed households. The move from the natural state to civil society is, for feminist scholars, suspect. As Susan Okin states:

> Having taken the fatal step of admitting women to that basic human equality upon which his system of politics is built, the only way in which Hobbes could justify their exclusion from political life, and the obvious inequality in contemporary society, was to substitute the male-headed family for the individual as his primary subject matter.[18]

For these reasons some feminists have concluded that the whole notion of contract theory is fundamentally flawed and impossible to apply without excluding at the very least the 'wives' of free men, and could have application to the female servants of whom Locke, at least, speaks of in terms of contract. Virginia Held states:

> To see contractual relations between self-interested or mutually dis-interested individuals as constituting a paradigm of human relations is to take a certain historically specific conception of 'economic man' as representative of humanity. And it is, many feminists are beginning to agree, to overlook or to discount in very fundamental ways the experience of women.[19]

While many feminists have attacked social contract theory, others have seen it as providing the basis for women's rights. By going back to the state of nature and the arguments made by Hobbes and Locke that all women and men are equal and free in their natural state, early feminist writers asked how liberals can conclude that civil society meant such a difference between men's and women's rights and freedoms in practice. In the words of Mary Astell: 'If All Men are born Free, how is it that all Women are born Slaves?'[20] Melissa Butler argues that early liberal attacks on partiarchalism lay the basic groundwork for later advances by writers like Mary

Wollstonecraft and John Stuart Mill, who argued in favour of women's rights.[21] Some feminists today still argue that is not only possible but desirable to use contract theory.[22]

The third and fourth tenets of liberal theory are a belief in the rule of law and the protection of universal human rights. The first challenge that feminists have made to these claims in liberal theory is the assumption of a political system based on abstract notions of justice. Carol Gilligan in her ground-breaking *In a Different Voice* argues that women understand ethical issues in a different way from men.[23] In essence, Gilligan makes two claims. Feminine reasoning tends to view interpersonal relations as critical to understanding any problem among a group of people. Second, feminine moral reasoning is concrete rather than abstract. In coming to a resolution about any issue, feminine reasoning will examine the context, the interrelationships of the people involved, the concrete details. Gilligan terms this type of moral reasoning 'the ethics of care', as opposed to the more traditional abstract moral reasoning, which Gilligan describes as 'the ethics of responsibility'. The former has historically, at least in moral psychology, been either ignored or seen as less evolved than the latter. Gilligan argues that we have been trained to listen to the masculine voice, which exhibits a Cartesian style of reasoning that limits context and specific details, and a desire to find abstract general principles to govern unspecified individuals. Thus the contrast between male abstraction and female specificity is critical to the liberal ideas of justice being fundamentally about an abstract rule of law and universal sets of rights.

A second critique of the rule of law that has been raised by feminist scholars concerns the public/private divide. Given that liberal laws were initially set up to protect and preserve the private sphere from interference by the government, many of the problems faced by women in the private sphere have traditionally not been subject to public discussion or legislation, but instead left to the authority of the head of the household. Issues ranging from the rearing of children to domestic violence to marital rape have until relatively recently been viewed as outside the purview of society or the state to address.

Equality is the last tenet of liberal political theory, in particular the equality of opportunity. Feminists are divided on their approach to the liberal notion of equality. On the one hand, liberal feminists have tended to argue that equality is the key goal for women – men and women should be treated essentially in the same manner by the state. Other feminists have argued that women are essentially different, and this difference must be respected. As Phillips comments, 'There has been a perennial see-saw between the universalizing aspirations of equality ("my sex does not matter, for I am human just like you") and the assertion of sexual difference ("I am a woman, and that does not make me less equal").'[24] Thus equality has been seen as the goal for liberal feminists and a potential pitfall for difference feminists. The latter argue that in demanding simple equality with men, without challenging more fundamentally the gendered nature of the political system, women will end up relinquishing what is different about them, what makes them women, in order to compete with men in the existing structures. The former would respond that in arguing in favour of difference, women risk falling back into biologically determined categories, roles and functions and accepting the definitions given to them by history and society rather than fighting for equal space and time alongside individual men.

If we look at the distinctions drawn between classical and welfare liberalism, we can begin to see how some of the questions that feminists have posed in liberal political theory, about the division between public and private, the abstract and the concrete, between equality and difference, actually play themselves out in the formulation of public policy. For classical liberals, the divide between public and private is held more strongly and what is encompassed by the private sphere is much greater (not just the family but the market and perhaps even healthcare and certain educational institutions), and therefore beyond the touch of political life. Classical liberals also believe that equality means nothing more than removing any political or legal obstacles to individuals achieving their goals – every individual citizen should be treated in exactly the same way. Any notion of affirmative action is thus seen as the state interfering in the private market. Finally, classical liberals often justify their views on the basis of abstract principles of freedom or individual autonomy. On the other hand, welfare liberals embrace a blurring of the public and private roles, where the state becomes involved in education, health, care for children and the elderly and social assistance to the poor. Over the past two decades welfare liberalism has also promoted a recognition of difference in the social and economic well-being of different groups within society. Groups which have historically been marginalized should be treated differently – for example, through affirmative action programmes – in order to address these inequalities. Thus welfare liberalism has tended to see individuals in their specific concrete social and economic context.

As the 1996 Presidential elections in the USA demonstrated, American women were more likely then men to embrace a welfare liberal vision and vote for Bill Clinton rather than Bob Dole. There are several reasons to explain this gender gap. First, the Democrats defended the state's role not in abstract terms but in areas which concern the concrete and specific needs of individuals and their families (health, education, social security for the elderly, family leave). Second, and related to the first point, is the perception that the Democrats were more concerned with the least well-off (and women fall disproportionately within this category or have responsibilities to care for those who do). This conclusion has been reinforced by polling results. For example, one poll of voters found 'when they were asked if they or anyone in their family would be likely to use a safety-net program a plurality of white men said no, but a strong majority of white women said yes'.[25] This sense of concern for the poor also relates to the perception of Clinton as someone 'who cares' and Carol Gilligan's thesis that women's moral decision-making tends to centre on questions of 'care' rather than abstract theories of rights or responsibilities. Third, the policies to support childcare and elderly care demonstrate that as women have moved from the private to the public sphere, they are more likely to support the notion that society and the state must take on more responsibilities traditionally associated with the family. 'A large majority of women would like to see some form of eldercare program, since they see themselves as facing the prospect of caring for aging parents or in-laws.'[26] Finally, on affirmative action programmes women are far more likely to be supportive than men. In a *New York Times*/CBS poll released one month before the election, the widest gap between men and women in a series of political views was on the question of abolishing affirmative action programmes. Some 52 per cent of men felt affirmative action programmes should be abolished compared to 36 per cent of women. Women are consequently more likely to support candidates and platforms which recognize difference in the status of different groups in society and respond with programmes to address those differences.

Thus the questions raised by feminists about the assumptions made in liberal political theory have important implications in our daily political life. From the question of the size of the public sphere, its role in the private sphere, to the concrete ways in which people are cared for in society, to support for a recognition of difference in affirmative action policies, the gap in views on politics is not simply between feminists and non-feminist political thinkers but, as the 1996 presidential election demonstrates, between women and men.

Socialism/Marxism

Socialism, as much as liberalism, is a product of modern political thought. Karl Marx, in particular, believed that his form of socialism was scientific in its understanding and universal in its application. While socialism and Marxism have, since the late 1980s, become less influential in the practice of politics, they nevertheless continue to be important to analyse as theoretical frameworks. Socialism dates back to the nineteenth century and the reaction of some French and British political thinkers to the industrial societies of their day. Robert Owen, Charles Fourier, Henri Saint Simon and William Thompson all argued in favour of a socialist vision of society. Their views were combined with German idealist philosophy and English political economy by Marx to create his own theory of 'scientific socialism'. Within this broad framework, socialist thought developed.

The first tenet of socialism is the focus on material production as the basic engine of history. Individuals are born into a given economic and social structure. In essence, while liberalism begins with the individual in order to explain the existence of government and society, socialism begins with the economic and social underpinnings of society in order to explain the existence of the individual. Production, and the conflicts which emerge as a result of the different relationships groups of people have with the means of production, lies at the heart of both history and politics, properly understood, according to Marx.

The second tenet of socialism is the division of labour. Throughout history, the production of material goods has created divisions depending on the labour of different individuals and the economic basis of society. Marx argues that labour is divided between the industrial and agricultural sectors and further between commercial and industrial labour. Furthermore, there are divisions within these branches. Throughout history, Marx argues that the division of labour has resulted in different classes of people who eventually come into conflict with each other.

The third tenet of socialism is a class analysis of society. Unlike liberals, socialist thinkers cannot see human beings as atomistic individuals, outside of the social and economic contexts within which they live and work. Thus, rather than a state of nature in which individuals clash with each another as individuals, the socialist, particularly the Marxist, believes that the most fundamental conflict in society is between economic classes. This conflict, as it evolves through history, is called 'dialectical materialism'. Thus, underlying Marx, like all western thinkers, is a fundamental duality. Nowhere is this more evident than in his analysis of class struggle. Ultimately, in capitalist society, there are two classes: the workers or proletariat who labour for wages and the capitalists who own the means of production. For Marx, the class struggle, while a central feature of history, will eventually lead to the overthrow of capitalist society in favour of control by the workers in a communist society.

A fourth tenet of socialism, particularly Marxism, is alienation. Unlike liberalism, which from its earliest roots believed that human beings through their labour expanded not only their own private property but the sphere of cultural knowledge in arts and sciences, Marxism believed that labour within a capitalist system resulted in alienation for workers from both the process and the product of their labour. Work was not an end in itself, but a compulsory activity to sustain mere life. Industrial labour, therefore, instead of being the most human activity possible, turned people into animals.

> Labour is exterior to the worker ... it belongs to another and is the loss of himself. The result we arrive at then is that man (the worker) only feels himself freely active in his animal functions of eating, drinking and procreating, at most also in his dwelling and dress, and feels himself an animal in his human functions. Eating, drinking, procreating, etc. are indeed truly human functions. But in the abstraction that separates them from the other round of human activity and makes them into final and exclusive ends they become animal.[27]

Marx argues that what is required to end alienation is for workers to be engaged in labour which produces a product of his own consciousness and will. 'Conscious, vital activity differentiates men immediately from animal vital activity... Alienated labour reverses the relationship so that, just because he is a conscious being, man makes his vital activity and essence a mere means to his existence.'[28]

A final tenet of socialism is a belief in the communal ownership of production. In its most extreme form, this means communism or the abolition of private property and the nuclear family. In other cases, this means national or state ownership of key economic sectors (steel, transport, oil, communications). For the utopian socialists, this means the application of the principle of communal ownership to individual companies.

As liberalism was critiqued by liberal feminists, so too Marxism and socialism has come under fire largely from feminists sympathetic to many of its tenets. The issue, as with liberal feminists, is to analyse the often implicit assumptions made about gender in this theory and the implications for women and to ensure that the future imagined in socialist theory responds to the concerns and interests of women as well as men.

We will look at each tenet in turn, but some general observations can be made in relation to the two basic dualities we have discussed, which define socialist political theory as much as liberal, namely the division between public and private, and culture and nature. Feminists' central critique of Marx and other socialists has been the almost exclusive focus on 'production' rather than reproduction. Like liberals, Marxist political theory has made the same division between public and private, analysing the former at the expense of the latter, failing to see the degree to which such an analysis explains only the history of men's labour rather than that of women in the household. Similarly, Marx assumes a duality between culture and nature where human beings must use their reason and industry to subdue nature.

> Nature does not construct machines, locomotives, railways, electric telegraphs, self-acting mules, etc. These are products of human industry; natural material transformed into organs of the human will to dominate nature or to realize itself therein. They are organs of the human brain, created by human hands; the power of knowledge made into an object.[29]

Like the 'politics' of liberalism, the 'economics' of Marx are those of the masculine public realm of industry and labour defined against the private realm of reproduction and the sphere of nature. As with liberalism, a set of key tenets can be found at the heart of socialism/Marxism.

The first tenet, namely material production as the fundamental engine of history, has been at the heart of many feminist critiques of Marxism. The first problem with Marxist analysis is its failure to explain why women are 'oppressed' as women, regardless of class. Heidi Hartmann comments: 'The early marxists failed to focus on the *difference* between men's and women's experiences under capitalism . . . how and why women are oppressed as women. They did not, therefore, recognize the vested interest men had in women's continued subordination.'[30] Consequently, Engels's solution for the emancipation of women, namely incorporating women into public employment, was doomed to failure. 'Patriarchal relations, far from being . . . rapidly outmoded by capitalism, as the early marxists suggested, have survived and thrived alongside it. And since capital and private property do not cause the oppression of women as *women*, their end alone will not result in the end of women's oppression.'[31]

Many of the Marxist feminists, in tackling this issue, developed a 'dual systems theory'. On the one hand, workers were oppressed by capitalism; on the other hand, women were oppressed by patriarchy.[32] For feminists like Hartmann, Iris Young and Juliet Mitchell, patriarchy becomes as central and fundamental a feature of history as the analysis of capitalism and production. While Marx identified both spheres of labour (production and reproduction) as worthy of analysis, the vast bulk of his work was concerned with only the former. Mitchell argues that one must understand both the material conditions of oppression in capitalist production and the non-material conditions of oppression in the family. Both must be attacked simultaneously: 'As the elimination of economic classes requires the revolt of the economic "underclass" (the proletariat), so the overthrow of the sexual classes similarly demands the revolt of its underclass (women). In both cases the revolution is not to conquer privilege but to eliminate distinction.'[33] It is worth noting that Mitchell is arguing, consistent with most second wave feminists, that men and women are essentially the same; the goal is to eliminate any kind of difference which currently exists between them.

Hartmann, while also a dual systems theorist, argues unlike Mitchell or Millet that patriarchy is not simply a matter of socialization and psychoanalysis, but has a real material basis, as much as capitalist production does. Feminists, she argues, have been too quick to accept the notion of Marxists that 'labour' or 'work' is something which can only be done outside the home. Thus Hartmann defines patriarchy as 'a set of social relations between men which have a material base, and which, though hierarchical, establish or create interdependence and solidarity among men that enable them to dominate women'.[34]

Iris Marion Young argues that dual systems theories are fundamentally flawed.

> However one formulates it, the dual system theory allows traditional marxism to maintain its theory of production relations, historical change, and analysis of the structure of capitalism in a basically unchanged form. Thus, not unlike traditional marxism, the dual systems theory tends to see the question of women's oppression as merely an additive to the main questions of marxism.[35]

Young's solution is to move away from notions of production and reproduction or class analysis and use instead the division of labour within any society as the basis of analysis. As the second tenet of Marxism and socialism, it is transformed by Young, who argues that through examining how labour is divided both within and outside the family, one can explain not only gender but racial inequalities, which traditional Marxist categories could not. Young concludes that women's labour forms a secondary labour force in capitalist society and therefore the marginalization of women is a fundamental characteristic of capitalism.

Marx himself states that 'the division of labour . . . was originally nothing but the division of labour in the sexual act . . . which develops spontaneously or "naturally" by virtue of natural predisposition (e.g. physical strength), needs, accident, etc. etc.'[36] What is curious about this statement is Marx's repeated references in his work to the 'natural' division of labour in the family, a claim he does not make about the division of labour outside the home under capitalist production. Marx goes on to say that this 'natural' division of labour only becomes a 'real' division of labour when distinctions are drawn between 'material and mental labour' in the realm of production outside the family.

One of the important outgrowths of the feminist critique of Marxist analyses of labour, and one which challenges the Marxist notion of classes, is the debate which has emerged around housework. In trying to define labour, many feminists, both liberal and Marxist, have analysed the peculiar nature of work within the home, and in particular why it is not paid for. In some cases, feminists have argued that housewives should be conceived of as a class. Thus Margaret Benston talks about a new class constituted by those responsible for the production of 'simple use-values in those activities associated with the home and family'.[37] Some feminist critics argued that women should be paid a salary for the labour they do in the home, a campaign which came to be known as 'wages for housework'. Interestingly, other Marxist feminists argued against such a strategy. This debate has evolved and emerged in mainstream economic debates about what is now called 'unpaid work'. Marilyn Waring, author of *If Women Counted*, argues that much of the productive labour which is done in the world is simply not counted in the calculation of national accounts.[38] Governments have begun to accept this analysis and at the UN Conference on Women in Beijing in September 1995, the governments represented there agreed to the principle that unpaid labour should be accounted for in the national accounts of their finance ministries.

The fourth tenet of socialism, namely alienation, is a concept which appeals to many feminists. The notion that labour can be controlled by someone else, is uncreative and is only done to maintain one's existence, is something which resonated with many of those feminists analysing women's labour in the world. Alison Jaggar uses 'alienation' as the central concept in her analysis, *Feminist Politics and Human Nature*.[39] For Jagger, the difficulty with Marx was not so much his notion of alienation as his failure to explain it in 'gender-specific' ways.

Jagger's project, therefore, is to remedy this by applying the concept of alienation to women's experience. She does this under three categories – sexuality, motherhood and intellectuality – concluding that women are alienated from their own sexuality in conforming to their roles as sexual objects or commodities, from motherhood through the process of obstetrics and scientific experts and from her own intellectuality by a world of ideas whose terms have been set down by men.

Finally, feminists have taken aim at the 'communist society', envisioned in particular by Marx. First and foremost, following from the general analysis above, Marxist feminists argue that the overthrow of capitalism and beginning of communist society alone may be a necessary but is not a sufficient condition to ensure women's emancipation. Second, the abolition of the family has drawn criticism from feminist critics. In *Public Man, Private Woman*, Jean Bethke Elshtain was critical of the Marxist depiction of family as a creature of capitalism, instituted for the sole purpose of reproducing labour and enslaving women. For Elshtain, the family was the single place in capitalist society where one could escape the uglier sides of a profit-driven economy. Elshtain was firmly against the abolition of the family, to be replaced by communal childrearing. She argued that children deprived of daily contact with parents would be much worse off. Finally, Elshtain, like critics of liberal feminism, takes aim at the abstract logic and language which feminist Marxists have adopted, resulting in a language and point of departure alien to women in general, but in particular mothers.

> Ask any mother whether she would accept 'producing the future commodity labour power' as an apt characterization of what she is doing. One's fears and love for children are drained of their meaning, their emotional significance . . . By their choice of an abstracted, reductionist language, marxist feminists confound ordinary language and evade the serious questions that arise when one attempts to express and examine the depth and complexity of family relations. Within the boundaries of econometric discourse, issues that emerge when one takes the human subject and her relations as a starting point simply disappear.[40]

Communitarianism

In response to the political frameworks postulated by both socialist and liberal thinkers, a group of thinkers, known as communitarians, have recently posed an alternative basis for political analysis. Sceptical of what they perceive to be the unbridled individualism and the free market embraced by classical liberals on the one hand, and the bureaucratic state reflected in both welfare liberalism and state socialism on the other hand, the communitarians put the 'community' at the heart of their political theory instead. Communitarianism begins with a critique of John Rawls's *Theory of Justice* and the 'unencumbered individual' which underpins it. Because every person is born into a community with certain goals and purposes, one's identity and relationship to others in the society can only be understood in this context. As Michael Sandel states:

> Communitarian critics of rights-based liberals say . . . certain of our roles are partly constitutive of the persons we are – as citizens of a country, or members of a movement, or partisans of a cause. But if we are partly defined by the communities we inhabit, then we must also be implicated in the purposes and ends characteristic of those communities.[41]

Thus, 'community' takes on both analytical and normative forms: analytical in the sense of simply recognizing and taking account of the historical and geographical context within which any individual is living; normative in the sense that communities are perceived to have a common purpose or good which has implications for individuals and how they live together. In essence, individuals are seen as citizens of a community as well as being individuals with rights. Communitarianism, as we shall see in looking at its basic tenets, is both an ethical and a political response to liberal democracy as it is practised in the second half of the twentieth century.

The first tenet of communitarianism is, thus, the notion of a 'situated self', as opposed to the 'unencumbered self' of liberal thought. Communitarians begin by challenging the liberal premise that an individual can be conceived of outside of society and history, namely in the pre-social state of nature of early liberal thought or John Rawls's 'original position', arguing that human beings can only be understood, even in the abstract, within a given historical and geographical context. Within this concept of a situated self are several related ideas.

The first challenge that communitarians make to the liberal notion of 'self' is the relationship between the self and its 'ends'. Thus Sandel and MacIntyre take exception to the existentialist and liberal notion that an individual can exist first as a 'self' who then chooses the purposes or ends for his or her individual life. In the words of liberal theorist Rawls, 'The self is prior to the ends which are affirmed by it; even a dominant end must be chosen from among numerous possibilities.'[42]

Sandel's response to this free-floating rational self is to assert that communitarians 'cannot conceive ourselves as independent in this way, as bearers of selves wholly detached from our aims and attachments'.[43] In the words of one commentator on Sandel, 'A self that is as open-ended as the liberal conception requires would be not so much free as *identityless*.'[44] Identity has become a critical aspect of political theory in recent years. The communitarians argue that a self without identity cannot be considered human, in any sense of the word at all. Alasdair MacIntyre makes a similar case, arguing a narrative conception of self with a *telos* or purpose in it. For MacIntyre, one's identity, or notion of 'self', is thus not independent of one's purpose, but constituted by it.[45]

The liberal notion of 'self' is also challenged by communitarians on the basis of its relationship to others. From its inception, liberal theory has argued that the self is completely independent of others. Communitarians believe that the self is 'situated' not only in terms of the values and ends of its own personal narrative but in terms of its relationship to others in the community in which it develops and the overall purposes to which the community itself aims. MacIntyre states: 'I am part of their story, as they are part of mine. The narrative of any one life is part of an interlocking set of narratives.'[46] The purposes which inhere in any community are critical to who we are. 'If we are partly defined by the communities we inhabit, then we must also be implicated in the purposes and ends which characterise those communities . . . the story of my life is laws embedded in the story of those communities from which I derive my identity – whether family or city, tribe or nation, party or cause.' Finally, as Sandel goes on to argue, the 'situated self' has moral, not just psychological, import. 'On the communitarian view, these stories [of communities] make a moral difference . . . They situate us in the world, and give our lives their moral particularity.'[47]

This brings us to the second tenet of communitarianism, namely a republican belief in 'public good' and civic virtue. MacIntyre writes that justice is to be found in 'a community whose primary bond is a shared understanding both of the good for man and the good for the community'. It is the thought of Aristotle and Hegel which underlies the communitarian commitment to a public good, but shaped in the second half of the twentieth century to challenge the most basic of liberal premises: protection of individual rights. Sandel and MacIntyre, in particular, juxtapose the notion of the common good against the liberal defence of rights. Sandel is enough of a liberal, however, to state: 'individual rights cannot be sacrificed for the sake of the general good'.[48]

Michael Walzer gives some specific shape to what these public goods might look like. 'Membership is important because of what the members of a political community owe to one another and to no one else, or to no one else in the same degree. And the first thing they owe is the communal provision of security and welfare.'[49] This means that within a community, need and membership must be recognized, and responded to.

The third and final tenet of communitarianism, which follows from the first two but has fundamental implications for the way political goods are distributed in society, is the belief in the local community as tending to the needs of the people from that community. Communitarians thus wish to move away from dependence on either the welfare state, a remote and bureaucratic means of looking after citizens' needs, or the liberal market, for the distribution of society's goods. Sandel comments:

> Where the liberal regards the expansion of individual's rights and entitlements as unqualified moral and political progress, the communitarian is troubled by the tendency of liberal programmes to

displace politics from smaller forms of association to more comprehensive ones. Where libertarian liberals defend the private economy
and egalitarian liberals defend the welfare state, communitarians
worry about the concentration of power in both the corporate
economy and the bureaucratic state, and the erosion of those inter-
mediate forms of community that have at times sustained a more
vital public life.[50]

Thus, communitarians have a tendency to look towards the family,
cultural communities and local neighbourhoods for the service of
needs.

The feminist response to communitarianism has been mixed. On
the one hand, some feminists have found in communitarianism
tenets which concur with their own suspicions about liberalism
and the unencumbered individual. In particular, the notion that
one can only be understood within a given historical and social
context and not as a free-floating individual is appealing to many
feminist analyses. Similarly, the claims on behalf of communities to
limit certain 'rights' or freedoms has created strange bed-fellows
between conservative communitarians and some feminists on issues such as pornography, prostitution and the value of unpaid
work. Finally, the challenge by some communitarians to the libertarian ideology of the 1980s and the overarching belief in free
markets as the solution to many of our political problems has been
shared by many feminist writers.

On the other hand, feminists have found great dangers in the
communitarian framework. First and foremost is the potentially
conservative nature of the ideology, appealing to an overly romanticized view of a traditional community, where the status quo is
not only given but often embraced. Second, feminists have questioned the potentially profound implications of the communitarian
search for a common purpose or unity. In particular, concerns are
raised about diversity and difference in such a theoretical framework. Women of colour, lesbians and other historically marginalized
groups may be the victims of this denial of difference. Third, many
feminists argue that the move towards 'community' as the locus
of politics has often shifted many important political tasks from
federal and regional governments to local groups. This has meant,
in practice, that more work falls upon the shoulders of unpaid
women, either in their homes or through volunteer work. Finally, for
liberal feminists, the curtailing of rights by some notion of a public
'good' tends to undercut women's capacity as individuals to challenge an overall system on the grounds of individual discrimination.

Such challenges in the past have resulted in important gains for women.

If we begin with the first tenet of communitarianism, namely the notion of a situated self, we begin to see the variety of feminist responses. While feminism has challenged, like communitarianism, the liberal notion of a rational and disembodied self, as we have discussed in the critique of liberalism, the communitarian approach is equally problematic to the extent that it views the self or subject as the product rather than the generator of social reality. If individuals do not have any ontological status – that is, existence – outside of the social relations which constitute them, then how can anyone seek to challenge the culture into which he or she is born? As Elizabeth Frazer and Nicola Lacey comment, 'On this communitarian view of personhood, the woman who lives in a sexist and patriarchal culture is peculiarly powerless. For she cannot find any jumping-off point for a critique of the dominant conception of value: her position as a socially constructed being seems to render her a helpless victim of her situation.'[51]

Many feminists, however, agree with the second argument made by communitarians about the unencumbered liberal self, namely that it does not account for the relationship of the self to others in any given community and the extent to which one's reality is shaped by one's social and political relations. The difficulty in communitarianism for many feminist thinkers is when traditional models, such as the family, are used as the model for the larger community. It is at this point that communitarianism is in danger of becoming conservative and romantic, and of constructing a new form of female oppression. Amy Gutmann comments in a critical comparison of both Marxist (old) and communitarian (new) critiques of liberalism:

> The political implications of the new communitarian criticism are . . . more conservative . . . the good society of the new critics is one of settled traditions and established identities. For many of the old critics, the role of women within the family was symptomatic of their social and economic oppression; for Sandel, the family [is] a model of community and evidence of a good greater than justice.[52]

It is the idea of 'settled traditions' and 'established identities', coupled with a drive towards unity, which poses a key problem for feminists regarding respect for difference and diversity. Iris Marion Young warns that to the extent feminists take on communitarianism, as a framework, they must recognize its tendency towards unity and repression of difference:

> The striving for mutual identification and shared understanding among those who seek to foster a radical and progressive politics . . . can and has led to denying or suppressing differences within political groups or movements. Many feminists groups, for example, have sought to foster relations of equality and reciprocity of understanding in such a way that disagreement, difference and deviation have been interpreted as a breech of sisterhood, the destruction of personal relatedness and community.[53]

Communitarianism, in other words, in seeking to find unity may continue to repress those who have historically been marginalized on the basis of their colour, class or sexuality.

The second tenet, namely a belief in the notion of a public good realizable only through membership in a community, which precedes any idea of rights in society, is a direct challenge to liberalism's reliance on a charter or bill of rights as the basis of any society. For feminist communitarians, like Jean Bethke Elshtain, liberalism's greatest flaw is the tendency towards fragmentation as a result of ever more virulent demands for individualistic rights.

> Rights cannot stand alone. Rights cannot come close to exhausting who and what we are. Should we try to understand why we stay up all night with a sick child . . . or spend hours helping to provision the victims of a natural disaster (like a flood or a hurricane) in and through 'rights talk' we would seriously distort these socially responsible and compassionate activities. We know this in our bones. Yet each time we feel called upon to justify something politically, the tendency is to make our concerns far more individualistic and asocial than they, in fact, are by reverting to the language of rights as a 'first language' of liberal democracy.[54]

Such a belief in a public good existing outside of a rights framework has allowed for strange political alliances between radical feminists like Andrea Dworkin or Catharine MacKinnon, communitarians and even the Christian right on an issue like pornography. For different reasons, these groups believe that the community's sense of public good (in not degrading women through pornography) is more important than the right of free expression for those who wish to consume pornographic material.[55] Similarly, in sexual assault cases, the right of the accused has often come up against the idea that there are other greater goods at stake if his rights are left uncurtailed by legislation for the good of society. For example, the right of an accused rapist to conduct his own trial (which has happened recently in the UK and Canada), and thereby to cross-examine and potentially harangue the very person he may have raped, has been defended by civil rights advocates but challenged by many feminists as violating a sense of public or moral good.

The tension between the rights of the individual and a public good is present in both liberal and communitarian thought. While feminists like Elshtain tend to support the latter, there are some liberal feminists who argue that in giving up rights in favour of some notion of a general good, women risk losing one of their most powerful tools, namely challenging individual cases of discrimination in court. If there is one tool that liberal feminism gives women, beyond the sense of a free and choosing self described above, it is the idea of having rights through which a woman may challenge discrimination. As Fraser and Lacey comment:

> For liberal feminism, women are free and choosing subjects who have been discriminated against. They exercise their individual subjectivity by asserting their rights and pointing out the injustices of their situations. Liberal feminism, indeed, has operated as a powerful critique ... To the extent that, for example, job segregation, low pay or sexual harassment constitute discrimination, in the sense of adverse and differential treatment of women on sexual grounds, the liberal feminist can identify and oppose these phenomena.[56]

Finally, placing a public good before individual rights has been critiqued by liberal feminist thinkers for its tendency towards authoritarianism. 'The only really envisagable world which is sufficiently homogenous to keep the communitarian subject together is an authoritarian one.'[57]

The public good can be defined in any number of ways. Michael Walzer, as we have discussed, provides a compelling argument that the communal provision of security and welfare is the one public good that must be upheld. If this definition is taken to be 'care', than many feminists would endorse Walzer's claim that the 'care' of society's members from the youngest to the oldest must not exist strictly within the private sphere, as this creates the double burden experienced by women in today's world. Rather, the welfare and security of individuals in society must be the concern of the community as a whole. The question of 'care' as a public and political, as opposed to private, issue has been the subject of considerable feminist writings since the 1970s. Care for children, elderly parents and disabled family members has traditionally been thought of as a private concern. As women have moved from the private sphere into the working world, there has been pressure to find answers within the public sphere for such individuals.

The final tenet of communitarianism is the belief in the community, rather than the welfare state or free market, as the best mechanism for the distribution of goods in society. Feminists have argued that such a view of community as the benefactor and caretaker of society's social ills is both romanticized and lacking in a gender analysis. It has been noted, by some critics, that both Margaret Thatcher and Ronald Reagan used the idea of community to devolve many government responsibilities – for example, 'community care' for the mentally ill, or 'community service' for minor criminal offences, or the voluntary sector for everything from food to healthcare – assuming that there was a community to fill the gap. 'The relevant communities were often fragmented or nonexistent, as former prisoners, victims of mental illness and other homeless people now sleeping on the streets of American and British cities can readily testify.'[58] Moreover, it is argued, in turning over these responsibilities to the community, either in theory or in practice, it is often unpaid women, either as family members or as part of voluntary organizations, who become particularly responsible for filling the vacuum.

Examining the main theoretical frameworks for modern politics and the feminist critique of these frameworks has provided an analysis of how gender and politics intersect, at the level of ideology. Specifically, this chapter has shown how feminism has challenged the precepts of the existing theoretical frameworks on the basis that they excluded, distorted or ignored women in their analysis. So far, we have examined feminism in terms of the history of western political thought. In the following two chapters, we will examine the evolution of feminism in its own terms. Rather than simply trying to incorporate women into an existing framework – that is, pushing women into the spheres from which they have been excluded (cultural and public) – feminism can be seen as increasingly a challenge to the underlying structure of politics itself, and the boundaries by which it has been demarcated. In short, feminism has its own perspectives, its own voices, its own histories. Thus, having examined the feminist response to traditional political theory and the amended frameworks consequently produced, we will now turn to look at the development of feminism in its own terms, from first wave, through second wave and eventually to a third wave of feminism(s).

6

First and Second Wave Feminism: Challenging the Dualisms

Throughout the history of feminist thought, the relationship between western politics, or more particularly political theory, and feminism has largely been reflected in the way in which the latter has been, until recently, categorized by the former. Feminism, in other words, was hyphenated: liberal feminism, socialist feminism, Marxist feminism, psychoanalytical feminism and radical feminism. More recently, postmodern feminism has been added to the list of feminist schools of thought. Such categorization has always been dependent on a marriage between a school of thought outside of feminism and the feminist variation of that school. As such, feminism is a modifier, and always the second term, to the larger, referent, theoretical framework.[1] Furthermore, second wave feminism found itself, by virtue of these marriages, both ideologically discordant and often rigid, as each branch of feminism held to the theoretical framework with which it was partnered. Any contradictions which arose as a result, either with other feminists or with their larger theoretical framework, were the source of great tension, as second wave feminists struggled to make their world coherent, consistent and unified; as their view of feminism demanded.

The practice of politics – that is, the changes which feminists argue must be made in order to meet their objectives – has varied with each theoretical framework. In the case of liberal feminism, it has been the fight for equal rights with men within a liberal democratic framework in both first and second wave feminism; for socialist or Marxist feminists, it has been the push for fundamental changes to the economic system through a collectivization of both the production and reproduction of life; for psychoanalytical feminists, it has been a reworking of the ways in which children and parents interact from the beginning of life. In each case, the goals of another framework have been adapted to those of feminism.

Such marriages between mainstream political theory and feminist thought have, in recent years, been challenged by feminists themselves. Indeed, many feminists have come largely to reject the need to attach themselves to a mainstream school of thought, beginning instead with their own premises (based on a different set of experiences and perspectives) and then incorporating those aspects of other theories (whatever their label) which add to their analysis. Feminism, in its current multiple forms, often cuts across a variety of theories exactly because it begins with different premises from any of them. Thus a lesbian feminist might simultaneously defend the right of privacy (traditional liberal tenet), the social constructedness of identity (postmodern tenet) and materialism as the basis of political power (socialist tenet). Internal consistency and with it the sense that there is 'one' form of feminism free from contradiction has been challenged, in particular, by a new generation of feminists who celebrate multiplicity and reject, from their point of view, the rigid 'ideals' of second wave feminism.[2]

In examining contemporary feminist thought and its evolution, I would argue that we have entered the age of third wave feminism(s). In order to recognize this shift, feminists themselves must look afresh at where they are now, as well as their own history. Rather than continuing to try to categorize different theorists within the various forms of hyphenated feminist thought (which always tended to box individuals into categories they were not entirely comfortable with), feminism must be seen from the perspective of its *own* evolution, not that of its theoretical partners, and include the diversity of voices which have been present throughout its history. The historical development of feminism is an evolution from being largely subsumed within another framework, namely liberalism (first wave feminism), to a marriage with traditional political theoretical frameworks, which involved inserting women into a modified male world of politics, to a period of separation and renegotiation of the marital contract (second wave feminism), to an independent position or rather set of positions (third wave feminism(s)) which try to define politics from an overlapping and even contradictory set of women's perspective(s).[3]

First wave feminism was a period where feminists largely argued from a position completely contained within liberalism. The second wave of feminist thought is hyphenated feminism, with different theoretical frameworks but united by a commitment to sameness, equality, universality and scientific understanding. The third wave of feminism(s) begins by questioning these basic premises, yielding up instead ideas like difference, particularity, embodiment, multiplicity, contradictions and identity. With it has come a destabilization of the dualities inherent in the second wave, from culture/nature to public/private to man/woman. The roots of this critical shift can be found in the adoption of the motto 'the personal is political', which challenged not only the public/private divide but also the scientific distance always assumed as between culture, mind and subject versus nature, matter or object, as will be discussed. The new wave has hit not only the shores of academia, but the wider world of women and politics, as expressed succinctly in the overarching theme for the UN World Conference on Women, held in Beijing in 1995: 'Seeing the world through a woman's eyes.'

The dualities that have underpinned political theory, as described in the previous chapters – between culture and nature, and between public and private, and even between man and woman – have evolved and to a great extent unravelled as feminism has developed through the three waves. Beginning with the first wave of feminism, dualisms remained unchallenged, the values attached to each assumed by early feminist thinkers. In many ways, as we shall see, the first wave feminists who fought for civil rights on behalf of white middle- and upper-class women, accepted women's role in the private sphere as a given; indeed, they used the ideal of 'motherhood' and the 'lady of the house' to further their claims that women were more attached to the cultural and civil realm than men. It was exactly her role in the private sphere which made her uniquely qualified to contribute to the political sphere in the form of her vote.

Second wave feminism continued to accept the dualities inherent in modern political theory, but broadened the arena to which women should gain access. Not only was the 'cultural realm' under attack, but now too the 'public realm' of work and politics was equally being challenged for its exclusion of women. The goal, therefore, was primarily to get women (again primarily white middle-class women) 'in' – inside the spheres of the political and cultural realms – and make them the 'equals' of men, no longer outside or marginalized, or 'the other', by their relation to the natural or private spheres. The means by which this movement and therefore 'equality' would be achieved varied according to different schools of hyphenated feminist thought. At the heart of second wave feminism has been the question of 'reproduction'. Reproduction in terms of both childbearing and childrearing is central to the traditional political definitions of 'natural' and 'private', and therefore outside the boundaries of political theory. As feminists made inroads into both the theoretical and practical worlds of politics (the cultural and public realms), it was recognized that the spheres being vacated by many women (the private and natural) were becoming difficult to sustain, in their existing forms. As feminists encouraged women to leave the former spheres, the movement simultaneously created a need to reconstruct the latter. Rather than, at this point, fundamentally challenging the dualisms themselves, feminism, particularly liberal feminism, has instead argued that as certain groups of women move into the public/cultural spheres, men have simultaneously to move into the private and natural spheres. This has not been entirely successful. Instead of men filling the spaces vacated by these women, they have been increasingly filled by poor women of colour. By taking on the role of 'wife' and 'servant', these women, defined along racial and class lines, have, as discussed, continued to maintain the private and natural spheres which underpin politics from Aristotle's *oikos* to Rawls's original position. Finally, because second wave feminism, in all its theoretical manifestations, claimed for itself a universality of both historical cause and the goals for the potential future, its adherents have believed that it could both accommodate and transcend individual differences, by uniting women in the goal of entering the cultural and public realms. This would only be achieved, however, if feminists brought down these barriers as a unified force.

Third wave feminisms have come to question second wave feminism and, with it, the categories themselves, the dualisms inherent in political theory and the way in which they structure not only gender and politics, but race, identity and sexuality. At the same time, feminists have questioned the values attached to the cultural realm over the natural, the public over the private and the assumed duality of man/woman. The earliest roots of second wave feminism can be found when feminists began to revel in their role as 'other' or 'outsider' rather than setting as their goal getting 'inside' the realms of either public or natural. As feminists celebrated the differences between men and women, they reaffirmed the categories of nature, sexuality and motherhood which have been devalued by political thought for so long. At the same time, third wave feminisms are marked by the attempt to break down the duality of men/women. The assumption of man/woman as a binary whole not only assumed a heterosexual model, but made other divisions (for example, 'race' or 'class') marginal.[4] To what extent 'difference' and 'woman' can be reconciled with 'differences' and 'women' lies at the heart of many current feminist debates about 'the political'. Third wave feminism, particularly the younger generation feminists, as we shall see in the next chapter, argue that attempts at seamless unity are pointless; instead, we must learn to live with contradiction and multiplicity.

In order to understand the debates which are now occurring in contemporary feminist thought, it is necessary to trace this evolution in its own terms. The movement from incorporation in liberalism, to marriage with traditional political theory, to trial separation, to newly found independence can best be understood in terms of feminism's relationship to the dualities used throughout this book, between man/woman, public/private and culture/nature. We begin in this chapter with first and second wave feminism.

First Wave Feminism

The goal for most of the first wave feminists was largely to get white middle- and upper-class women inside the public and cultural world from which they were excluded.[5] In keeping with liberal tenets, they argued that women were rational, differences between men and women were largely social rather than natural in origin and therefore education and training could make women citizens in the same way men were. The goal was equality. The general themes of this early movement were virtue, equality, rationality and nurture over nature. Most of these feminist writings did not fundamentally challenge the public/private divide. It was assumed that this distinction must be made and that it would be divided along gender lines. Indeed, in some cases an argument was made that women's role within the private sphere enhanced their claim to be both more cultured and more rational than men, and therefore worthy of citizenship. It was only during the latter part of first wave feminism and the early part of second wave feminism that feminists began to challenge women's exclusion from the public sphere and their role in the private sphere, as shall be discussed.

Mary Wollstonecraft was one of the first modern feminist writers. She published her essay *A Vindication on the Rights of Women* in 1792, in response to Rousseau's political and educational writings, which differentiated the roles of men and women based on 'nature'. In particular, Wollstonecraft challenges Rousseau's claims that women were irrational, or lacked rationality. She argues that in denying them the capacity for reason, Rousseau denies women not only the right of citizenship but their basic humanity. Her focus, therefore, was to ensure that white middle- and upper-class women were not excluded from the sphere of reason and language, for surely this is what differentiated all human beings, both men and women, from animals. At the heart of her theory is the very liberal premise that women have the capacity for reason by nature (as men do), but have not been properly educated to exhibit the right values and virtues. Citizenship is thus a matter of nurture rather than nature, and women must be included in cultural education in the same way that men are. Clearly Wollstonecraft does not see any need to challenge women's role in the private sphere. Indeed, she not only leaves the private sphere intact but argues that through education, women could fulfil this role even better, defining the familial functions as the duties of women's citizenship: 'Would men but generously snap our chains, and be content with rational fellowship instead of slavish obedience, they would find us more observant daughters, more affectionate sisters, more faithful wives, more reasonable mothers – in a word, better citizens.'[6]

John Stuart Mill and many of those who fought for women's right to vote in the nineteenth century joined Wollstonecraft in the reinforcement of women's role in the private sphere, while challenging the assumption that women should be excluded on the basis of her irrationality or closeness to nature, emotion and instinct. Like Wollstonecraft, Mill is mainly interested in writing about white middle- and upper-class women. Mill argues that while these women should have the option of working outside the home, he assumes that most of them will choose to fulfil themselves as mothers and wives.

> Like a man when he chooses a profession, so, when a woman marries, it may in general be understood that she makes choice of the management of a household, and the bringing up of a family, as the first call upon her exertions, during as many years of her life as may be required for the purpose; and that she renounces not all other objets and occupations, but all which are not consistent with the requirements of this.[7]

It should be noted that the first seeds of a breakdown in the link between women and the private sphere is provided by Harriet

Taylor Mill, who disagreed strongly with her husband on the issue of women entering the public realm. In terms of both work and politics, women must, if they are to be equals, share in the work associated with both the earning of money and the dispensation of that which is taxed. It becomes clear that Taylor's vision is limited to middle- and upper-class women, as she refers to the 'panoply of domestic servants' which would be necessary if the women to which she is referring are to combine marriage and work outside the home. Taylor's voice is a lone one in the nineteenth century. By and large, feminists are not challenging the exclusion of women from the public realm and their relegation to the private sphere.

Most of the white suffragists took up this dichotomy between public and private, within the context of Victorian morality, to bolster their case for white middle-class women being more closely associated with reason, culture, civility and men were more likely to fall victim to their animalistic side of their natures, through instincts such as passion, greed and lust.

> What was the response of the Suffragists to arguments that woman was pure, private and apolitical and man was immoral, public and political (because his sphere was)? Rather than rejecting the conceptual system from which these dichotomies were a predictable outgrowth, the Suffragists turned anti-Suffrage arguments upside down to serve as the basis for a pro-Suffrage plea. Yes, man was evil and bad and he had made something nasty out of politics. True, woman was purer and more virtuous; look at the way she had ennobled the private sphere. What must be done therefore is to throw the mantle of private morality *over* the public sphere by drawing women into it.[8]

In other words, it was her role in the private sphere, and the virtues associated with it, which made the white middle-class woman uniquely qualified to be part of the cultural, rational realm and, therefore, a citizen with the right to vote. Elizabeth Cady Stanton, one of the key figures in the suffragist movement in the USA, writes of men's attributes as belonging to the public world outside of reason and language: 'The male element is a destructive force, stern, selfish, aggrandizing, loving war, violence, conquest, acquisition, breeding in the material and moral world alike discord, disorder, disease and death.'[9]

The shift to virtuous woman meant that white women came to discount any connection they might have to the 'natural' sphere at all. Sexuality, indeed the body itself, was denied. 'Most white women eagerly absorbed sexist ideology that claimed virtuous women had no sexual impulses. So convinced were they of the necessity to hide their sexuality that they were unwilling to undress to expose sick body parts to male physicians . . . Forcing white women to deny their physical beings.'[10] And as white middle-class women became pure, asexual virtuous beings, the image of black women in America, for example, simultaneously changed to absorb the sexualized image of women.

> 19th century white women were no longer portrayed as sexual tempt-resses; they were extolled as the 'nobler half' of humanity. . . The shift away from the image of white woman as sinful and sexual to that of white woman as virtuous lady occurred at the same time as mass sexual exploitation of enslaved black women – just as the rigid sexual morality of Victoria England created a society in which the extolling of woman as mother and helpmate occurred at the same time as the formation of a mass underworld of prostitution.[11]

Thus white middle-class women fought to enter the political realm on the basis of their distance from the natural sphere. Their role in the private sphere, they argued, strengthened their claims to be part of the world of culture and reason. Black women, on the other hand, were cast as part of the natural world (through their sexuality as discussed), while, through their work as domestic servants in the private sphere, they were connected, in the minds of many white middle-class women, even more strongly with 'nature' and 'natural' needs.

Many in the white feminist movement in the USA, casting themselves as they did, used their role in the private sphere to denounce vehemently the right of black women or men gaining the vote before they did. Elizabeth Cady Stanton expresses her outrage, calling on the intimate relations of the white family to question the vote being granted to men of colour:

> If Saxon men have legislated thus for their own mothers, wives and daughters, what can we hope for at the hands of the Chinese, Indians, and Africans? . . . I protest against the enfranchisement of another man of any race of clime until the daughters of Jefferson, Hancock, and Adams are crowned with their rights.[12]

While Stanton and fellow white suffragist Susan B. Anthony openly opposed the Fourteenth Amendment to the American Constitution, which in 1866 gave black men the right to vote, Sojourner Truth, the only black woman present at the First National Women's

Rights Convention in 1850, stood throughout her life for the rights of black women to vote. In a famous speech at the 1850 convention, Sojourner Truth asked a question which would portend the debates within third wave feminism more than a hundred years later about a particular versus universal definition of 'woman'. In asking her famous question, 'Ain't I a Woman?', Truth not only questions how 'woman' is being defined but illustrates how white and black women were differentiated in the nineteenth century, as discussed above:

> That man over there says that women need to be helped into carriages, and lifted over ditches, and to have the best place everywhere. Nobody ever helps me into carriages, or over mud-puddles, or give me any best place! And ain't I a woman? Look at me! Look at my arm! I have ploughed and planted, and gathered into barns, and no man could head me! And ain't I a woman?[13]

Sojourner Truth was just one among many African American women who were involved in the struggle for the vote in the United States. Contrary to some white feminist accounts of the history of American suffragism, black women were very active in first wave feminism.

> Black women have always been at the center of the feminist struggle in this country . . . With the formation of the National Association of Coloured Women in 1896, black women activists, among them Frances Ellen Watkins and Mary Church Terell – engaged in the organized suffrage campaign with as much determination, and less race and class prejudice than white counterparts such as Susan B. Anthony.[14]

Black women were active in the struggle for those denied the vote on the basis of either gender or race. White feminists have often failed to incorporate this history into their generalized notion of 'feminist history', often constructing black women, instead, as marginalized or victims:

> Standard feminist histories of the first wave contain obligatory references to . . . Sojourner Truth and Harriet Tubman. Their feminism is depicted as 'exceptional' and not shared by other black women, whose deficiencies as producers and consumers of feminist theory have rendered them minor characters in the overall feminist drama. It then follows that Black women's historical role as objects of exploitation meant that they lacked the requisite political agency to be significant in the early feminist struggle . . . It is against such biased interpretations that Black Feminist scholars today are reacting.[15]

Revisiting history is critical to recent feminist analysis, which seeks to address the question of 'identity' and 'diversity' and difference in politics. If one is to embrace 'difference' in contemporary feminism, it is necessary to ensure that one's understanding of the history of feminism is similarly diverse. Caraway comments: 'This recent body of revisionist history explores just such questions as highly contestable subjects, with the aim of retrieving and reclaiming a *diverse* feminist identity.'[16]

In contrast to the white feminists Stanton and Anthony, Anna Julia Cooper was writing texts at the same time in support of an inclusive suffrage movement. She criticizes the white suffragists for failing to represent all women and men who are oppressed:

> Is not this hitching our wagon to something much lower than a star? Is not woman's cause broader, and deeper, and grander, than a blue stocking debate or an aristocratic pink tea? Why should woman become plaintiff in a suit versus the Indian, or the Negro, or any other race or class who have been crushed under the iron heel of Anglo-Saxon power?[17]

As women gained the vote in the first few decades of the twentieth century, feminism began to shift, laying the groundwork for the second wave.[18] With the First World War and its aftermath, feminism endorsed the universal humanism which pervaded institutions like the League of Nations, arguing that women were human beings like men, rather than women with a different or superior morality, as the Victorians saw them. Thus you see a new emphasis on sameness, humanism and universality. Second, with women working outside the home during the war, there is a new challenge to the gendered division of men and women in the private and public spheres. Finally, with the vote gained, the fight for equality, in terms of opportunities and work, will gradually gather force. The dualisms described above continue to be left unchallenged. However, feminists are arguing that all women should be equal to all men and therefore women must be equal partners in the public realm.

Vera Brittain, a British feminist writer and activist at the beginning of the twentieth century, begins the demand for men and women (largely white middle class) to share in and experience both a public and a private life in her 1927 tract, *Why Feminism Lives*.

> Women do their best work when they are allowed to do it, not as women, but as human beings. It is the urge behind women's growing

demand for employment unhandicapped by inadequate pay or unnecessary restrictions as whether she is married or whether her husband has an income. The right to separate her public and private affairs as every man is allowed to separate his is no 'minor grievance', but the test of a fundamental distinction – the distinction between a social chattel and an independent, responsible individual.[19]

As the welfare state begins to develop, more divisions appear in feminist thought in Britain. There is a dawning recognition of the distinctive needs of women as opposed to men in the creation and implementation of social programs. The idea of viewing women and men as human beings who should be treated exactly the same runs head long into a new feminism which argues that women have a different point of view and special needs. Brittain summarizes this division in an essay published in 1926:

[There are] two schools of thought – the Old Feminists, who view with misgiving a 'decline from the pure milk of the word' of 'equality of liberties, status and opportunities between men and women' and the New Feminists, who believe . . . that 'the time has come to look beyond them'. They have, therefore, included in their programme reforms such as family allowances, birth control and similar policies . . . The New Feminism emphasizes the importance of the 'women's point of view', the Old Feminism believes in the primary importance of the human being.[20]

Brittain concludes the article by describing herself as an 'old feminist with the motto Equality First'. Nevertheless, within this article one can begin to see the roots of later second and third wave questions about difference, reproduction and women's point of view. In calling for family allowances and birth control, the new feminism can be seen to presage the realignment of public and private spheres. The roots of second and third wave feminism are even more fully developed in the writings of Virginia Woolf. In particular, Woolf's description of women as the 'mirror' portends both de Beauvoir's notion of 'otherness' and Irigaray's speculum. Second, Woolf, unlike the Victorian feminists, argues that women's role in 'civilization' and culture, far from being central to, is in fact alien from or in opposition to, women's view of themselves: 'If one is a woman one is often surprised by a sudden splitting off of consciousness, say in walking down Whitehall, when from being the natural inheritor of that civilisation, she becomes, on the contrary, outside of it, alien and critical.'[21] Finally, Woolf argues that women, because they are isolated in the private sphere and alienated from the cultural realm, must have a place away from men, or in her own words, 'a room of one's own'. Her argument extended beyond the individual woman to the notion of what she called 'Outsiders' Society', women's groups that could meet to protect and preserve women's culture. As Naomi Black comments, 'Woolf's Outsider's Society presages second wave feminism's consciousness raising groups'.[22]

Second Wave Feminism

Simone de Beauvoir's classic text, *The Second Sex*, which many mark as the breaking point between first and second wave feminism, is important for a number of reasons. In many ways de Beauvoir is the final expression of the first wave feminist's belief in humanism, equality and reason. de Beauvoir accepts the argument that women are basically the same as men. As such, she absorbs the dualisms of western thought between public and private and culture and nature into her theory. Her basic argument is twofold: first that one is not born but rather becomes a woman, in other words 'gender' is socially rather than naturally constructed; second, woman plays the role of 'other' throughout history, she is defined in relation to men. It is in her final chapter on how women might become 'independent' that de Beauvoir makes clear the extent to which she continues to work within the categories of western political thought, particularly existentialism.

In this sense she is perhaps the first of the second wave, hyphenated feminists – namely, existentialist feminist. Consistent with the existentialist framework, de Beauvoir argues that if women are to be truly free they only have to make certain choices. First, they must overcome their biology, their bodies, in order to enter the cultural, rational realm of men; second, women should consider seriously their continued role in the private sphere, most specifically their role as mothers, which de Beauvoir sees as one of the greatest obstacles to independence. Unlike the earlier first wave feminists, de Beauvoir is the first thinker (since Plato and for very different reasons) to question women's role in the private sphere. Rather than seeing it, as the Victorian feminists did, as a positive aspect of women's lives, de Beauvoir sees the role as wife and mother as often in direct conflict with the role as an independent woman. If there is one distinction to be drawn between the earlier group of feminist thinkers in this category and later feminist thinkers it is their attitude to the public and private realms, and the role of men and women in each. de Beauvoir thus ushered in the era of hyphenated feminisms. With Betty Friedan began what has been called contemporary liberal feminism; with Sheila Rowbotham came socialist/Marxist feminism; with Juliet Mitchell came psychoanalytical feminism; and Kate Millet's *Sexual Politics* ushered in radical feminism. We can examine all these feminist thinkers not in terms of their relationship to their theoretical partners but in relation to each other, noting both the similarities and the differences in their approaches.

All these thinkers shared a common belief in the universality of women's condition, with little analysis of the differences between women on the basis of sexual or racial identity. The search for solutions had to begin with the link between gender and the dualisms of public/private and culture/nature. In particular, the connection between women and the private sphere is challenged and destabilized, for the first time, in this body of feminist thought in a sustained and critical manner. No phrase better encapsulates the new way in which feminists were introducing 'politics' into the private sphere than the phrase 'the personal is political'. What this phrase meant was a multitude of things to different women, but somehow it resonated with the time. It was, in part, a reference to the fact that within the family home, the private sphere, politics existed as the power relations between husband and wife; it also referred to the sense that power or coercion was something which affected women's everyday life: what they wore, what they ate, how they acted, all related to the way in which 'femininity' had been constructed. Third, it was a siren call to the legislators of western countries that politics stretched beyond the realm of the public sphere and it was time that the state began to consider their role in areas heretofore defined as private: domestic violence, childcare, senior care, family allowances and so forth. Finally, it was the underpinning for 'consciousness raising groups' – groups of women who discussed the politics of their personal experiences, thus transforming private experience into public concerns, and making women aware of the extent to which they shared common problems, which had to be solved in public, political forums as opposed to private ones.

The challenge of second wave feminists to the long-standing notion in western political theory that politics occurred and should occur in the public realm only is a central and critical development. Private family life, private property and the private rights of individuals were thought to be realms within which neither the state nor the community should be involved. As many second wave feminists pointed out, far from being apolitical, women were increasingly realizing that the private sphere was in fact the place where power was exerted over them the most. It has, therefore, to become central to political analysis rather than excluded from it. Each of the different 'forms' of feminisms developed its own ideas about how to break through this oppression of women in the private sphere.

Betty Friedan, the founder and first president of the American National Organization of Women, and author of *The Feminine Mystique*, wrote in 1953 of 'the problem that had no name' – the enormous psychological distress shown by a whole generation of women (mainly middle-class white) who did not have public careers or work outside the home, and were thus limited to the private sphere. Within their domestic homes, these women were trying to fulfil a mythological role imposed by 'the feminine mystique' – namely, women will reach the pinnacle of womanhood by being the perfect wives and mothers. Friedan's solution, in line with liberal feminists such as Wollstonecraft and Taylor, and with Simone de Beauvoir, was twofold: greater educational opportunities for women and re-entry into the work force. Friedan, and many liberal feminists who followed in her path, did not challenge the underlying structure of public and private; their main concern was to move women into the public realm of work and politics. Her arguments, as was discussed in previous chapters, were focused almost entirely on middle-class white housewives (although claiming to be universal to American women). Many lesbian feminists challenged Friedan and other liberal feminists to look beyond the quintessential heterosexual woman, the 'housewife', to the oppression faced by lesbian women. The challenge by lesbians to mainstream feminism in the USA was met by hostility, with Friedan herself calling lesbians within the feminist movement 'the lavender menace'.[23] Second, Friedan's solution was of limited value to women already working in exploitative, low paying jobs, which was the case for many women of colour and working-class women:

> White middle and upper class women like those described in Betty Friedan's *The Feminine Mystique* were housewives not because sexism would have prevented them from being in the paid labor force, but because they had willingly embraced the notion that it was better to be a housewife than to be a worker. The racism and classism of white women's liberationists was most apparent whenever they discussed

work as the liberating force for women. In such discussions it was always the middle class 'housewife' who was depicted as the victim of sexist oppression and not the poor black and non-black women who are most exploited by American economics.[24]

In recent years, the hyphenated liberal feminism has come to be challenged by liberal feminists themselves. And it is the liberal commitment to the private sphere which lies at the heart of the problem:

> It is when feminists talk of equality and equal rights that they most closely approximate the liberal tradition. When they talk instead of the personal as political, they are profoundly at odds with liberal ideas. The relationship between public and private has become the real bone of contention between liberal and feminist thinking, and it is the focus of most feminist critiques . . . If all aspects of our lives are up for question, then nothing is outside the political sphere. For liberals this is anathema, for to make no distinction between private life and public affairs is the very antithesis of their thinking.[25]

While many liberal feminists continued to hold on to a distinction between public and private, in order to pursue the goal of negative liberty and equal rights for women, the moment in which 'the personal is political' entered the feminist lexicon was the point at which liberal feminism began to shift towards feminism, and the public/private duality began to falter.

Socialist feminists attempted to address the issue of gender as well as class in their analyses. 'Reproduction' was at the heart of their critiques and challenged both the public/private duality and the nature/culture duality, as we shall see. For Marxist and socialist feminists, the family and private property were intimately related in both history and present day politics and economics; both provided the underpinnings for capitalism. Women's role in the private family, or 'reproduction', was essentially unpaid domestic labour. For feminists like Juliet Mitchell and Sheila Rowbotham, traditional Marxism and socialism was correct on the fundamental underpinnings of capitalist society, but had failed to account for either the role of patriarchy in history or the sexual as opposed to class division of labour.

Juliet Mitchell does not challenge the underlying belief by modern thinkers, feminist or otherwise, in the importance of science and technology to overcome or conquer nature. Indeed, she sees it as the basis for the 'ultimate revolution', for both socialism and feminism:

The material basis for sexual division being the reproductive system, the revolutionary means to its annihilation will be man's scientific ability to transcend it. Science conquers Nature. The ecological revolution will finally put an end to the biological base . . . Embracing the feminist and ecological revolution would mean that cybernation and other technological advances would end all joyless labour: the labour of the factory and of the child-bed . . . Culture would at last overcome nature and the 'ultimate revolution' would be achieved.[26]

While embracing the power of culture over nature, Mitchell did challenge the assumed link between biology, reproduction and the nuclear family. She did not question the assumption that maternity is a universal biological fact, just the type of family formed by nature:

The biological function of maternity is a universal, atemporal fact . . . however from it is made to follow the so-called stability and omnipresence of the family, if in very different forms. Once this is accepted, women's social subordination . . . can be seen to follow inevitably as an insurmountable bio-historical fact . . . The lynch-pin in this line of argument is the idea of the family.[27]

Mitchell concludes that the link between family and women is a social construct, resulting more from economics than biology.

Reproduction is seen as an apparently constant atemporal phenomenon – part of biology rather than history. In fact this is an illusion . . . It has been defined till now by its uncontrollable, natural character and to this extent has been an unmodified biological fact. As long as reproduction remained a natural phenomenon, of course, women were effectively doomed to social exploitation.[28]

Reproduction, in other words, is not purely biological, but the outgrowth of the sexual division of labour and patriarchy. The family serves two purposes, according to Mitchell: the economic function of reproducing a productive labour force and arena for the consumption of market goods; and the ideological function of reproducing the mythology surrounding the family and mystifying its economic reality. Mitchell's conclusion therefore is that while feminism must embrace the cultural world over the biological sphere, women's liberation will only be achieved when the family and private sphere is dissolved. 'It seems possible that within this dual contradiction lies the eventual dissolution of the "family", a future already visible with the conditions of capitalism. The social nature of production restores the family to its social form – a social group of individuals.'[29] While Mitchell is sometimes labelled a 'socialist feminist', the extent to which she incorporated psychoanalytical theory into her feminism should be noted, reminding us of how feminists during this period were routinely categorized according to theoretical boxes outside their premises and their making.

Like Mitchell, Sheila Rowbotham argues that arguments about biological determinism are highly suspect for women. She warns fellow feminists from searching for 'women's nature' as so much of the world is socially constructed. Like Plato, liberal and socialist feminists both believe that nature accounts for little in terms of differences between the sexes and through the right conditions they could be virtually the same:

> We have to recognize our biological distinctness but this does not mean that we should become involved in an illusory hunt for our lost 'nature'. There are so many social accretions around our biology. All conceptions of female 'nature' are formed in cultures dominated by men, and like all abstract ideas of human nature are invariably used to deter the oppressed from organizing effectively against that most unnatural of systems, capitalism.[30]

For Rowbotham, the public/private divide was critical. She argued that private property and the family had a tendency to separate women from themselves and their collective reality. She concluded, therefore, that socialist feminists needed to embrace the realm of personal experience while bringing together women, particularly working-class women, to create an alternative society.

> We perceived ourselves through anecdote, through immediate experience. The world simply was and we were in it . . . In order to create an alternative an oppressed group must at once shatter the self-reflecting world which encircles it and at the same time, project its own image onto history. In order to discover its own identity as distinct from that of the oppressor it has to become visible to itself . . . The first step is to connect and learn to trust one another.[31]

The hyphenation of Marxism or socialism with feminism was challenged by Marxist feminists themselves. In a collection of essays edited by Lydia Sargeant, and published in 1981, the lead essay by Heidi Hartmann puts the problem succinctly:

> The marriage of marxism and feminism has been like the marriage of husband and wife depicted in English common law: marxism and feminism are one, and that one is marxism. Recent attempts to integrate marxism and feminism are unsatisfactory to us as feminists because they subsume the feminist struggle into the 'larger' struggle

against capital. To continue the simile further, either we need a healthier marriage or we need a divorce.[32]

Hartmann and many of the other writers within this collection of essays believe that the marriage can be salvaged, through some kind of dual systems theory incorporating both patriarchy and capitalism as the underpinning structures for power in society. In the case of both patriarchy and capitalism there is a 'material' base upon which everything else is erected. The very sharp distinction between nature and culture, material forces and social forces, and sex and gender are adopted by Hartmann:

> The aspects of social structure that perpetuate patriarchy are theoretically identifiable, hence separable from their other aspects . . . We are both female and male, biological sexes, but we are created woman and man, socially recognized genders . . . How people propagate the species is socially determined. If biologically, people are sexually polymorphous, and society were organized in such a way that all forms of sexual expression were equally permissible, reproduction would result only from some sexual encounters, the heterosexual ones. The strict division of labor by sex, a social invention common to all known societies, creates two very separate genders and a need for men and women to get together for economic reasons.[33]

In other words, Hartmann is arguing, consistent with liberal thinkers, that we are born basically the same, but it is social structures which create the divisions and differences between people. Consequently, with a non-patriarchal communist society it would be possible fundamentally to change these divisions and differences and create wholly new 'genders'. Thus, while Hartmann is able to demonstrate the tensions inherent in hyphenated feminism, she continues to use the dualism of culture and nature (so central to Marxist thought) to underpin her analysis. This same collection of essays is also important to the development of feminism by introducing challenges to the concepts of 'reproduction' and 'gender' used so often in Marxist feminist analysis on the basis of sexual identity and race. To what extent are these analyses, which both emphasize the sameness between men and women and within the category called women, and refer to the importance of 'reproduction', reflective of women of colour or lesbians?[34] While Riddiough and Joseph are hopeful that the issues of 'identity' which they raise may be reconcilable with both socialism and feminism, the question of difference has been explicitly introduced, which will tend to undermine the elements of socialist thinking which are universalistic, essentialist and dedicated to the idea of equality and sameness.

Socialist feminists thus simultaneously hold on to some facets of dualistic modern thought while sowing some ultimately very corrosive seeds of criticism. Like Plato, Marxist feminists assume a public/private divide as given; and argue that for the good of all the latter must be destroyed, pushing for women basically to become proletariats like men, and with it revolutionaries for the working class. Any values attached to the domestic sphere, traditionally associated with 'feminine' work of nurturance and care, are seen as false consciousness, or in later versions should be validated through notions of 'wage labour' in the campaigns for 'wages for housework'. More importantly, socialist feminism is deeply committed to a nature/culture distinction in its concepts of materialism as the basis of society, over which technology must ultimately reign supreme. The dual systems theories, which take patriarchy and capitalism to be the underlying structures through which we live our 'material lives', demonstrate the extent to which 'dualism' is still inherent to Marxist and socialist feminist thought.

Some feminists began to realize that this commitment to materialism, in particular dialectical materialism, was difficult to reconcile with feminism. Catharine MacKinnon argues, in a similar manner to Anne Phillips's the 'personal is political' moment in liberal feminist thought, that 'consciousness raising' had created a similar fundamental groundshift in socialist feminist thought. It is one which challenged those aspects of socialism which were once considered sacrosanct, like dialectical materialism: 'Feminism is the first theory to emerge from those whose interests it affirms . . . As marxist method is dialectical materialism, feminist method is consciousness raising: the collective critical reconstitution of the mean of women's social experience, as women live through it.'[35] As MacKinnon herself makes clear, this new method closes the gap between subject and object, mind and matter, as previously conceived in scientific thought generally, but more specifically, scientific socialism:

> Marxism and feminism on this level posit a different relation between thought and thing . . . To the extent that materialism is scientific it posits and refers to a reality outside thought which it considers to have an objective – that is, truly nonsocially perspectival – content. Consciousness raising, by contrast, inquires into an intrinsically social situation, into that mixture of thought and materiality which is women's sexuality in the most generic sense.[36]

Thus MacKinnon has begun to question the 'scientific' premises of modern thought (specifically dialectical materialism) as irreconcilable with a feminist approach, and with it the relationship between subject and object as defined in science since the time of Descartes. While the commitment to the culture/nature divide is still under contestation in socialist feminism, the dualistic foundations of the public/private divide of modern political theory were firmly shaken by two powerful critiques in socialist feminism. First, they critiqued the assumed biological link between women, reproduction and families, arguing instead that there are ideological rather than natural reasons for the creation of families and women's roles in them. Second, they questioned the need for a private sphere at all. Through the dissolution of families in the long term, it is critical that women push the personal and the private into the public and the political realms.

Thus, like the liberal feminists, socialist feminists still accept the ideas of universal goals for all women and men, the fundamental sameness of men and women, and that the world can ultimately be changed; nothing is fixed in nature. But unlike the liberal feminist thinkers who find their liberalism and its commitment to a private sphere difficult to reconcile with feminism, the socialist feminists take as one of their goals the destruction of the private sphere. On the other hand, socialist feminists are unwilling to give up the notion of a material basis for reality which must be discovered through scientific thought; that is, a distinction between culture and nature, where the former overcoming the latter is the engine of history. In other words, while liberal feminists are more prepared to challenge the culture/nature divide, they nevertheless hold on to the public/private divide as central to the liberal framework. Socialist feminists are similarly prepared to give up on the public/private divide but need to hold on to the culture/nature divide as the backbone of their socialist tenets. In both cases, they realize the difficulty in trying to reconcile feminism with either one of these dualities and, as we shall see in the next two chapters, feminists have begun to move away from the traditional theoretical frameworks for politics, and towards new independent perspectives.

In response to socialist feminism and its emphasis on materialism and reproduction, the psychoanalytical feminists argued that the oppression of women must also be understood in terms of the development of the mind. Like all the other hyphenated modern feminisms we have looked at, psychoanalytical theory assumes a universality of human experience, a capacity for scientific understanding of the world around us (subject versus object) and an assumed sameness among women and difference from men. It differs from the other feminisms we have considered in that it questions the dominant role of 'reason' over 'nature' or body that socialist and liberal feminism largely accept. For psychoanalytical feminists, reason was the channel through which passions and instincts were conducted and made socially acceptable. In asserting the notions of superego, ego and id, psychoanalytical thought undermines the basic relationship between culture and nature or the rational and irrational sides of the human being first laid out in Plato's conception of justice in the *Republic*. At the heart of the psychoanalytical feminist's scientific analysis is the family, and in particular the role of mother and child:

> Psychoanalysis, exploring the unconscious and the constructs of mental life, works on the terrain of which the dominant phenomenal form is the family. In studying women we cannot neglect the methods of a science of the mind, a theory that attempts to explain how women become women and men, men. The borderline between the biological and the social which finds expression in the family is the land that psychoanalysis sets out to chart, it is the land where sexual distinction originates.[37]

Psychoanalytical feminists were attached to the 'science' of psychoanalysis because they wanted to use the method of Sigmund Freud, while simultaneously distancing themselves from his conclusions about men and women, which could be construed, *vis-à-vis* the science of his method, as simply an 'ideological' bias. Mitchell comments 'That Freud personally, had a reactionary ideological attitude to women in no way affects his science – it wouldn't be a science if it did.'[38] Mitchell and other psychoanalytical feminists were defending the Freudian method against attacks from feminists like Friedan, Firestone and Kate Millet. Friedan, for example, attacked Freud's biological foundationalism as expressed in the aphorism 'anatomy is destiny'. As a liberal feminist, she argued that one's biological role does not necessarily determine one's social role. Kate Millett also questioned the biological foundationalism of psychoanalysis. In particular, she challenged the argument that men's violence and sexual aggression against women arose from biological necessity rather than the way power was structured in society. Millet argued that underpinning the political power of men over women is either the threat of aggression or violence itself. Both Friedan and Millet ridicule the notion of 'penis envy', where women have babies as a concession prize for not having penises, as the most extreme form of male egocentrism. Shulamith Firestone, on the other hand, endorsed Freud's emphasis on the body and sexuality but criticized him for not fully accounting for power within the family (a focus, as we shall see, of radical feminism).

Feminists who adopted the psychoanalytical framework began by challenging or transforming some of the more objectionable aspects of Freudian analysis. They argued that Freud's biological foundationalism, that 'anatomy is destiny' or nature determines culture, is misguided. Feminists like Karen Horney and Clara Thompson conclude that 'development [is] a process of growth away from one's biology and toward mastery of one's environment'.[39] These feminists not only adopt the duality between sex and gender but most importantly incorporate the modern view of overcoming one's biology or transcending nature through social or cultural means, applying this concept to the development of the individual psyche. Second, the notion of 'penis envy' was broadened to include the idea of 'phallus', the power which men enjoy as men in society. This phallic power is what women envy. Mitchell comments:

> Notorious concepts such as 'penis envy' have come to suggest to most people a wish to seize the object itself. But what underlies this concept is, in fact, Freud's much more complex notion of the power of the image of the phallus within human society. It is its social, ideological and psychic power, embodied in the thing itself.[40]

The bodily part is thus transformed into a construct of power. Later feminists will come to use this idea of 'phallic power' as a fused notion of natural and cultural dominance of men over women.

Psychoanalytical feminism in the later 1970s and early 1980s began to focus on mothering and its role in the development of children. Dorothy Dinnerstein argues that women, because they are first and foremost mothers to all of us as children, are both 'nature' and 'object' at an unconscious level before we can recognize them as 'rational' and 'subject' at a conscious level. Even when children do begin to recognize their mothers and other women as 'persons' like themselves, these viewpoints continue to be saturated with earlier unconscious views of women, as described above:

> The earliest roots of antagonism to women lie in the period before the infant has any clear idea where the self ends and the outside world begins, or any way of knowing that the mother is a separately sentient being. At this stage a woman is the helpless child's main

contact with the natural surround ... She is the centre also of the non-self, an unbounded, still unarticulated region with which the child labours to define itself ... She is this global, inchoate, all-embracing presence before she is a person, a discrete finite human individual with a subjectivity of her own. When she does become a person, her person-ness is shot through for the child with these earlier qualities. And when it begins to be clear that this person is a female in a world of males and females, femaleness come to be the name for, the embodiment of, these global and inchoate and all embracing qualities, qualities very hard indeed to reconcile with person-ness as one has begun to feel it inside oneself.[41]

Men, Dinnerstein argues, thus grow up with a sense of women as representative of nature and inchoate to their subjective unity. The all-encompassing power of mother is still present, so as adults they seek to control women and by extension nature. Hence comes the description of women as 'mermaids' by Dinnerstein: 'seductive and impenetrable female representative of the dark and magic underwater world from which our life comes and in which we cannot live'.[42] Women, on the other hand, fear the power of the mother within them and seek to be controlled by men. The relationship of both men and women to their mothers is rooted in these early childhood experiences.

To recognize woman as subjective or as an 'I' is to return both men and women back to the traumatic moment in childhood when infants first recognize mothers as something other than an all-encompassing object against which they are defining themselves. This trauma prevents both men and women from defining women as subjects, in sexuality and society more generally. Fathers, on the other hand, are usually only encountered after the trauma of the infant defining itself free from the rest of the world. Consequently, it is less problematic for either men or women to recognize the man as a subjective 'I'. Dinnerstein also argues that the role of mother as bodily presence in infancy has created a strongly ambivalent attitude towards the body, particularly the female body. Women's bodies are powerful, for they represent life-giving (in birth and breast feeding) and therefore we are attracted to the female body, but on the other hand men and women are also repelled by the 'messiness' of women's bodies. Women in particular can come to hate their own bodies and try to control or hurt themselves. Finally, Dinnerstein argues that our early childhood development creates two spheres: the public for men and the private for women; the former marked by the need to control, the latter by relationships. Dinnerstein concludes that unless both men and women are involved in the nurturing of small infants, we will not escape our gendered identities.

Nancy Chodorow argues in a similar vein that the role of mothering should be central to our analysis of reproduction and social institutions. Chodorow claims that mothering is neither a natural instinct nor a socially constructed role; instead women develop the desire and capacity to mother through early pre-conscious childhood experience. Men, on the other hand, develop the need to distance themselves from their mothers, repressing their 'mothering' capacities and desires. 'The sexual and familial division of labour in which women . . . are more involved in interpersonal, affective relationships than men produces in daughters and sons a division of psychological capacities which leads them to reproduce this sexual and familial division of labor.'[43] Like Dinnerstein, Chodorow concludes that both men and women must be involved in the nurturing and early development of children if gender roles are to change.

Chodorow introduces two important concepts to feminist analysis which will have an enormous impact on feminism, moving it away from its hyphenated modern dependence on universality and sameness and towards independent feminist perspectives. First, she concludes that men and women are fundamentally different; second, she posits that neither nature nor nurture can explain this difference. This approach has been called 'object-relations theory', and with it feminism provides its own explanation for some of the dualities we have addressed in previous chapters. The implications for politics and political theory are profound, as Nancy Hirschmann argues:

> Because women, not men, 'mother' (that is have primary if not sole responsibility for the care and nurturance of young children) boys and girls will develop different senses of themselves as gendered subjects as well as different conceptions of their relation to the 'object-world' or world outside the self. The power of object-relations theory lies in its epistemological implications, for it suggests two very different ways of seeing and 'knowing' the world. One fits the dominant discourse of political theory . . . the other is at odds with it.[44]

As Jane Flax and Nancy Hirschmann argue, it is the 'reactive autonomy' of a boy's early childhood, the need to separate and be independent from mother, which underpins the male way of seeing the world. 'It produces a conception of agency that abstracts individual will . . . out of the context of the social relationship within which it develops . . . While autonomy is defined as independence, its reactive character ensures that others set the terms of one's identity.'[45] Hirshmann concludes that this viewpoint on the world is consistent with notions of agency, right, domination over nature and obligation (the very stuff of modern political theory and that which has been described as of the cultural or public realm). On the other hand, women exercise 'relational autonomy', 'wherein the self derives its strength from its context of relations'. A political theory from this perspective would be based around connection and responsibility and care (values associated with the private sphere).[46] As a result, men and women have very different views and roles in the world. Flax argues that these psychoanalytical differences have been ignored by political philosophy, with the consequence of assuming one perspective to be universal when in fact it is masculine and patriarchal:

> The denial and repression of early infantile experience has had a deep and largely unexplored impact on philosophy. This repressed material shapes by its very absence in consciousness the way we look at and reflect upon the world . . . adopting a feminist viewpoint that seeks to include infantile experience and women's activity within the realm of the social and knowable, permits and requires a critique of philosophy in which previously unacknowledged assumptions are revealed.[47]

In this 'object-relations' theory we begin to see a recognition of the masculine nature of the theoretical frameworks and their dualisms with which feminism has had to work, and the transition towards an independent feminist perspective. Thus Flax concludes:

> The apparently irresolvable dualism of subject–object, mind–body, inner–outer, reason–sense . . . are incomplete and abstract (that is, not adequately grounded in human experience). What is lacking is an account of the earliest period of individual history in which the self emerges within the context of a relation with a woman (or women) which is itself overdetermined by patriarchy and class relations. Only certain forms of the self and of philosophy can emerge under these conditions . . . It is necessary to develop an autonomous feminist viewpoint(s). Women's experience, which has been excluded from the realm of the known, of the rational, is not in itself an adequate ground for theory. As the other pole of the dualities it must be incorporated and transcended.[48]

Many have argued that psychoanalysis, like socialism and liberalism, ultimately stands in the way of a fully feminist analysis, on two grounds: first, that it is universalistic (and therefore antithetical to recognition of difference) and, second, that it is individualistic (ignoring larger social contexts).

> Repudiating psychoanalysis has become a familiar gesture of contemporary feminist discourse – and with some good reasons . . . The traditional indifference of psychoanalysis to insulate subjectivity from social practices and discourses all run contrary to a feminism increasingly attuned to the power of social exigencies and differences in the constitution of subjectivity.[49]

Thus, it is argued, psychoanalytical feminism and its progeny tend to ignore differences of race and class. Elizabeth Spelman and Toril Moi both critique object-relations theory as homogenizing different children into a scientific model, requiring a 'universal' white middle-class family.[50] Collette Guillaumin argues that psychoanalytical theory, in its reinforcement of individualism, was at odds with anti-racialist theories.[51] Other feminists have defended psychoanalytical theory, arguing that racial and class differences can be incorporated into a feminist reworking of the theory.[52] Finally, the new theories about 'mothering' by Dinnerstein and Chodorow are criticized by Adrienne Rich for their role in the entrenchment of 'compulsory heterosexuality'.

> Neglecting the covert socializations and the covert forces that have channeled women into marriage and heterosexual romance . . . [Chodorow,] like Dinnerstein, is stuck with trying to reform a man-made institution – compulsory heterosexuality – as if, despite profound emotional impulses and complementarities drawing women toward women, there is a mystical/biological heterosexual inclination, a 'preference' or 'choice' that draws women toward men . . . This assumption of female heterosexuality seems to me in itself remarkable; it is an enormous assumption to have glided so silently into the foundations of our thought.[53]

This is particularly surprising in psychoanalytical theory, Rich claims, given both authors' belief that the earliest sources of emotional nurturance and caring come from women (as mothers). What should be explained, therefore, is why women turn away from this first, profound and natural experience towards a socially constructed and, as Rich sees it, coercive relationship of heterosexuality. In other words, Rich was challenging the mainstream feminist practice, in this case reflected in psychoanalytical thought, of assuming a duality between 'men' and 'women', based on a natural, biological relationship between men and women, rather than attempting to explain it as a social construct.

Thus, the two sets of dualisms (culture/nature; public/private) are adopted but transformed in psychoanalytical thought. The cultural/natural divide is adopted in the scientific method, as described above, but the assumed relationship between mind and body is turned upside down where the bodily instincts (the unconscious) are the forces underpinning what goes on in the 'rational' part of the mind. Unlike traditional political theory, which understands the roles of men and women in relation to the public needs of the civil state or *polis*, psychoanalytical feminism looks for the differentiation between sexes in the family and most particularly in the relationship between mothers and their infant children (a subject which until recently was considered to be well outside the domain of political studies). Psychoanalytical feminists argue that you cannot begin to understand a society until you understand and incorporate the way in which men and women are differentiated in their pre-conscious infancies. Moreover, roles and dualities will only be overcome when men and women share in the nurturance and care of their children, thus arguing for a fundamental transformation of the private sphere.

The final form of second wave feminism is radical feminism. Like the other schools of thought in this category, radical feminism believes in culture overcoming biology, in a category of 'women' versus 'men', and in universal solutions to the problem faced by all women. The concept universal to all cultures and all times, and therefore lying at the heart of radical feminism, is 'patriarchy'. Unlike socialist and liberal feminists, however, many of the radical feminists were not interested in women becoming either the same as or equal to men; the objective was to break down patriarchy and emancipate women. Some argued that this would involve the separation of men and women. This group of feminists, including Kate Millet, Shulamith Firestone, Adrienne Rich, Mary Daly, create enormous challenges for other forms of hyphenated feminism. First, in their introduction of difference among women, particularly in terms of sexual identity, they challenge the underlying heterosexual assumptions in the public/private split accepted by both socialist and liberal feminists within their analyses. Second, radical feminism begins to tackle the question of power and its relationship to politics exclusively in terms of men and women. 'Patriarchy' was the power men had over women. Underpinning it at all times was a possibility of violence or coercion. 'Politics' therefore cannot simply be seen as the process for people, through reason and language, to come to collective decisions, as western political theory has long argued. Politics is fundamentally the exercise of power in whatever form, including violence.

Shualmith Firestone published her *Dialectic of Sex* in 1970. Perhaps more than any other feminist thinker, Firestone adopts the fundamental distinction between nature or biology and technology or culture. 'We have assumed the biological division of the sexes for procreation to be the fundamental "natural duality" from which grows all further division into classes.'[54] The goal for feminists, according to Firestone, is to overcome their own biology. 'The material of women's body is the source of her enslavement but . . . technological change would give women the chance to seize control of reproduction.'[55] Only when women have control over their biology through technology can they be truly emancipated. 'The end goal of feminist revolution must be, unlike that of the first feminist movement, not just the elimination of male privilege but of the sex distinction itself: genital differences between human beings would no longer matter culturally . . . The tyranny of the biological family would be broken.'[56] Firestone goes on to argue that women will only be free when sexuality is liberated from the confines of the nuclear family. 'Abolition of the family, would have profound effects: sexuality would be released from its straight jacket to eroticize our whole culture, changing its very definition.'[57]

Linda Nicholson argues that this notion of 'biological foundationalism' is central to radical feminism as a whole. It grew, she argues, out of a need to make all women the same and fundamentally different from men:

> Biological foundationalism . . . represents . . . a major tendency within second-wave theory, particularly in that tendency known as radical feminism. This of course is not surprising. Since the early 1970s, radical feminists have tended to be in the vanguard of those who have stressed the similarities among women and their differences from men. But it is difficult justifying such claims without invoking biology in some way or other. During the 1970s, many radical feminists explicitly endorsed biological determinism.[58]

The 'sameness' as each other and 'difference' from men as universals would be increasingly challenged, as has been discussed, by feminists who wanted to allow for both differences among women and links between given groups of women and men. Radical feminism is thus often accused of excluding the perspective of women of colour in particular.

Kate Millet's *Sexual Politics*, published in 1970, was also a groundbreaking work. Perhaps the most important contribution of this work was the new definition of politics introduced by Millet, and its implications for the view in political theory that 'politics' only occurs among groups of people (as opposed to animals) and only when reasoned argument and negotiations as opposed to violence or war are occurring (in simple seventeenth-century terms the apolitical state of nature versus the political civil society). Millet's argument is basically that politics is the exercise of power in whatever form. Patriarchy is the root of all other forms of power:

> In introducing the term 'sexual politics' one must first answer the inevitable question, 'Can the relationship between the sexes be viewed in a political light at all?' The answer depends on how one defines politics. This essay does not define the political as that relatively narrow and exclusive world of meetings, chairmen and parties. The term 'politics' shall refer to power-structured relationships, arrangements whereby one group of persons is controlled by another . . . Our society, like all other historical civilizations, is a patriarchy.[59]

Thus politics is not just about institutions and meetings in public or cultural spheres, as the liberals claim; politics is also about violence and the private sphere. Neither is power just about economics and class, as Marxists claim. Politics exists in nearly every relationship and between groups of people, but the most fundamental form of power is that of men over women, namely patriarchy. In one sentence, Millet concludes that gender, more than race, caste or class, is the fundamental form of politics in western society: 'However muted its appearance may be, sexual domination obtains nevertheless as perhaps the most pervasive ideology of our culture and provides its most fundamental concept of power.'[60] This claim, made often by radical feminists, created divisions among feminist thinkers, for it does not account for different forms of domination which occur to different groups of women and their own sense of which feels most oppressive. bell hooks and others argue that radical feminists have little understanding of the ways in which racism was an equally or more powerful form of domination than patriarchy.

Millet's idea of power, and her definition of politics, is the basis of many arguments made by radical feminists about the violence of men towards women. Andrea Dworkin, Susan Griffin and Susan

Brownmiller, to a greater or lesser extent, all argue that sexual violence underpins patriarchy and allows men to control women. Through pornography, domestic violence, prostitution and sexual assault, all women are afflicted by the potential threat of violence. And all this violence, as the radical feminists point out, occurs on the female body. Patriarchal history, in other words, is the history of the exploitation of women's bodies by men. Such violence would be described in most of traditional political theory as outside the scope of politics: first, because it occurs in the private home (domestic violence, sexual assault within the home) or the private market (prostitution, pornography); or, second, because it is an individual criminal act (sexual assault outside the home) brought on by a sexual impulse. The first is within the authority of the private sphere and therefore not a subject for political consideration; the latter is covered under criminal laws. Neither needs to be elevated to the level of public discourse. For the radical feminists, if violence is to recognized for what it is, our notions of politics, private versus public and power need to be redefined.

One of the key developments within radical feminism was a further erosion of the private sphere of women in western political thought. Consciousness raising groups were one of the ways in which women were overcoming the isolated, private, personal sphere and beginning to connect with other women and their shared problems, while searching for common solutions. A new concept was introduced into feminist thought, 'the woman-identified woman' and the 'lesbian continuum'. First used in the essay published in 1970 by the New York Radicalesbians, it attempted to broaden the notion of 'lesbian' from what was currently a sexual and psychological category to a broader definition incorporating politics, identity and ideology. Charlotte Bunch comments: 'Woman-identified lesbianism is ... more than sexual preference; it is a political choice. It is political because relations between men and women are essentially political; they involve power and dominance. Since the Lesbian actively rejects that relationship and chooses women, she defies the established political system.'[61]

Adrienne Rich goes even further, to include any relationship of 'primary intensity between and among women, including the sharing of a rich inner life, the bonding against male tyranny, the giving and receiving of practical and political support.'[62] Lesbianism, in other words, must reinvent the meaning of 'lesbian'. 'Lesbians' are particularly dangerous to western political theory and politics because they fall outside of the private sphere of family and heterosexuality and therefore cannot be controlled by those institutions. Given that women have historically been defined as close to nature and sex, a lesbian becomes, when she is recognized at all in modern thought, sexualized. It is this connection between sexuality and lesbianism which Bunch, Rich and other lesbian feminists seek to break down and redefine.

The discord between the notions of family and lesbian becomes vividly clear in the lesbian feminist's analysis of mothering. In the courts of the USA, 'lesbian' and 'mother' have often been, in custody battles, mutually exclusive categories. Many adoption agencies until recently adopted a similar policy. 'Mother' has been constructed in the dualities between public and private, men and women, culture and nature, in such a way as could not be recognized as anything other than heterosexual. While this is now changing, feminists like Ruthann Robson argue that lesbians must still jump over several more hurdles than heterosexual women in order to win custody of their children. In other words, the bias in favour of mothers in American courts (in keeping with the notions of women's role in the private sphere) is much different when the mother is lesbian.[63] Adrienne Rich argues that part of the reason why lesbianism and motherhood are so difficult to reconcile is because 'lesbian' is defined in exclusively sexual terms and motherhood is simultaneously defined as 'divested of sexuality'.

> The divisions of labor and allocations of power in patriarchy demand not merely a suffering Mother but one divested of sexuality: the Virgin Mary, *virgo intacta*, perfectly chaste. Women are permitted to be sexual only at a certain time of life, and the sensuality of mature – and certainly of aging – women has been perceived as grotesque, threatening, and inappropriate.[64]

Thus lesbian feminism challenges the public/private dichotomy in particular in both western liberal thought and some of the mainstream feminist theory, first by pulling women out of their private, isolated homes, where they identify with their families and husbands, to recognize the identification they have with other women. From conscious raising groups to the call for separation from men, lesbian feminists have challenged the compulsory nature of the heterosexual private family underpinning political theory. Second, the discord between lesbianism and traditional or mainstream notions of family has come to a head in the developing literature, politics and judicial decisions around 'motherhood'. Even recent psychoanalytical feminist analysis of motherhood has been taken to task for assuming a certain model of family as natural or given.

The scientific model of knowledge, which assumes a rational mind objectively dissecting the material world around 'him', has also been challenged by lesbian feminist writers. Mary Daly, for example, in her *Gyn/Ecology*, argues that women must reinvent a whole new language and way of looking at the world in order to avoid the 'phallic culture' embued by science.

> The Journey of this book, therefore, is . . . for the Lesbian Imagination in All Women . . . Since *Gyn/Ecology* is the Un-field/Ourfield/Outfield of Journeyers, rather than a game in an 'in' field, the pedantic can be expected to perceive it as 'unscholarly' . . . Since *Gyn/Ecology* Spins around, past, and through the established fields, opening the coffers/coffins in which 'knowledge' has been stored, re-stored, re-covered, its meaning will be hidden from the Grave Keepers of that tradition.[65]

Mary Daly's book was the subject of a critical letter written by Audre Lorde, who argued that while Daly attempted to celebrate women, and specifically lesbian difference, she had depicted black women as almost entirely victims of history, ignoring the positive cultural images African American women had developed for themselves. With this critique, Lorde sows the seeds of the newer forms of feminism which will attempt to undermine Aristotle's original claim of women as 'passive' recipients of history, and instead uncover the many ways in which women have been 'active' actors, who are subsequently distorted by the theoretical frameworks of passivity and victimhood imposed by Aristotle and subsequent historians and political theorists. Her critique of Daly is that she has fallen into this same pattern in her work, by minimizing the differences in the experience of black and white women and by positing the former only as victims:

> What you excluded from *Gyn/Ecology* dismissed my heritage and the heritage of all other non-european women, and denied the real connections that exist between all of us . . . Have you read my work, and the work of other Black women, for what it could give you? Or did you hunt through only to find words that would legitimize your chapter on African mutilation in the eyes of the other Black women?[66]

Thus, first wave feminism and second wave feminism, or hyphenated feminism, have evolved over time. Within them we find not only the tensions between traditional political frameworks and feminism developing but simultaneously the seeds of a new form of feminism being sown. Throughout this evolution we have seen the two dualities we have used throughout this book as defining politics also evolve. They are initially embraced by feminism, then critically analysed by feminism and eventually destabilized by the necessities of feminist thought. We began with early first wave feminism, the struggle for the vote, where suffragists embraced women's role in the private sphere, while simultaneously trying to push for women's inclusion in the cultural sphere. It becomes clear from the historical writings that the 'women' referred to in this feminist struggle were middle- and upper-class white women. The later first wave feminists continue to hold on to the categories of public/private and culture/nature as necessary to an understanding of politics, but begin to challenge women's exclusion from both spheres. Simone de Beauvoir's great contribution to feminist thought, at the end of the first wave, was the understanding that these categories were not mutually defined in terms of one another, but rather that public defined what was 'private' and culture defined 'nature'. Men similarly defined 'women'. In each case, private, nature, woman were the 'other', understood only in terms of the referent term. de Beauvoir also ushered in the beginnings of second wave feminism, the hyphenated feminisms: liberal feminism, Marxist feminism and psychoanalytical feminism. All of them share, with regard to the culture/nature divide, a commitment to universality, science and a distinction between sex and gender and, with regard to the public/private duality, a focus on and thorough analysis of what constitutes the 'private sphere', often referred to as 'reproduction'. The need to hold on to one set of dualities, while challenging another, depends very much on the traditional framework that the feminist aligns herself with. While none of them ultimately eschews the dualities involved, the feminism half of their analysis will eventually force a great destabilization of the spheres as given by political theory.

Beginning with liberal feminism, it was critical that the liberal feminist hold on to the notion of 'private', for without it liberal thought means little, but feminists like Betty Friedan and others analysed this central principle from a feminist perspective. Socialist feminists, on the other hand, needed to hold on to the 'materialism' inherent in a culture/nature divide between the material underpinnings of history and the ideological or cultural justifications for them. Once again, however, socialist feminists, in holding on to 'materialism', applied a feminist analysis to this central concept and developed theories around both production and reproduction. In addition, Marxist feminists in particular supported the abolition of the private sphere as fundamentally opposed to women's interests. Psychoanalytical feminism embraced the 'private' sphere as central to our understanding of all aspects of life, including the political sphere. They ultimately argued that both men and women must be involved in childrearing. At the same time, psychoanalytical feminism held on to the scientific nature of its inquiry while turning the culture/nature divide upside down by arguing that reason serves only to channel the more powerful natural instincts into socially acceptable ways of behaving. Finally, radical feminism challenged and destabilized both the public/private divide and the cultural/natural divide. Many of the radical feminists argued that heterosexual and family relations must be fundamentally altered, while simultaneously challenging the claims of science to be something other than an ideology. At the same time, some of the early radical feminists argued strongly for a theory of biological foundationalism which had to be overcome by technology. Perhaps most important of all was the radical feminists' redefinition of politics. At the moment when the 'personal is the political' was taken to be the motto for the feminist movement, the dualities and hyphenations described above began to disintegrate and yield to the new form of contemporary feminisms which we see today. Thus we turn to examine the third wave of feminism(s).

7

Third Wave Feminism(s): the View at, of and from the Border(s)

The late 1980s and 1990s have witnessed the emergence of a new, third wave of feminism(s).[1] It began as feminists came to realize that the theoretical frameworks they had been using, built on the foundations of universality, sameness and scientific methodology, were becoming increasingly difficult to reconcile with where feminism had led them: to notions of identity, difference, particularity and embodiment. This new wave of feminism(s) has posed a fundamental challenge to western dualisms in particular. Rather than simply adopting the dualistic categories created by western political thought, as second wave feminism has done, and dividing the world into just two groups of people – namely men and women – and then attempting, in turn, to move men and women around within the dualistic categories of public/private or nature/culture, as has been discussed, there is a growing recognition that the way the categories themselves have been constructed is flawed. At the heart of third wave feminism(s) is the deconstruction of dualistic theoretical frameworks on two grounds. First, the dualisms which have been analysed in previous chapters by definition break the world into two, rather than a multiplicity. Second, such dualities have always meant there must be an 'other' against which the reference point, concept or perspective is defined. Third wave feminism(s) take (a) new perspective(s): beginning with 'women's' points of view, this new wave embraces the diversity and differences in perspectives among 'women', ultimately straddling both the 'one' and the 'other'.

Thus third wave feminism(s) begin with a breakdown in the marriages between feminism and other theoretical schools and a fundamental questioning of the categories that up until now have been adopted by feminists as their own theoretical underpinnings.

> Feminist theories today no longer feel compelled to carry their allegiances 'on their sleeves' (*Marxist* feminism, *liberal* feminism) in order to signal their authority to speak . . . Many contemporary feminist theorists no longer have faith in the utility of existing socio-political theories to explain or clarify the socio-political status of women. This 'loss of faith' in what has variously been named malestream, phallocentric or simply masculinist theories signals that many feminist no longer believe that these theories are marred by only a superficial sex-blindness or sexism. The problem is now located at a much more fundamental level. It cannot be simply a matter of removing superficial biases from socio-political theories, since the bias is now understood as intrinsic to the structure of the theories in question.[2]

These new feminisms begin with concepts of difference rather than sameness, identity and particularity rather than universality, celebrating the status of other or outsider rather than wanting inside, embodiment rather than the view from nowhere and, finally, a relational rather than binary approach. At the core of this approach is an attempt to base the analysis of politics on the experience and perspective of women rather then men. Elizabeth Grosz comments:

> Feminists of autonomy, on the other hand, undertake the challenge to the foundational reliance of knowledges on phallocentric norms, methods and paradigms. In questioning the 'contents' and unspoken assumptions, the preferred methods and ideals of phallocentric knowledges, these feminists are committed to the development of new or different forms of knowledge and intellectual inquiry. . . This, for many, is only the first step in the development of entirely new forms of theory based on women's experiences and perceptions rather than men's.[3]

Grosz distinguishes between what she calls 'feminists of autonomy' and conservative and liberal feminists, who continue to 'bolster and place beyond question the domination of masculine intellectual paradigms'.[4] I would argue, however, that every area of feminist thought, as has been shown above, has been destabilized by the necessities of feminism to rethink their marriage to traditional political and theoretical paradigms. In this sense, the third 'wave' is washing over all feminists, as they are forced to grapple seriously with the central issue of women's perspectives, and its implications for previous formulations of politics, history and knowledge. Thus, it is not that feminism has broken down into a continuation of a second wave feminism (untouched by 'third wave' considerations of difference, perspective and contradiction) on the one hand, represented by conservatives and liberals, and an 'autonomous feminism' (among them, self-declared third wave feminists) on the other, but an evolution in feminist thought generally, as it grapples towards particular, embodied, women's perspective(s).[5] As with any shift in thinking, there is not a clear demarcation, but shifting positions within feminist texts, so one finds allusions to second wave feminism's commitment to universality, sameness and unity in the same work as the defence of difference, embodiment and contradiction. As we shall see, feminists have largely left behind the theoretical frameworks to which they were attached in second wave feminism, but have incorporated as a central debate in third wave feminism the degree to which a unity and/or universality of 'women' as different from 'men' can be reconciled with the construction of identity and 'differences' among women.

'Generation X' Third Wave

One aspect of the 'third wave' has come from a younger generation of feminists. Since the mid-1990s there has been an important movement developing among some 'generation X' feminists, self-described 'third wavers'.[6] In 1995, two books – Listen Up: Voices from the Next Feminist Generation and To Be Real: Telling the Truth and Changing the Face of Feminism – were published.[7] They posed some new questions and challenges to a previous generation of feminists. These collections of essays were followed in the summer of 1997 with a special issue of Hypatia, dedicated entirely to examining the possibility of a new wave:

> Looking back and looking forward, there are generations of feminism forming in new ways and reforming the old . . . this special issue of Hypatia will refocus such a dialogue within feminist philosophy in an effort to speak across generations as we learn to speak, write and theorize across and through our many other relational differences.[8]

What distinguishes this group of younger feminist writings is first the very personal and popular nature of these narrative essays.

This is a deliberate choice, as editor Rebecca Walker makes clear, because personal stories are the most truly political (in the 'personal is political' sense of feminism) and more accessible, and because they respect the difference of perspectives among women.

> My requirement was that the pieces be personal, honest, and record a transformative journey taken. I prefer personal testimonies because they build empathy and compassion, are infinitely more accessible than more academic tracts, and because I believe that our lives are the best basis for feminist theory... we lay the groundwork for feminist theory that neither vilifies nor deifies, but that accepts and respects difference.[9]

Second is a recognition of the question of identity and, in particular, the multiplicity of identity and difference among women and the difficulties in categorizing oneself. Findlen comments:

> Generation X... one of the characteristics we're known for is our disunity. Maybe we're not as unified as the generation that preceded us. Maybe we're just not as categorizable... What may appear to be a splintering in this generation often comes from an honest assessment of our differences as each of us defines our place and role in feminism.[10]

Third, and linked to the second characteristic, is the desire to be 'real' or 'honest' about the contradictions feminists face every day in their lives, and to challenge the perceived rigidity in the ideals of second wave feminist politics.

> The complex, multi-issue nature of our lives, the instinct not to categorize and shut oneself off from others, and the enormous contradictions we embody are all fodder for making new theories of living and relating... rather than allowing ourselves and others to be put into boxes meant to categorize and dismiss, we can use the complexity of our lives to challenge the belief that any person or group is more righteous, more correct, more deserving of life than any other.[11]

The question that arises for these feminists, given the fragmented nature of the project which they are undertaking, is expressed by Rebecca Walker herself: 'What about the politics? What about the activism?'[12] of simply bringing together collections of essays which are highly individualistic, contradictory yet, in their own terms, more 'real'? Has this new generation of feminists redefined politics? In many ways, they have added a new dimension to a process already under way. More than anything else, the new generation feminists are calling for a new understanding of the 'personal is the political', what one writer calls a 'new subjectivity': a subjectivity not based around gender alone, but which must include all aspects of identity (sexuality, race, class, ability). This subjectivity, as it comes across in the pages of these new anthologies, in cyberspace, and from a new generation of 'grrl' music, is edgy and 'in your face'. The writings of Kate Roiphe, Naomi Wolf and Rene Denfeld (who argue that women in the 1990s must recognize, explore and use their untapped power and not accept what they describe as the 'victim' mentality of some second wave feminism) have been both incorporated and rejected by the new third wave.[13] Rejected, in part, for being too conservative and status quo, their thrust has simultaneously been incorporated in the new generation's feminism, through notions of individuality, strength and female power (the subjectivity described above). The idea of speaking from a position of strength has found its voice in the angry and individualistic world of a new generation of young female singers. From the 'Riot Grrls' to the Spice Girls to Alanis Morrisette to Mc'Shell NdegeOcello, the world of both mainstream and alternative music has been filled, in the 1990s, with the songs of young women claiming a sense of their own power.[14] As one website describes the concept of Riot Grrls:

A music movement that has its roots in punk rock . . . it is activist music, zines, and other activity that builds a supportive environment for women and girls and is concerned with feminist issues . . . The network of zines that are produced by girls and young women who identify with the music that is associated with RIOT GRRL. The zines are often intensely personal, but that personal outlet is translated to larger political action when the zines are available to the public . . . the ethos of RIOT GRRL is about supporting each other, empowering each other.[15]

This alternative movement has been overtaken by popular culture, creating, among other things, the phenomenon known as the Spice Girls, who are seen by some as a watered down, consumer driven version of the original Riot Grrl movement:

Their [the Spice Girls'] Girl Power message . . . is a sanitized version of the antimedia Riot Grrrl movement, which developed several years ago in the US. The Riot Grrrls were unsightly teen feminists, iconoclasts who scrawled graffiti on their stomachs . . . Less girl groups than gender terrorists, these bands originated Girl Power, and then demonstrated it every time they picked up an electric guitar . . . Bad Sisters. Unphotogenic. And virtuosic in the male-dominated sphere of hard-core.[16]

The contradictions in this brand of American third wave feminism, between embracing and rejecting both second wave feminism and 'power feminism', are best reflected, it is argued by some third wave feminists, in figures like punk rocker Courtney Love:

> One public figure who demonstrates some of the contradictions that third wave feminism brings together is Courtney Love, the punk rock musician who bridges the opposition between 'power feminism' and 'victim feminism'. She combines the individualism, combativeness, and starpower . . . with second wave critiques of beauty and male dominance.[17]

Finally, many young third wave feminists are questioning the confines of feminist academia, particularly the media chosen for the dissemination of feminist ideas. Rather than scholarly papers in 'refereed' journals, many have taken to communicating with one another through zines; that is, photocopied pages passed along through informal networks and hybrid publications, and through cyberspace (e-mails, web pages and chat groups). There are often connections between these different forms of communications, as zine networks create their own websites.[18] This new generation of women is taking over areas which have often been dominated by men, and their numbers appear to be growing exponentially. For example, in 1995, a group of six New York women formed a group called 'Cybergrrls'. Through the power of the Internet it has blossomed into a global network.[19]

Young academic feminists are also exploring the possibilities of cyberspace, for both communication and dissemination. For example, the first article in the special issue of *Hypatia* is written in the form of an e-mail dialogue. Catherine Orr argues that this reliance on information technology poses a profound challenge for all feminists:

> The term 'third wave' within contemporary feminism presents some initial difficulties in scholarly investigation. Located in popular-press anthologies, zines, punk music and cyber space, many third wave discourses constitute themselves as a break with both second wave and academic feminisms . . . the emergence of third wave feminism offers academic feminists an opportunity to rethink the context of knowledge production and the mediums through which we disseminate our work.[20]

While the 'generational' aspect has been the focus of much of the discussion within academia of 'third wave feminism', a few feminists have questioned whether this new wave can be reduced to a matter of age and medium. Rita Alfonso argues that is not just a generation based on age, but includes women across different age groups, what she calls a 'political generation', defining this to be: 'a group of people (not necessarily of the same age) that experiences shared shaped formative social conditions . . . and that hold a common interpretive framework shaped by historical circumstances'.[21]

It is clear, however, as will be shown, that many of the ideas adopted by this new generation of feminists were first articulated a decade ago by, in particular, feminists of colour, lesbian feminists and queer theory. As Orr comments:

> [The] definitional moment of third wave feminism took place on the terrain of racism in the 1980s rather than age in the mid-1990s . . . The contradictory characteristic of the third wave emerged not from the generational divide . . . but from the critiques of . . . feminists of colour who called for a 'new subjectivity' in what was, up to that point, white, middle-class, first world feminism. These are the discourses that shaped and must continue to shape, third wave agendas in the years to come.[22]

Heywood and Drake also conclude that the 'third wave's roots' are to be found in the work of earlier 'US third world feminism'. For it is their analysis which seems more 'real' at the end of the millennium:

> Although we also owe an enormous debt to the critique of sexism and the struggles for gender equity that were white feminism's strongest provinces, it was US third world feminism that modeled a language and a politics of hybridity that can account for our lives at the century's turn. These are lives marked by the realities of multicultural exchange, fusion, and conflict, lives that combine blackness, whiteness, brownness, gayness, bisexuality, straightness.[23]

Thus, third wave feminism(s) are rooted in the questions raised by feminists of colour and lesbian and queer theorists about the nature of identity, the meaning of 'gender' and working through some of the contradictions elicited by such questions. It is these challenges, posed by feminists a decade ago, that created the momentum for a wave which is now beginning to crest, and wash over feminists across the board. It may be the new generation of young feminists who show the rest of us how to surf it.

Given that third wave feminism(s) is something whose roots stretch back into the 1980s and whose force will be felt into the next millennium, beyond this generation and the next, let us consider what has emerged as the central themes or ideas in third wave feminism(s), how they developed and the ways in which they challenge the dualistic frameworks which preceded them.

Difference

First and foremost is the notion of difference(s). Some have argued that differences have become the singular focus of feminism. 'Many feminists now contend that difference occupies center stage as *the* project of women studies today.'[24] Elizabeth Fox-Genovese comments: 'Difference has replaced equality as the central concern of feminist theory.'[25] Difference is seen in two senses of the word: difference between men and women as opposed to the sameness embraced by second wave feminism; and difference among 'women', so often ignored by second wave feminism. Both of these ideas of 'difference' will be discussed at length. As we shall see, the dualities inherent in western political theory are not only challenged but destabilized by difference(s). The boundaries which have demarcated politics for most of its history are under attack, and the dualities themselves are being redefined.

'Difference' between men and women represents an important shift from second to third wave feminism(s). As we have discussed, many of the universalistic hyphenated feminisms adopted the notion provided by their theoretical frameworks that every person is basically the same by nature but that society (for liberals), the mode of production (for Marxists) or early childhood rearing (for psychoanalysts) creates differences. The goal, for the most part, was to find ways that men and women could be equal and the same, as has been discussed, by attempting to move women into the public, cultural realms. The only exception to this would be some of the second wave 'radical feminists' discussed in previous chapters. Their work provides some of the foundations for the third wave of feminism(s). Radical second wave feminism and third wave feminism(s) share the idea of difference, but the latter, as will be discussed, does not necessarily consider gender prior to all other notions of identity and is more willing to live with the contradictions inherent in bridging the boundaries between different identities. Thus, the roots of embracing woman's difference are found in second wave feminism's celebration of that which makes her different; that is, women *as* 'the other'.

The first step towards third wave feminism(s) was thus an identification with, and celebration of, 'otherness'; the embracing of

women's connection with nature and the private sphere. By looking at the world from 'a woman's point of view', the natural and
private spheres which had been traditionally devalued are suddenly extolled: women's sexuality, their bodies, their relationship
to the environment on the one hand, and the values and activities
associated with nurturing and motherhood on the other. The celebration of women's otherness not only challenged the power bal-
ance inherent in the dualities of political thought, but began to
destabilize the whole structure of dualistic western thought. At the
same time, difference cut across what had previously been distinct
schools of hyphenated feminist thought, seeping into all the vari-
ants of second wave feminism.

Towards the end of second wave feminism, the roots of this
notion of 'difference' in perspective were being sown. Nancy
Chodorow and Carol Gilligan were two key figures in the introduction of difference into Anglo-American feminist literature. 'The
enormous attention given . . . to books such as Carol Gilligan's, *In a
Different Voice* (1980) and Nancy Chodorow's, *The Reproduction of
Mothering* (1978) can be said to follow from the usefulness of the
former in elaborating difference between women and men and of
the latter in accounting for it.'[26] Although Gilligan herself was
explicit about not necessarily identifying the different moral voices
she discovered in her work as explicitly male and female, she
nevertheless identified a different morality she called 'the ethics of
care' which heretofore had been ignored in traditional psychological studies of ethical development. Specifically, Gilligan was challenging Lawrence Kohlberg's sixfold scale of moral development,
moving from a early stage of obedience and reciprocity, to interpersonal concordance, law and order and eventually acceptance of
rights, social contracts and ultimately a universal principles orientation. Gilligan found that such a scale reflected the general perspective of men on ethical issues but not women. Instead, women's
approach to moral reasoning was less dependent on an individualistic moral self legislating universal laws as on someone already
engaged in a variety of human relations who was trying to work
out, with other individuals, an agreed upon solution which would
minimize the pain to both the individuals and relationships involved in the issue. The development pattern for women is therefore from self-directed care to altruism, or care for others, and finally
to a relational, caring position, where everyone's needs must be
taken into consideration in relation to all others.[27] Gilligan, like
many second wave feminists, has been criticized for her failure to

address racial and class differences among her subjects, assuming that gender was the most critical variable.[28]

Nancy Chodorow not only describes the differences between men and women but attempts to provide an explanation for them. Her argument, as has been discussed, is that men and women develop very different personalities from early childhood because women are the nurturers:

> Women's mothering, then, produces ... crucial differences in feminine and masculine personality, and the relational capacities and modes which these entail ... Feminine personality comes to be based less on repression of inner objects, and fixed and firm splits in the ego, and more on retention and continuity of external relationships ... Boys come to define themselves as more separate and distinct, with a greater sense of rigid ego boundaries and differentiation. The basic feminine sense of self is connected to the world, the basic masculine sense of self is separate.[29]

Chodorow concludes that men must be more involved in the task of 'mothering' – that is, early childhood development and nurturance – if men and women are to overcome these differences. Chodorow, having identified and celebrated women's role as mother, nevertheless has as her goal, like much of second wave feminism, that men and women will become more or less the same. Unlike earlier feminists, however, she is arguing that men need to become more like women, need to enter the private and natural spheres of reproduction more fully, rather than the other way around. Other feminist thinkers, like Jean Bethke Elshtain and Alice Rossi, have questioned the assumption by both Chodorow and Dorothy Dinnerstein that men need only be more involved in early childcare for the differences between men and women basically to disappear and for the problems associated with gender to be solved.[30]

Difference between men and women has also been central to the French feminists, such as Helene Cixous, Luce Irigaray and Julia Kristeva. All of them challenged the dualities inherent in western thought, by beginning their writing and thinking from the point of view of women's bodies and sexuality. Cixous believed that the dichotomous pairs of western thought all originated in the most fundamental duality between men and women. Cixous argued that women must begin writing in 'different' ways from what is 'allowed' under the rules of masculine thinking and writing. Such writing is intimately tied to the difference in women's sexuality. Unlike western thought, Cixous thus begins with the body. 'Woman will confirm woman in a place other than that which is reserved [when] she physically materializes what she's thinking; she signifies it with her body'.[31]

Luce Irigaray took on 'sameness' directly, arguing that for too long women have adopted a masculine femininity imposed upon them by a world constructed by men. Women need to find the 'feminine feminine', namely that which makes them different. She provides several strategies. The first is to avoid becoming the 'neutral voice' of science. The falsely objective voice of scientific analysis is inconsistent with the feminine feminine. Instead, woman should speak in an active subjective voice, taking responsibility for her words and thoughts. Second, women's sexuality is plural, as opposed to men's, which is singular and linear. All human expression until now has reflected the latter. Women must begin to express themselves in terms of the former: to celebrate their sexual and subjective difference.

> One must listen to her differently in order to hear *an 'other meaning' which is constantly in the process of weaving itself, at the same time ceaselessly embracing words and yet casting them off to avoid becoming fixed, immobilized* ... Moreover, her statements are never identical to anything. This distinguishing feature is one of contiguity. They touch (upon). And when they wander too far from this nearness, she stops and begins again from 'zero': her body-sex organ.[32]

Irigaray argues that if sexual difference were truly recognized, whole new horizons of knowledge would be possible: 'Sexual difference would constitute the horizon of worlds of a still unknown fecundity... Fecundity of birth and regeneration for amorous partners, but more the production of a new epoch of thought, art, poetry, language.'[33]

Kristeva distinguishes a difference between masculinity and femininity rather than men and women. This difference originates at the time when mother and child bond, called the 'semiotic' – a time preceding language and marked by the omnipresence of the mother's body. With the acquisition of language, one enters the paternal sphere, what Kristeva calls the 'symbolic'. The symbolic attempts to repress the semiotic in language but it is nevertheless present. When the feminine, or semiotic, writing is freed it will embrace rhythm, sound and the maternal body.

> Memories of bodily contact, warmth, and nourishment: these underlie the breast of the newborn body as it appeals to a source of support, a fulfillment of care ... Voice is the vehicle of that call for

help ... and this is undoubtedly significant for the acquisition of language, which will soon be articulated along the same vehicle.[34]

While she acknowledges both difference and the importance of women's bodies to the construction of this difference, Kristeva's refusal to identify masculine with men and feminine with women arises from her contention that ontologically women simply cannot 'be'. Her argument both picks up the question articulated by Sojourner Truth a century earlier and presages the debates which were yet to occur among feminists about the meaning of 'woman'. Kristeva concludes that while there is no ontological meaning to 'woman', there is a political meaning:

> The belief that 'one is a woman' is almost as absurd and obscurantist as the belief that 'one is a man'. I say 'almost' because there are still many goals which women can achieve: freedom of abortion and contraception, day care centres for children, equality on the job, etc. Therefore we must use 'we are women' as an advertisement or slogan for our demands. On a deeper level, however, a woman cannot 'be'; it is something which does not even belong in the order of being.[35]

These notions of difference are central to contemporary third wave feminism(s), and both destabilize and turn the dichotomy between nature and culture in particular on its head. Rather than playing into the devaluing or domination of the body, sexuality and reproduction by the mind, reason and culture, third wave feminists begin with the body and embodiment as central to the development of political theory from a woman's point of view. One of the most fundamental problems in western political thought, including second wave feminism, has been the negation of the body, in particular the female body. The notion of 'difference', as we have seen in French feminist thought, begins with the celebration of the female body. Third wave feminism has made the body and 'embodiment' a central feature of its analysis.[36]

The female body and embodiment

From the second wave feminists' account of difference and celebration of woman's connection with nature, and in particular her own body, we arrive at one of the key themes in third wave feminism(s), namely 'embodiment'. Embodiment or the situated body is first and foremost a challenge to scientific methodology; that is, both the view from nowhere and the distance assumed between subject and object, between mind and body. Women and men are thus situated in a particular place and time, demarcated by their bodies. This cannot simply be eschewed, as is done in political theory from Thomas Hobbes's state of nature to John Rawls's original position. Grosz comments: 'This idealized space, the prerequisite for the knowing, objective, rational subject, is the space based on the male disavowal of his body and his sex, and the assumption that he occupies a neutral position. Feminist theory on the other hand readily accepts the complicity of subject and object in knowledge-production.'[37] Donna Haraway talks of 'situated knowledges' and the need for 'political accounts of constructed embodiments'.[38] Such accounts, however, must incorporate different cross-cutting bodily identities, including race, class and sexuality. 'Necessarily political accounts of constructed embodiments, like feminist theories of gendered racial subjectivities, have to take affirmative *and* critical account of emergent, differentiating, self-representing, contradictory social subjectivities, with their claims on action, knowledge, and belief.'[39]

For many feminists, the focus on women's bodies destabilizes the duality of culture/nature in another important way. The body and one's 'sex', within western political thought, has long been seen as a 'biological' entity. Many mainstream feminists adopted this point of view, arguing that one's sex is given, immutable, while one's gender is the socially constructed identity which develops on top of this biological 'reality'. As Linda Nicholson points out, the body was held to be biologically common; that is, foundational but *not* determinative, so that second wave feminists could reconcile difference between men and women (biological common ground) with difference among women (cultural diversity) and the belief that change was possible (non-determinative biology or nature). She adds that such a view undermines women's understanding of themselves:

> If one thought of the body as the common rack upon which different societies impose different norms of personality and behavior, then one could explain both how some of those norms might be the same in different societies and how some others might be different . . . the coat rack view of identity in general stand[s] in the way of our truly understanding differences among women, differences among men, and the differences regarding who gets counted as either.[40]

To break down the duality between gender and sex, it is necessary, according to Jane Flax, to deconstruct the larger categories of culture and nature:

Thus, in order to understand gender as a social relation, feminist theories need to deconstruct further the meanings we attach to biology/sex/gender/nature. This process of deconstruction is far from complete and certainly is not easy. Initially some feminists thought we could merely separate the terms *sex* and *gender*. As we became more sensitive to the social histories of concepts, it became clear that such an (apparent) disjunction . . . rested upon problematic and culture-specific oppositions, for example, the one between nature and culture or body and mind.[41]

Thus the constructed relationship between culture and nature, where the latter is taken to be the unchanging foundation upon which the former is built, is false, particularly the belief that there is some pre-cultural biological body. Butler concludes:

> There will be no way to understand 'gender' as a cultural construct which is imposed upon the surface of matter, understood either as 'the body' or its given sex . . . Sex is thus, not simply what one has, or a static description of what one is: it will be one of the norms by which the 'one' becomes viable at all, that which qualifies a body for life with the domain of cultural intelligibility.[42]

Collete Guillaumin and Avtar Brah agree with Butler but argue that the construction of identity must incorporate race and gender. Brah concludes that Butler's question about the construction of the body must be more inclusive:

> Her question: 'To what extent does the body come in to being in and through the mark(s) of gender?' may be reformulated as: 'To what extent does the body come in to being in and through the mark(s) of gender, "race", or class?' There is then an implosion of boundaries between the physical and social body.[43]

Shane Phelan argues that, for lesbian feminists, this recognition of the cultural, as opposed to biological, construction of sex and sexuality is often difficult but necessary: 'Relinquishing lesbianism as a state of nature may seem baffling or incoherent . . . Convinced that sexuality is symptomatic of being, that is its "prior to" convention . . . lesbians have called upon ourselves and one another to decipher the truth of our bodies and to attune our politics to that truth.'[44] Jeannine Delombard concurs with Phelan, concluding that lesbian 'femmenists' must relinquish the dualities of culture and nature, and accept that the truths which ensue are rife with contradictions. This is the heart, she claims, of third wave 'femmenism':

Waves – which by definition, curve alternately in opposite directions – embody contradiction. For me femmenism is where the third wave of Western feminism and the third wave of American lesbianism intersect. Femmenism is the riptide that drags nature and nurture, essentialism and constructivism, and all other binary oppositions out to sea. Femmenism is nothing if not contradictory. Femmenism is looking like a straight woman and living like a dyke.[45]

'Embodiment' and situated perspectives are also critical to the analysis of traditional political theory. If women's bodies are considered in the way one conceptualizes politics, it is clear that the body politic of political theory excludes women's bodies. This is critical in understanding why second wave feminists, who attempted to begin their own analysis from within such frameworks, have run into difficulties. The underlying duality between mind and body, between culture and nature, between the body politic and women's bodies, must be completely rethought if women are to be truly part of the political world. Gatens comments:

> It is not so much that women are biologically unsuited to political participation, as political participation has been structured and defined in such a way that it excludes women's bodies. If this is so then fighting to have women included in the present body politic will be counterproductive unless it is accompanied by some analysis of the exclusions of women's corporeality that still define that body politic and a working framework from which to think and live other ways of being.[46]

Carole Pateman provides a specific example of such exclusion. The embracing of the body by feminists undercuts the possibility of thinking in liberal democratic terms of a social contract, she argues. This seventeenth-century device, which has continued to underpin the rights and obligations of liberal political theory, is simply irreconcilable with women's bodies as understood from a feminist perspective:

> The logic of contract as exhibited in 'surrogate' motherhood shows very starkly how extension of the standing of 'individual' to women can reinforce and transform patriarchy as well as challenge patriarchal institutions. To extend to women the masculine conception of the individual as owner, and the conception of freedom as the capacity to do what you will with your own, is to sweep away any intrinsic relation between the female owner, her body and reproductive capacities. She stands to her property in exactly the same external relation as the male owner stands to his labour power or sperm; there is nothing distinctive about womanhood.[47]

Pateman's critique of liberal democratic citizenship as a whole is directed towards the exclusion of women's bodies from the current understanding of politics. Her solution is to develop a 'sexually differentiated' notion of citizenship. In particular, it would give equal political significance to the bodily capacity which women have and men lack; namely to give birth. The problem with current liberal democratic theory is that giving birth is not given the same weight in defining citizenship as the willingness to die for one's country, which is the traditional and ultimate test for citizenship among men. Pateman concludes that the two underpinning dualities of modern political thought must be renegotiated, both the culture/nature divide represented in the disembodied 'view from nowhere' and the public/private dichotomy. Such a reconceptualization of politics, which 'gives due weight to sexual difference in a context of civil equality, requires the rejection of a unitary (i.e., masculine) conception of the individual, abstracted from our embodied existence and from the patriarchal division between the private and public'.[48] Anne Phillips concurs: 'Those who seek to deny the body, who deal only in the abstraction of "the individual" or "the citizen", who it think it should make no difference whether these individuals are women or men, will be writing in one sex alone as their standard.'[49]

Motherhood

One aspect of women's bodies which became a central debate in second wave feminism was 'motherhood'. Traditional political theory and some feminist writers, such as Simone de Beauvoir and Shulamith Firestone, sought to devalue the role of women as mothers, as has been discussed. Adrienne Rich also denounced the patriarchal form of motherhood. It is the denunciation of motherhood that some third wave feminists have take exception to, while embracing the writings of bell hooks and Jean Bethke Elshtain, who see mothering as a strength rather than a weakness of women. Elshtain, for example, argues that women as mothers should be the starting point of feminist political analysis; providing a new political ethics to replace the individual utilitarianism of liberal democracies. Elshtain concludes:

> For women to affirm the protection of fragile and vulnerable human existence as the basis of a mode of political discourse, and to create the terms for its flourishing as a worthy political activity, for women

to stand firm against cries of 'emotional' or 'sentimental' even as they refuse to lapse into a sentimental rendering of the values and language which flow form 'mothering' would signal a force of great reconstructive potential.[50]

hooks states: 'Had black women voiced their views on motherhood, it would not have been named a serious obstacle to our freedom as women.'[51] Allison Abner, a new third wave feminist, concludes in response to her reading of Adrienne Rich that there is 'something more' to motherhood than second wave feminists, such as Rich, have allowed:

> For me, that 'something more' means being part of another tradition, the eternally connective tradition of motherhood. For me, having this child won't be an impediment, but a channel through which I feel connected to other women, other mothers, other wives who have placed family at the heart of their self-concept without feeling they've lost themselves.[52]

Another young feminist writer speaks of the many contradictions in her life as a stay at home mother, and the struggle to accept 'motherhood' as part of her strength and one aspect of her multiple identities:

> As an educated, married, monogamous, feminist, Christian, African American mother; I suffer from an acute case of multiplicity. Each identity defines me; each is responsible for elements of my character; from each I derive some sustenance for my soul . . . I now know that it is not necessary to shun marriage and family. Instead we must redefine these concepts and break the narrow traditional encasings . . . We can make the roles fit our identity instead of deriving our identity from these labels.[53]

Challenges to ecofeminism

While the body is one aspect of the 'natural sphere' which has been reanalysed in third wave feminism, the 'environment' is another. Second wave ecofeminism, which had sought to 'strengthen the bonds between women and nature by critiquing their parallel oppressions and encouraging an ethic of caring and politics of solidarity', has also been challenged by third wave feminism(s).[54] Perhaps the greatest critic of ecofeminism is Donna Haraway, whose work attempts to break down the distinction between nature and culture and technology. Nowhere is this clearer than in her notion of the 'cyborg'. Haraway argues that many of the views embraced by ecofeminism, in failing to destabilize the categories of nature and culture, are completely compatible with continued male oppression. She uses Japanese primatology to demonstrate how values that have been embraced by ecofeminists can indeed serve to support masculine power:

> Holism, appreciation of intuitive method, presence of 'matriarchal' myth systems and histories of women's cultural innovation, cultivation of emotional and cognitive connection between humans and animals, absence of dualist splits in objects of knowledge, qualitative method subtly integrated with rigorous and long-term quantification, extensive attention to the female social organization as the infrastructure grounding more visible male activities, and lack of culturally reinforced fear of loss of personal boundaries in loving scientific attention to the world are all perfectly compatible with masculinism in epistemology and male dominance in politics.[55]

The problem with simply embracing the dualities as they exist between culture and nature, and then validate the 'natural' side of that distinction, is that it fails to question the underlying politics or power dynamic inherent in the duality itself, thus leaving ecofeminism open to the possibility of being used to reinforce traditional patriarchal assumptions, and leaving women as 'passive' and without agency. The solution for some feminists is to create an alliance rather than identification between women and nature, and assert the political agency of both. This will necessarily involve the deconstruction of the passive category within which women and nature are both constrained, in both traditional political theory and ecofeminism. Stacey Alaimo concludes:

> Although ecofeminism attempts to rearticulate the age-old associations of woman and nature in order to make them comrades in a struggle that would benefit them both, many of the connections it affirms can be readily deployed to support patriarchal capitalism and the domination of Others . . . By envisioning women and nature as political allies, an environmental feminism would emphasize the importance of women as political activists and stress the agency of nature. Focusing on the agency of women and nature can help keep environmentalism in the political arena and can oppose the appropriation of nature . . . by breaking down the nature/culture divide, thus undermining the system of domination.[56]

Haraway uses the image of a cyborg, straddling nature and culture, to centre her feminism, and to argue for a stronger agency on behalf of women. 'At the centre of my ironic faith, my blasphemy, is the image of the cyborg. A cyborg is a cybernetic organism, a hybrid of machine and organism.'[57] Her argument will be taken up in more depth in the final section of this chapter.

The celebration of difference in all the forms we have discussed (the breakdown of dualisms, beginning afresh from women's perspective(s), the centrality of women's bodies to political theory, the agency of women and the contradictions which emerge) is thus found in a wide variety of writings which taken together create the intellectural force behind the third wave. This first theme of third wave feminism (namely 'difference' in all of its manifestations) necessarily leads feminism into the second general theme (namely 'differences'). For in taking seriously the notion of difference, and thereby the points of view from which women look at the world, the question of identity, or the specific and unique perspective of different individual or groups of women, immediately arises.

Difference(s)

Difference and differences, while implied in each other, do not necessarily sit easily together. Indeed, the two terms introduce any number of contradictions which strike at the very heart of what second wave feminism called either 'gender' or, indeed, 'feminism' as one unified term. At the crux of the current debates about politics and political activities, among feminists today, is the question of whether it is possible, or desirable, to maintain a unified force of 'women' and their different perspective(s) in order to resist the historical oppression of women, as women, while simultaneously incorporating, in a serious way, the 'differences' among women in both theory and practice. Third wave feminism, in grappling with these questions, is engaged in debates not so much with other political frameworks and their proponents, as among themselves over this question of women's (womens') perspective(s). We must turn, then, and examine the second important aspect of third wave feminism(s), namely 'differences', which will include a discussion of identity (including the debate between postmodern and standpoint feminists), contradiction, hybridity, affiliation and locality.

This latter notion of 'differences' poses an even more profound challenge to the dualistic conception underpinning much of political theory and second wave feminism. Rather than assuming two categories in any given analysis – for example, man and woman or black and white – third wave feminism(s) acknowledge(s) the greater complexity of a multiplicity of differences between individuals and groups. In a phrase, the politics of identity. The origins of these questions about identity and difference are to be found in the writings of lesbians and women of colour, who have challenged the assumed 'sameness' of women, as articulated in first and second wave feminism.

Identity

Some lesbian feminists argued that the beginnings of the recognition of their difference(s), their identities, by mainstream second wave feminism really came with the motto 'the personal is the political'. Once you begin analysing the 'personal', notions of 'identity' are immediately introduced, which not only makes differences more explicit but may simultaneously propel the identification of those group members with each other rather than with 'outsiders'. Shane Phelan comments:

> Feminist theorizing about lesbianism began with the premise that the personal is political. This framework was used to legitimate lesbianism as 'feminist theory in action' . . . as visible, integrated love of women, and therefore of oneself . . . the early recognition of the connection between the personal and the political was often transformed into overarching explanations of every aspect of lesbian lives. Whether explicitly or not, these theories have worked to turn our communities inward rather than to propel us toward alliances and coalitions with others.[58]

Some feminists also challenged the 'racial' biases inherent within mainstream second wave feminist discourse, as has been discussed in previous chapters, most particularly the notion of 'woman' as universal. Martin and Mohanty argue that the recognition of class and 'racial' identity has exposed 'the extreme limits of what passes itself off as simply human, as universal, as unconstrained by identity, namely the position of the white middle class . . . Change has to do with the transgression of boundaries, those boundaries so carefully, so tenaciously, so invisibly drawn around white identity.'[59] The recognition of differences has not come easily for some feminists. Haraway comments: 'White women including Euro-american socialist feminists, discovered (i.e. were forced kicking and screaming to notice) the non-innocence of the category "woman".'[60]

At the heart of third wave feminism(s)' focus on identity is thus a challenge to the notion of 'woman' as a unified self with one perspective, albeit different from traditional masculine political theory. Multiple viewpoints and identities must be a starting point for third wave feminism(s). Contradictions and conflicts must ultimately emerge. 'We learn that feminists speak in different voices and from multiple historical, cultural, racial, economic and sexual locations. We learn of the shaping power of overlapping allegiances and oppressions which intersect in often conflicting modes.'[61]

Three concepts with regard to identity enter the feminist lexicon: one is fluidity rather than fixed identity; the second is multiple rather than singular identity; the third is contradiction. The first comes in part from French feminist arguments about the nature of the unconscious and how it lies outside the grasp of our unified sense of rational self. Identity or the 'self' is not fixed, but fluid and unstable:

> A fixed identity is perhaps a fiction, an illusion – who amongst us has a fixed identity... All identities are unstable: the identity of linguistic signs, the identity of meaning and, as a result, the identity of the speaker. And in order to take account of this de-stabilization of meaning and of the subject I thought the term 'subject in process' would be appropriate.[62]

Beyond the idea of a unified self, feminists have also challenged the notion that there is such a thing as 'women', with some essential singular identity. Instead, women exist as a multiplicity of identities, defined in terms of our differences to others. Haraway argues that feminism must begin from this recognition of multiple identities: 'Identities seem contradictory, partial and strategic. With the hard-won recognition of their social and historical constitution, gender, race, and class cannot provide the basis for belief in "essential" unity. There is nothing about being "female" that naturally binds women.'[63] Thus, one must be careful not to 'essentialize' or universalize 'women' as a single entity, for in doing so, one must immediately exclude certain groups of women who do not see themselves reflected in the concept of 'woman' which feminism has claimed for itself. Judith Butler comments:

> Feminist theory has taken the category of women to be foundational to any further political claims without realizing that the category effects a political closure on the kinds of experiences articulable as part of a feminist discourse ... This move has created a problem both theoretical and political, namely that a variety of women from various cultural positions have refused to recognize themselves as 'women' in the terms articulated by feminist theory with the result

that these women fall outside the category and are left to conclude that either (1) they are not women as they have perhaps previously assumed or (2) the category reflects the restricted location of its theoreticians and, hence, fails to recognize the intersection of gender with race, class, ethnicity, age, sexuality and other currents which contribute to the formation of cultural (non) identity.[64]

Many feminists argue that the incorporation of differences into feminist analysis must fully address not just multiplicity, but the relationship between *power* and difference. As Zinn and Dill argue, this is not always the case: 'Despite the much-heralded diversity trend within feminists' studies, difference is often reduced to pluralism: a "live and let live" approach . . . The major limitation of these approaches is the failure to attend to the power relations that accompany difference.'[65]

For Haraway and Butler, among others, power is critical. Indeed, differences of identity exist only in relationship to the historical oppressions which created them: 'Gender, race, or class consciousness is an achievement forced on us by the terrible historical experience of the contradictory social realities of patriarchy, colonialism, racism and capitalism.'[66] It is for this reason that Butler claims that lying at the heart of 'politics' for feminism must be the 'deconstruction' of identity. 'The deconstruction of identity is not the deconstruction of politics; rather, it establishes as political the very terms through which identity is articulated.'[67] The question immediately arises: how do feminists practise this new form of politics? How has feminism incorporated these ideas of power, identity and difference in order to recognize the ways in which gender is constructed through 'a matrix of domination', including race, class and identification, to create a unified force against such domination, while ensuring that the voices of those who were marginalized by second wave feminism are heard?[68]

Iris Marion Young and Anne Phillips have attempted to incorporate differences into their analysis of politics by focusing on how to create practices and institutions which will ensure that previously marginalized voices are heard. For Young, this 'openness to difference' must become the very stuff of politics:

I am asserting an ideal, which consists in a politics of difference . . . The relationship among group identities and cultures in our society is blotted by racism, sexism, xenophobia, homophobia, suspicion and mockery. A politics of difference lays down institutional and ideological means for recognizing and affirming differently identifying groups in two basic senses: giving political representation to

group interests and celebrating the distinctive cultures and characteristics of different groups.[69]

Standpoint feminists, who have been criticized by Donna
Haraway and others for their tendency to essentialize 'woman's'
perspective or standpoint and consequently ignore the differences
between women, have also begun to address seriously the question
of differences.[70] In a 1997 issue of *Signs*, Susan Hekman confronts
this issue in an article responded to by Nancy Hartsock, Patricia
Hill Collins, Sandra Harding and Dorothy Smith. Hekman claims
that standpoint feminism is the perfect vehicle for a feminism which
embraces differences:

> I assert that this theory remains central to contemporary feminism
> because the questions it raises are crucial to the future development
> of feminist theory and politics. Recently there has been much discus-
> sion among feminists of the parameters of a 'politics of difference'.
> I believe that feminist standpoint theory has laid the ground-
> work for such a politics by initiating the discussion of situated
> knowledges.[71]

Hekman's argument is that within the epistemology of standpoint
theory itself is the basis for the inclusion of difference. The price of
it must be to eschew the 'privileged' claim of Hartsock:

> The original formulations of feminist standpoint theory rest on two
> assumptions: that all knowledge is located and situated, and that
> one location, that of the standpoint of women, is privileged because
> it provides a vantage point that reveals the truth of social reality. It is
> my thesis that the deconstruction of this second assumption is im-
> plicit in the first and as the theory developed the problematic nature
> of the second assumption came to the forefront.[72]

In her response to Hekman, Hartsock admits in the original formulation of standpoint theory: 'I failed to allow for the importance
of differences among women and differences among other various
groups – power differences all.'[73] Hartsock, in subsequent writings,
and in the response to Hekman, is seeking ways in which to incorporate difference without losing the notion that there is still a
privileged position based on ethical and political grounds for the
'women's standpoint'. Hartsock criticizes Hekman's attempt to make
standpoint theory into pure epistemology, arguing that it is necessary to hold on to the notion of women's standpoint as privileged
on 'ethical or political rather than purely epistemological' grounds.[74]
Similarly, Patricia Hill Collins argues that standpoint theory refers

to historically shared '*group*-based experiences', and has its 'moorings in a knowledge/power' framework. Thus Collins concludes that Hekman, by making a purely epistemological argument, 'depoliticizes the potentially radical content of standpoint theory'.[75]

Postmodern feminism and the third wave

While third wave feminism(s) have embraced differences among women as central to their analysis, concern has been expressed that this new form of identity feminism(s) may lose its (their) capacity to resist the monolith of sameness and universality represented by modern political thought and practice. This question is central to the debate between standpoint and postmodern feminists. For standpoint feminists, it is still necessary to make a political claim on behalf of privileging 'woman's' standpoint. For postmodern feminists such a privileging of a 'woman's' standpoint is to marginalize aspects of one's identity other than gender.

Whether postmodernism, as an approach, best incorporates 'differences' into feminist analysis has also generated some debate among feminists. Christine Di Stefano, Sandra Harding and Seyla Benhabib, in a collection of essays on postmodernism and feminism, all argue in different ways that the 'relativism' and 'difference' of postmodern feminism may ironically tend to exclude those individuals it claims to want to include, while making resistance to the current paradigms of science and politics more difficult.

> In our efforts to find ways to include the voices of marginal groups, we might expect helpful guidance from those who have argued against totalizing and universalistic theories such as those of the Enlightenment ... Despite their apparent congruence with the project I am proposing, these theories, I contend, would hinder rather than help its accomplishment ... At their worst, postmodern theories merely recapitulate the effects of Enlightenment theories – theories that deny marginalized people the right to participate in defining the terms of interaction with people in the mainstream.[76]

bell hooks has made the same point about postmodern discourses. hooks's greatest concern, despite her embracing of the idea of a 'politics of difference', is that postmodern discourse has failed to interest African American intellectuals while completely excluding those who are not part of its 'specialized audience'.

> Postmodernist discourses are often exclusionary even as they call attention to, appropriate even, the experience of 'difference' and

'Otherness' to provide oppositional political meaning, legitimacy, and immediacy when they are accused of lacking concrete relevance. Very few African-American intellectuals have talked or written about postmodernism . . . Radical postmodernist practise, most powerfully conceptualized as a 'politics of difference', should incorporate the voices of displaced, marginalized, exploited, and oppressed black people. It is sadly ironic that the contemporary discourse which talks the most about heterogeneity, the decentered subject, declaring breakthroughs that allow recognition of Otherness, still directs its critical voice primarily to a specialized audience that shares a common language rooted in the very master narratives it claims to challenge.[77]

Patricia Hill Collins concurs with hooks, adding what is really missing from postmodern analyses of differences is the recognition of power in our society against different groups and a clear idea about how to oppose that power:

> To recast race, class, gender politics as an issue of postmodernist difference is indicative of some problems of the politics of post-modernist discourse overall. The construct of difference emerges from social constructionist views of self/other where the self is constructed against the difference of the other . . . Social institutions, especially analyses of the institutional bases of power shaping race, class, and gender, are dropped form the analysis, leaving a plethora of post-modernist representations in their wake . . . Studies with post-modernist notions of difference leave us on dangerously thin ice. What type of oppositional politics emerge from a focus on difference devoid of power . . . Quite simply, difference is less a problem for me than racism, class exploitation, and gender oppression. Concep-tualizing these systems of oppression as difference obfuscates the power relations and material inequalities that constitute oppression.[78]

For many of the critics of postmodern feminism it often comes back to the notion that there must be something about 'gender' which unites feminists despite the differences among women, and provides them with a unified force to resist gender oppression.

> By reference to postmodernism's own championing of an alternative to unified theoretical coherence, we should insist that the theoretical and political dilemmas of difference are well worth pondering. As yet they remain stubbornly persistent and elusive, suggesting that gender is basic in ways that we have yet to fully understand, that it functions as 'a difference that makes a difference', even as it can no longer claim the legitimating mantel of *the* difference.[79]

There are other feminists who argue that, not withstanding the attractions to universality and subjectivity, and resistance, contained in modernist theory, feminism is by definition postmodern, if it is to take 'differences' seriously. Jane Flax comments: 'Despite an understandable attraction to the (apparently) logical orderly world of the Enlightenment, feminist theory more properly belongs in the terrain of postmodern philosophy. Feminist notions of the self, knowledge, and truth are too contradictory to those of the Enlightenment to be contained within its categories.'[80]

Rita Alfonso and Jo Triglio, in trying to define a new generation of self-described 'third wave feminists', argue on either side of the postmodern as requisite to third wave feminism debate. Triglio argues in favour: 'Third wave feminism seems to be more of an academic construction, used to mark the development of postmodernist critiques of second wave feminism. I cannot help feeling that one must be a postmodernist to be a third waver.'[81] Alfonso disagrees, concluding that postmodernism is too heterosexual and white to include all the voices which can be included in the third wave:

> I certainly do not hold either that you have to be a postmodernist ... in order to identify as a third wave feminist ... Consider the critiques of women of colour ... a better example may be found within the grassroots AIDS activists working under the rubric 'Queer Nation'. These are two examples of feminist positions that are not necessarily postmodernist nor second wave.[82]

It is curious that third wave feminists who have eschewed their marriages to other theoretical frameworks (Marxism, socialism, liberalism) have chosen, at times, to argue out their differences by engaging in a debate about yet another theoretical framework outside of feminism, namely postmodernism. Feminists' engagement in the critical debate around 'difference' and unity versus 'differences' must begin with their own premises and incorporate whatever aspects of other theories help them either to solve these tensions or to live with the contradictions. This is beginning to happen.

Living on the Borders: Third Wave's Answer to Dualism, Difference and Differences

The first way in which third wave feminisms have attempted to deal with identity and differences is by simply living with the contradictions they create; that is, straddling the borders which are supposed to differentiate or exclude women from men, black from white, culture from nature or heterosexual from homosexual. Given a theoretical world of dualities constructed from a political world of multiplicities, many feminists disengage from any theoretical framework other than their own. Rather than engaging in an abstract battle to enter one dualistic sphere and leave the other, or to transform the value ascribed to one side of the dualism at the expense of the other, or even to attempt to deconstruct the dualisms themselves, feminists are increasingly adopting a position of straddling these dualities as they exist and as they live them in particular contexts. Perhaps more than anything else, this creates a real agency for feminism: by not simply accepting a dualistic either/or world, but by actively becoming the boundaries themselves, the connections between seemingly exclusive spheres, feminists put themselves at the very heart of 'politics'. In the words of Janine Brodie, 'We are not only responsible for these boundaries, but, in a very real sense, "we are they".'[83] The future of third wave feminism(s) is thus to be found in straddling and connecting: in hybrids, affinities, coalitions, contradictions and localized politics.

Hybrids

Donna Haraway provides the image of the cyborg as a means to reconceive our world in terms of straddling, 'connected thinking' or networks rather than dualities: 'an ironic political myth faithful to feminism'.[84] The cyborg itself is a deliberate attempt to overcome the disconnection between nature and culture, or biology and technology. 'By the late twentieth century, our time, a mythic time, we are all chimeras, theorized and fabricated hybrids of machine and organism; in short, we are cyborgs. The cyborg is our ontology; it gives us our politics.'[85] In creating the cyborg, Haraway is looking to the future for feminism; it is 'a creature in a postgender world'. As such, it is 'no longer structured by the polarity of public and private, the cyborg defines a technological polis based partly on a revolution of social relations in the oikos, the household. Nature and culture are reworked; the one can no longer be the resource for appropriation or incorporation by the other.'[86] Thus the cyborg straddles, forms the border between, different dualities:

> The cyborg is a condensed image of both imagination and material reality, the two joined centers structuring any possibility of historical

transformation . . . the relation between organism and machine has
been a border war. The stakes in the border war have been the
territories of production, reproduction, and imagination . . . This chapter is an argument for pleasure in the confusion of boundaries and
for responsibility in their construction.[87]

Replacing the public/private dichotomy in Haraway's cybernetic
world is women as part of a network which weaves what had
traditionally been conceived of as the public and private worlds:

> If it was ever possible ideologically to characterize women's lives
> by the distinction of public and private domains . . . it is now a
> totally misleading ideology, even to show how both terms of these
> dichotomies construct each other in practice and in theory. I prefer
> a network ideological image, suggesting the profusion of spaces
> and identities and the permeability of boundaries in the personal
> body and in the body politic. 'Networking' is both a feminist prac-
> tice and a multinational corporate strategy-weaving for oppositional
> cyborgs.[88]

Zines and cyberspace have become one feature of this 'networking' by the new generation of feminists. As the Japanese site of
Webgrrls states of the cyber-weaving potential of this organization:

> The original chapter of Webgrrls began meeting in New York City in
> April of 1995, founded by Aliza Sherman. What started off as six
> women meeting together to network, discuss, support and help each
> other in the exciting field of new media quickly blossomed. In less
> than three years it has become an international organization consist-
> ing of more than 4,000 members in over 80 chapters around the
> world. Now that's networking power![89]

In contrast to this enthusiastic support for technology as an underpinning of third wave feminism(s) are the questions raised by some
young feminists about living in 'McJobdom'. Michelle Sidler comments of the two-edged sword of technology manifested in the
'cyborg' imagery:

> [While] Haraway advocates using the power of technology in the
> postmodern era to promote a new feminist agency . . . the current
> economic plight of twentysomethings complicates [her] insistence
> on the power of technology. Haraway simplifies . . . the privilege of
> class as a basis of acquiring knowledge of technology, particularly
> for young workers. As the importance of technology rises, so does
> the pay gap between those with and those without the economic
> means to attend college.[90]

Sidler concludes: 'In short, third wave feminism needs a new economy.'[91]

In the individual, the renegotiation or straddling of borders, which Haraway describes in her 'cyborg' metaphor, becomes described, in many feminists texts, as hybridity. The idea that everyone is a multiplicity of identities which both come together and continue to exist as contradictions within one's sense of self is a central feature of third wave feminism(s). The connection between these identities and power relations with others and society as a whole creates the energy of 'hybridity' or the borderlands.

Hybridity begins with a recognition that one's identity is called into question the moment one begins to write, and cannot write from the perspective of 'universality' assumed by the dualistic world of political theory. Critically, the dualistic notion of man versus woman does not begin to cover the multiple boundaries of identity. Trinh T. Minh-ha, in her book *Woman, Native, Other*, opens by describing the questions a woman of colour faces in beginning to write:

> No matter what position she decides to take, she will sooner or later find herself driven into situations where she is made to feel she must choose from among three conflicting identities. Writer of color? Woman writer? Or woman of color? . . . As focal point of cultural consciousness and social change, writing weaves into language the complex relations of a subject caught between the problems of race and gender and the practice of literature as the very place where social alienation is thwarted differently according to each specific context.[92]

Gloria Anzaldua, in her book *Borderlands/La Frontera*, a work which crosses the borders between history, poetry and autobiography, writes of the life of *mestizas*, people who live on the border: borders between nations (Mexico and the United States), borders of identity (race, sexuality, gender) and borders of language and culture. Her preoccupation is with the 'self', specifically with 'the inner life of the Self, and with the struggle of that Self amidst adversity and violation'.[93] 'The Borderlands are physically present wherever two or more cultures edge each other, where people of different races occupy the same territory, where under, lower, middle and upper classes touch, where the space between two individuals shrinks with intimacy.'[94] Her concept of *mestiza* fully recognizes the reality of today's society, where individuals are constituted by many different identities which exist in conflict with each other:

To live in the Borderlands means you
are neither *hispana india negra espanola*
ni gabacha, eres mestiza, mulata, half-breed
caught in the crossfire between camps
while carrying all five races on your back
not knowing which side to turn to, run from;
. . .
In the Borderlands
you are the battle ground
where the enemies are kin to each other;
you are at home, a stranger,
the border disputes have been settled
the volley of shots have shattered the truce
you are wounded, lost in action
dead, fighting back.[95]

To survive, she concludes, 'you must live *sin fronteras* [without borders]; be a crossroads'.[96] Thus, the borderlands, as crossroads, provide a way in which feminists of colour have theorized both within and outside western political theory:

> Theorists-of-colour are in the process of trying to formulate 'marginal' theories that are partially outside and partially inside the Western frame of reference (if that is possible), theories that overlap many 'worlds'. We are articulating new positions in these 'in-between', Borderland worlds of ethnic communities and academies, feminist and job worlds. In our literature, social issues such as race, class and sexual difference are intertwined with the narrative and poetic elements of a text, elements in which theory is embedded. In our *mestizaje* theories we create new categories for those of us left out or pushed out of the existing ones.[97]

One of the first steps is to challenge the dualisms inherent in much of western thought:

> The work of *mestiza* consciousness is to break down the subject–object duality that keeps her a prisoner and to show in the flesh and through the images in her work how duality is transcended. The answer to the problem between the white race and the colored, between males and females, lies in healing the split that originates in the very foundation of our lives, our culture, our languages, our thoughts. A massive uprooting of dualistic thinking in the individual and collective consciousness is the beginning of a long struggle, but one that could, in our best hopes, bring us to the end of rape, of violence, of war.[98]

Zillah Eisenstein comments: 'To create a feminist theory of women of color requires straddling a multiplicity of contexts. Often it requires rejecting the culture that oppresses women to affirm a once-colonized culture.'[99]

Queer theory reflects a similar rejection of dualities or binary opposites in favour of a multiplicity of identities. Anzaldua remarks on her *mestiza* lesbian and racial identity in the following way: 'As a *mestiza* I have no country, my homeland cast me out, yet all countries are mine because I am every woman's sister or potential lover. (As a lesbian I have no race, my own people disclaim me; but I am all races because there is the queer of me in all races.)'[100] Queer theory rejects the notion that the world can be divided into the dualistic notions of man/woman and homosexual/heterosexual. The word 'queer' in itself represents a plurality of identities: 'When you're trying to describe the community, and you have to list gays, lesbians, bisexuals, drag queens, transsexuals . . . it gets unwieldy. Queer says it all.'[101] The conclusion that many queer theorists have drawn is that the recognition of multiple identities necessitates the straddling of many positions and a challenge to traditional political theory's distinctions between public and private: 'Queer theory's postmodern conception of identity as an ensemble of unstable and multiple positions contests traditional formulations of sexuality as a personal issue . . . collectivity is reduced to a group affiliation defined according to the standard of authentic embodiment.'[102]

Borders and borderlands exist in different ways for all women. Feminist theory must require that all feminists (even white, middle-class, heterosexual feminists) recognize their *particular* mixture of identities, as opposed to claiming a 'universal' identity which historically has been so often assumed in feminist discourse. It is critical, however, that we understand and analyse the relationship between a 'multiplicity of contexts' and the power bestowed by different 'identities'. As we come to terms with the intersection of self, identity and power, it may be that it will be possible to begin to recognize our mixed roles, in varying degrees, as oppressed and oppressor. As Alice Walker writes of what it is to be a 'mestizo':

> We are the African and the trader. We are the Indian and the Settler. We are the oppressor and the oppressed . . . we are the mestizos of North America. We are black, yes, but we are 'white' too, and we are red. To attempt to function as only one, when you are really two or three, leads, I believe, to psychic illness: 'white' people have shown us the madness of that.[103]

It is the contradictions articulated by Alice Walker that are taken up by her daughter Rebecca Walker, in her collection of essays, for a younger generation: a generation which has grown up in a world full of multiplicities and contradictions. It is for this reason that younger feminists find it particularly difficult to operate in the dualistic world imposed by both western political theory and second wave feminism:

> This way of ordering the world is especially difficult for a generation that has grown up transgender, bisexual, interracial and knowing and loving people who are racist, sexist, and otherwise afflicted. We have trouble formulating and perpetuating theories that compartmentalize and divide according to race and gender and all of the other signifiers. For us the lines between Us and Them are often blurred, and as a result we find ourselves seeking to create identities that accommodate ambiguity and our multiple positionalities.[104]

The notion of hybridization involves not only the recognition of the multiplicity of one's identities, but the power relations involved in the construction of identity. For feminists like Patricia Clough and Chela Sandoval, hybridization also involves border warfare at the site of dualistic boundaries, and oppositional resistance to oppressive powers at the 'local' level: '[This feminism] valorizes the hybrid rather than the unified subject-identity figured in the dominant fiction of Western discourse; it foregrounds the multicultural rather than the unified identity of the nation-state and it insists on locally articulated criticisms of the globalization of relations of power/knowledge.'[105]

Sandoval has developed a theory of 'oppositional consciousness' to underscore the way in which 'US third world feminists' might break through the 'hegemonic structure' of white feminist theory and practice. This model provides a way, Sandoval argues, for feminists to work together. 'In mapping this new design, a model is revealed by which social actors can chart the points through which differing oppositional ideologies can meet, in spite of their varying trajectories.'[106] Sandoval concludes that opposition to different forms of power creates the need to shift or transform identity as required to oppose the particular and local form of oppression at hand. Like Anzaluda, Sandoval is waging warfare on the boundaries:

> The differential mode of oppositional consciousness depends upon the ability to read the current situation of power and of self-consciously choosing and adopting the ideological form best suited

to push against its configurations, a survival skill well known to oppressed peoples. Differential consciousness requires grace, flexibility, and strength: enough strength to confidently commit to a well-defined structure of identity for one hour, day, week, month, year; enough flexibility to self-consciously transform that identity according to the requisites of another oppositional ideological tactic if readings of power's formation require it; enough grace to recognize alliances with others committed to egalitarian social relations and race, gender, and class justice, when their readings of power call for alternative oppositional stands.[107]

In other words, because one's multiplicity of identities is created by the forces in history which have tended to marginalize, ignore or distort certain groups of people to varying degrees, oppositional consciousness, according to Haraway, 'marks out a self-consciously constructed space that cannot affirm the capacity to act on the basis of natural identification but only on the basis of conscious coalition of affinity or political kinship'.[108] Or, as Heywood and Drake put it:

A third wave goal . . . is the development of modes of thinking that can come to terms with the mutiple, constantly shifting bases of oppression in relation to the multiple, interpenetrating axes of identity, and the creation of a coalition politics based on these understandings – understandings that acknowledge the existence of oppression, even though it is not fashionable to say so.[109]

Coalitions

Third wave feminism(s) has (have) also come to embrace the notion of coalitions and affinities; that is, of different individuals and groups working with others in opposition to particular and local political conflicts.[110] Critical to this notion of 'affinity' is the idea that 'oppositional politics' must shift depending on the composition of the individuals and groups involved, on the nature and structure of the forces which are being opposed and on the tactics and strategies of the local political struggle.

Anna Yeatman describes such a politics of affinity within feminism as critical to any real notion of representation. 'A politics of representation becomes a genuine politics only when it is played out as a context of debate, reciprocal accountabilities . . . locally anchored to whatever jurisdictional boundaries permit those who "speak for" and self advocates to come together . . . making possible the acknowledgment of the hybrid realities which are lived out every day by minority as well as majority peoples.'[111] Janine Brodie, in the Canadian context, argues that other movements, such as the labour movement, have lost their political strength because they have been unable to adapt and incorporate other oppositional movements (from the environment to the women's movement to anti-racist groups). This should be a lesson to the future of coalition building in feminism. Coalitions must be inclusive yet fluid, to allow groups to decide among themselves the oppositional tack to take. 'A feminist politics of restructuring necessarily entails broad based alliances across gender, race and class, but the foundations for these coalitions defy an *a priori* determination.'[112] The writers of a third wave web page concur with this notion of fluid coalition building:

> Third Wave practice seeks to create what Angela Davis calls 'unpredicted coalitions.' That is to say that several smaller organizations exist, each with its own agenda and approach, and rather than replacing each other with bigger or better, we need to synthesize and use each other as resources, pulling together our strengths and abilities in order to be effective and efficient in reaching our goals – long term and short. Simultaneously, we need to strive to move beyond the boundaries that exist between us. We must challenge our own fears of difference, whatever the shape, size, color or name.[113]

At the heart of these arguments is a fundamental questioning of the underlying structure of western political thought and practice. Whereas traditional political theories and second wave feminism, to the extent that it became hyphenated to them, are based on a fixed separation and opposition so succinctly demonstrated in the dualities of public/private, culture/nature, man/woman, white/black, heterosexual/homosexual, third wave feminisms think and write in terms of the fluid *relation* between different identities, people and spheres. 'Relational thinking' is a recognition that the world is composed not of binaries but of multiplicities, and each thing within the world is defined in terms of not just the 'other' but many others. Moreover, these identities are not fixed, but shift in relation to their own evolution and that of others. Frazer and Lacey argue that feminism must go beyond the essential unity of the subject in liberal and communitarian thought, and instead begin with a 'relational theory of the self', which, 'in recognizing itself through its relation to others . . . embraces both connection and separation, and retains the potential for a reflective and critical stance towards itself and the world it encounters.'[114]

Susan Friedman writes of 'relational thinking' in terms of overcoming the binary between 'white/other':

> Within a relational frame work, identities shift with a changing context, dependent always upon the point of reference. Not essences or absolutes, identities are fluid sites that can be understood differently depending on the vantage point of their formation and function ... Stressing that individuals are constituted through many group identities and cannot be reduced to any one collectivity, they are able to be flexible in dealing with global variation in forms of otherness and contradictory subject positions ... Scripts of relational positionality still open the door for dialogue, affiliations, alliances, and coalitions across racial and ethnic boundaries.[115]

Unlike Sandoval, Friedman argues that coalitions must be built not on a joint enemy alone but 'unions based on common experience and need'.[116] Similarly, R. Radhakrishnan writes that 'coalitional politics' must be based on 'relationality as a field in process'.[117] Finally, Rebecca Walker concludes that feminism must accept multiplicity and look outward rather than inward in its attempts to create a strong political force:

> My hope is that this book can help us to see how the people in the world who are facing and embracing their contradictions and complexities and creating something new and empowering from them are important voices leading us away from divisiveness and dualism. I hope that in accepting contradiction and ambiguity, in using *and* much more than we use *either/or*, these voices can help us continue to shape a political force more concerned with mandating and cultivating freedom than with policing morality.[118]

Heywood and Drake argue that the model of coalitional politics is Walker's Third Wave collective, which has as its mission statement:

> Third Wave is a member-driven multiracial, multicultural, multisexuality national non-profit organization devoted to feminist and youth activism for change. Our goal is to harness the energy of young women and men by creating a community in which members can network, strategize, and ultimately, take action. By using our experiences as a starting point, we can create a diverse community and cultivate a meaningful response.[119]

Local politics

Third wave feminisms argue that feminist politics must be 'localized'. Feminists must engage at the local rather than abstract levels, engaging women from different perspectives in the resistance to different types of power in the specific historical and geographical contexts in which they occur. Linda Nicholson comments:

> Within contemporary European-based societies there is a strong tendency to think in either-or ways regarding generalities: either there are commonalties that tie us all together or we are all just individuals . . . A feminism of difference uncovered many important social patterns of gender . . . My argument against a feminism of difference does not mean that we should stop searching for such patterns. It is, rather, that we should understand them in different and more complex terms than we have tended to do so, particularly that we should become more attentive to the historicity of any patterns we uncover . . . My argument thus points to the replacement of claims about women as such or even women in patriarchal societies with claims about women in particular contexts.[120]

Shane Phelan also concludes that feminist politics must be local:

> The politics that I am calling for is 'local' in two senses. In its first, 'postmodern' sense, it is a politics which eschews universal narratives of oppression that base all oppressions on one 'most basic' one . . . The second sense . . . [of] local politics is a return to the original formulation of identity politics by the Combahee River Collective . . . we need to work on what is in front of us rather than on agendas given by someone else. Valuing local politics restores the theoretical priority of seeing the obvious – the injustice that is in front of our noses . . . Local politics is participatory politics, perhaps modest in each particular location, but forming in the end a situation discretely different than the one(s) preceding it.[121]

Finally, with all the emphasis on difference, hybridization, local contexts, affinities and coalitions, one is left to wonder what has happened to either 'women' or 'feminism'. Is there any coherence at all in either concept? The answer from third wave feminisms is in the affirmative, but defined almost exclusively in political terms. Some feminists, like Gaytari Spivak and Julia Kristeva, argue that while there may not be an ontological category of women, one must allow for a political category identified as 'women' in order to advance feminist ends.[122]

Anne Phillips argues that the struggle in recognizing the differences among women and the 'aspiration towards universality' of feminism can only be addressed by embracing both. She concludes that feminists, in order to change the way in which politics and gender are currently constructed, must be prepared to straddle the two and live with the tension: 'In the reworking of contemporary political theory and ideals, feminism cannot afford to situate itself *for* difference and *against* universality, for the impulse that takes us beyond our immediate and specific difference is a vital necessity in any radical transformation.'[123] Judith Butler, on the other hand, concludes that 'gender coherence' must be 'understood as the regulatory fiction it is – rather than the common point of our liberation'.[124]

This central debate among third wave feminists, between the 'difference' of women from men which tends towards duality and the unifying of women on the basis of some common attributes, on the one hand, and 'differences' among women which tend towards embracing diversity, contradiction, multiplicity and hybridity, on the other, will continue to be the basis of struggle and dissent in the development of feminism(s). That contradictions both within individual feminist's lives and work, as well as feminism(s) as a whole, may emerge is the sign of a healthy debate, brought on by the forces unleashed by the third wave. For ultimately, as was stated at the outset of this chapter, the most important development of third wave feminism(s), and one which is bound to elicit as many viewpoints as there are individual feminists, is the recognition of difference(s) in perspective.

Thus, if one considers the dualistic framework of western political thought, there is both the subjective point of reference or perspective of the observer (which, it is claimed, represents an objective view from nowhere) and the mirroring image of the other (the world modelled around that subject) which constructs what we call 'politics'. So, for example, the state of nature of Hobbes, Locke and Rousseau is nothing more than the negative image of how they view their own civil society. In the case of Hobbes, civil society is good and ordered, the state of nature must consequently be bad and anarchical; if, on the other hand, Rousseau wishes to argue that the origins of inequality begin with civil society, suddenly you have the image of the noble savage and a decadent and deteriorating civil society. In both cases, the state of nature exists in order to mirror, in an opposing fashion, what these writers wish to prove about civil society. The salient point here is that the writer, within civil society, is the referent point or perspective from which the natural state and 'natural man' is then reflected. In the same way, western thought has repeatedly begun with men, reason, culture, the public sphere, and constructed from those points of reference what women, non-reason, nature and the private sphere, respectively, will be.

Third wave feminisms have 'decentred' this seemingly 'universal' perspective by insisting on seeing the world from women's point(s) of view. All the clearly delineated boundaries, in turn, begin to break down as women increasingly provide their own perspectives on the world of politics. Culture/nature, public/private, even men/women, become more fluid at the traditional borderlands between the two coupled concepts. In terms of power, this shift in perspective may ultimately be the most potent change which third wave feminism(s) have brought into the western lexicon. For, as liberal philosophers have discovered, one cannot introduce into the world of political theory certain radical concepts and hope to limit their impact to selected targets. 'Rights', as they were first articulated for white male property-owning citizens, became the rallying call and opening for many other groups of people to claim their own place in the western political world. In the same way, opening the door to a multiplicity of perspectives in knowledge, or 'situated knowledges', brings with it enormous possibilities. It is this decentring of individual subjectivity, 'universal' scientific laws and fundamental dualistic categories which could prove to be the greatest challenge posed by third wave feminism(s) to western political thought.

8

Conclusion

In the first chapter of this book we began with a newspaper, as the gendered snapshot of the political world around us, and asked the question: why? In the search for an answer, we have instead begun to rethink the question. Rather than finding a singular cause for the gender imbalance, we have discovered that the way the western world is constructed over time and through history makes possible particular kinds of claims to 'universal' or 'objective' knowledge from specific perspectives and delineated within certain boundaries, as reflected on both the front pages of newspapers and within the words of the classic texts of western political theory. At the same time, one can also find the counterclaims or resistance to this 'universal' and 'objective' voice. Feminism, along with other dissenting voices, has formed part of the resistance to these claims to knowledge, the perspectives taken and the boundaries imposed by western political thought and practice. Such challenges have, as discovered in chapter 7, begun to have an impact and the newspapers themselves have begun, in turn, to change; in response not to any simple cause and effect, but to a shifting set of colliding forces and perspectives, creating, on a daily basis, a new distilled constellation of the political world around us.

Second, the newspaper as our 'snapshot' of the political world has been challenged not simply for its content. The new generation of third wave feminists has also begun to challenge the medium through which we communicate with one another. Eschewing traditional venues, such as the elite academic press on the one hand or the populist newspaper on the other, third wave 'generation X' feminists are both surfing the Internet and infiltrating, and in some cases subverting, the music industry to communicate among themselves and with others about their perspective on the world. The question, therefore, is not so much why are women excluded from politics in these newspapers, but how has the modern western world of political ideas and practice been constructed in our mass media and in what ways is it being challenged or resisted?

The initial definition of politics in chapter 1 – *the exercise of power, through reason and language, to achieve a particular outcome within a group of people* – would still encompass the world of politics that has been constructed by modern political theory. Most modern theorists would thus accept the notion that reason and technology (scientific understanding) is central to the unfolding of political history on the macro-scale. For many contemporary feminists, however, such a definition is far too narrow and dualistic. As we have discovered, since the emergence of second and third wave feminism(s), it is 'the personal' that 'is the political', meaning that politics can exist wherever power is exercised over someone, be that in the bedroom, on a women's magazine cover or in legislation passed in a national assembly. Politics cannot be contained within the world of reason and language and within the public sphere, because ultimately power cannot be contained within those worlds. Politics is the contestation for power in all its manifestations.

Thus, if we return to the newspaper described above, power does not simply exist in the headline about the latest development at the United Nations (although surely it does occur in that forum), but politics also exists in the sports section, where male activity dominates both the subjects chosen for coverage and the reporters doing the writing. It also exists in the ads where extraordinarily thin women are used to sell everything from cars to deodorants. It occurs in the world contained in the sections on entertainment and the arts and in the business pages. The perspective taken, the words chosen, the pictures included are all 'political' in the sense of whose voice is heard, whose view is represented, whose words are written and the nature of the boundaries constructed to contain each of the sections described. It is this 'political world', simultaneously personal and global, which feminists have begun to challenge; and finally, at the end of the twentieth century, have begun to crack.

The preliminary definition of 'feminism' is equally problematic. *The recognition that, virtually across time and place, men and women are unequal in the power they have either in society or over their own lives, and the corollary belief that men and women should be equal; the belief*

that knowledge has been written about, by and for men and the corollary
belief that all schools of knowledge must be re-examined and understood
to reveal the extent to which they ignore or distort gender. Third wave
feminism(s) have challenged us to rethink our preliminary definition of feminism on three counts. First, whatever oppression exists
in the world, it exists across a multiplicity of relations and must be
localized in terms of both geographic space and historical context.
Second, universal equality as a goal has been recognized as assuming a dualistic (man versus woman) and 'essentialist' (not taking
into account the different historical experiences of the diverse groups
of men and women in relationship to each other) view of the world.
Third, as the question of perspective becomes central to feminism,
the contradictory nature of 'identity' must be acknowledged in our
re-examination of knowedge.

While both of these definitions provided us with starting points
to examine the intersection between politics and gender, the analysis within the chapters which followed has obliged us to deconstruct
the very definitions we began with. There are a plethora of definitions for both politics and feminism, beginning from different perspectives and therefore different assumptions about the nature of
both. It might be more helpful to think of a gradient of definitions
in relation to politics and the contestation for power, from narrow
definitions around the activities of the state and citizen to an almost all-encompassing view of politics as both the construction of
power in all aspects of global and personal life and the corollary
points of resistance to such power. Feminism(s), similarly, may be
seen as a cluster of theories and/or views which now largely attempt to see and analyse the world from women's perspective(s).
In other words, there are different and contested definitions of
how broad politics is and what is/are women's perspective(s). It
is perhaps these two axes (that is, the scope of politics and the
'perspective(s)' of women), more than anything else, which define
the debate going on among feminists writing about politics today.

If we return to the newspaper once again, and introduce some of
the questions raised by second and third wave feminists about the
nature of the boundaries imposed by western political theory, we
can begin to see how this snapshot of our world contains within it
a contradictory picture. Thus, simultaneously, one can find both
the dualities described in the previous chapters (including the power
relations inherent within them) and the challenges made by feminists to this constructed world. Rather than looking at the business
pages or political news stories of a given newspaper and simply

pushing to have more women included in these worlds, many feminists have dug deeper to ask what it is about the way in which the economy and business (the private sector) or government (the public sector) have been constructed that by definition excludes women from these spheres. And so they return to John Locke's seminal piece on private property to examine how the property-owning citizen of civil society is originally differentiated from and reflected, like a mirror, by both the private sphere of the family and the non-European 'Indian' of the state of nature.[1] As the social contract cannot exist without the sexual contract, so civil society cannot exist without the state of nature, or the citizen without a household to preserve and protect. The private economy, the private family and the public state are all created at the same time and in relation to one another. Thus women are excluded, not because they are women *per se*, but because of the way in which politics in liberal democracies were delineated in their theoretical origins to exclude the spheres within which women lived and worked (as wives, servants, non-Europeans and so on). At the same time, the private property-owning citizen is also defined in relation to his family. Thus, in terms of liberal economics, as well as politics, the private sphere of the family constrained women (as wives, servants and slaves) within the domain of the male property owner (and thus outside of either political or economic life). This is why feminism has only got so far in arguing for the inclusion of women in the public sphere; it is not simply who inhabits which sphere that is at stake in the definition of the spheres themselves. Politics, thus, is beginning to be redefined, in both newspapers and academic journals. While the dualities of public and private still remain, many questions are raised, simultaneously, to challenge the notion of a political or public sphere constructed in opposition to the 'private sphere' of either family or the business sector.

For example, if you turn to the 'lifestyles' or 'family' sections of newspapers, you can see the two sides of public and private play themselves out. There are the stories about 'superwomen' and 'parenting tips for the working mother'; stories which construct a world in which women, while moving in greater numbers into government and business, continue to fulfil the 'private role' of wife and mother. Some better off parents have hired 'nannies' to maintain the sense of a private sphere with a full-time, albeit surrogate, 'wife and mother'. As we have seen in previous chapters, the disproportionate number of women coming from poorer parts of the world to look after other people's children has created very different realities, *vis-à-vis* the private sphere, for different groups of women.

On the other side of the public/private divide, cracks are beginning to appear. Questions are raised about the values of life in the fast lane for both men and women. Men write about the joys of fatherhood. On occasion now, one sees articles on the working conditions of domestic servants, or, in the United States, questions raised about the number of people who engage illegal immigrants in domestic service. Some of these stories have broached the divide set by the 'lifestyles' or 'family' sections of newspapers, and instead appear in the front section. Almost all the stories on public/private have assumed a heterosexual version of the family. Yet even here we have begun to see the cracks appearing, as increasing numbers of gay men and lesbians make their presence known in popular western culture. Thus, you read stories about coming out within one's family; or children raised by two mothers or two fathers. Different perspectives are seeping into our newspapers and challenging the boundaries around gender and politics.

The private sector, through the business pages, has faced a similar struggle over borders and perspectives. While the front sections and financial pages of newspapers have embraced the notions of growth, GDP, GNP and general economics – that is, the cultural world expanding by extracting more from the natural world – there have been, more recently, questions raised about the impact on the environment, on our natural world, of such development; of the assumption that science and technology must go on forever extracting the maximum possible from our natural world. Front page stories about the negotiations in Kyoto in December 1997 over global warming bring home to us the strength of the debate over such questions. Nurturing and protecting our natural environment have become increasingly important aspects of political debate towards the end of the twentieth century. Maintaining the basic belief in history as the movement from nature to culture (as articulated by both liberal thinkers and Marx and Engels) has become difficult in the face of such questions. Cracks within the assumed dualities and the relationship between them have begun to appear. Ecofeminism, as discussed in earlier chapters, has been an important force in challenging the assumptions made in the business pages about economics and growth in relationship to the natural environment.

The sports section has been the hardest to crack and there is no doubt that even today in most newspapers in the western world, one would be daunted by the overwhelmingly masculine nature of the subject, object and language of the coverage. But even here there may be some changes under way, to which the experience in other news media may attest. In the electronic media coverage of the 1996 Olympic Games in Atlanta, much was made of the major television networks' decision to individualize and make personal narratives about given athletes, rather than focusing on the conflict or competition *per se* of given sporting events. Particular focus was given to the personal obstacles which were overcome in order for a specific athlete to be present at the games themselves. Such a shift in coverage was due to the testing networks had done, about both the demographics of the watching audience and the type of coverage which would engage those people. Women constituted an important constituency of the audience watching the Olympics, and networks concluded from their polling that women's preference was to know the stories behind the actual sporting events, the relationships, the personal trials, the tragedies which went into the development of any particular athlete or team. The public world of the athletic event and the private world of the individual were thus blurred by major news networks as they relayed their programmes to communities around the United States and beyond. On the other side of the coin, stories of private abuse within athletics (of coaches towards their athletes) are increasingly the subject of sports pages. Over the past year or two in Canada, for instance, the sexual abuse of junior hockey players by coaches or officials in the ice arenas have been given extensive coverage as the survivors themselves come forward and make public previously private events, which heretofore had been impossible to do in the masculine world of sports. The private world of sexuality became the public world of news and politics as Sheldon Kennedy, a hockey player who went public with his story of abuse while a junior hockey player in Canada, was named 'newsmaker of the year' for 1997 by Canada's major media outlets.

The most extreme example of gendered politics in the newspapers has, of course, to be the 'page 3 girl' of the tabloid press. Not only is the woman made into a sexual object and so often stereotypically exaggerated in physical features, but the most profoundly political and out of date aspect of these pictures is the fundamentally heterosexual male gaze which is implied in the readership of the newspaper. The perspective assumed, in other words, is very closely linked to a particular identity. It is the question of perspective, as has been argued, which is so fundamental to both the history of western politics and the feminist challenge to that perspective. No part of the paper so starkly illustrates the 'politics' of our world than one which can exclude the perspective of so many of its readers without even realizing what it is doing. In other words, it is not simply that women are objects in these pictures, but that they *cannot be subjects* as readers of the newspapers in question, which is fundamentally at the heart of feminists' challenges to these photos. Even here, however, there are a few cracks appearing, as papers have begun to include pictures of 'boys', usually on about page 46, for their 'female' readership. The heterosexual assumptions, needless to say, are left unchallenged.

Finally, as feminism has become increasingly pluralistic and diverse, so too the challenges to the perspective assumed in the newspapers expand. While women as a whole are underrepresented in the political world around us, and in the papers which both cover and construct that world, women of colour are particularly absent, in terms of subject, coverage and those doing the writing. Their perspectives, in other words, are simply not part of these newspapers. In an increasingly global and multicultural society, such a limited perspective is once again under pressure, as individuals and groups challenge the assumed views and begin to enter the ranks of writers and commentators.

I have used the newspaper as a tool. It is, as I stated at the outset, a snapshot of the political world around us, but it does not simply 'reflect' the political world, but constructs it. Within the newspaper you can see all the different aspects of 'politics', not simply in the headlines or the front section of the newspapers but in the perspectives assumed, the lines drawn and the stories told. From the 'private' or personal world of the 'lifestyles' section, to the hardened and 'public' world of 'sport' and 'business', gender is critical to the way in which we look at our world and how others look at us. Assumptions are beginning to change and the stories, lines and perspectives are beginning to crack, as new voices insist on being heard and new eyes are being allowed to show others the world from their perspective. Feminism is one of those voices which has begun to break down our previous understanding of politics within these pages: first, by broadening politics to include every place where power is exerted to define, exclude or control women, and the resistance to that power; second, in demanding that the 'objective' viewpoint assumed within the political world, including newspapers, yields to allow a 'multiplicity' of viewpoints, including those of women; third, by increasingly using other media to communicate, with both themselves and others, ideas and messages which are not constrained by the nature of the newspaper itself. Thus, as was mentioned, cyberspace (including web pages and e-mail); musical videos, all-female musical tours (like Lilith Fair) and recordings provide alternative venues for many third wave feminists.

Over the past seven chapters I have tried to demonstrate how politics and gender intersect not just at the surface level of simply trying to increase the number of women in politics, but at the deeper level of boundaries and dualities within political theory: analysis which third wave feminists have increasingly demonstrated is necessary to their ends. Thus the construction of politics through the history of political thought has been historically demarcated by the distinctions between culture and nature and public and private. Such distinctions have, in the very construction of the western notion of politics, excluded, misrepresented or controlled women. Western politics grounds itself in the public rational realm, which assumes the objective view from nowhere; that is, the universal identityless voice of science. Recent feminism(s), at their best, have challenged this notion of one viewpoint on the one hand and its universality on the other. Instead, having begun, towards the end of second wave feminism, with the idea that there are at least two identities or two viewpoints, namely male and female, which need to be incorporated into knowledge and history, this has evolved in third wave feminism(s) to a multiplicity of identities and viewpoints which must be heard and seen. The many perspectives which exist in our world have only begun to break through, in a multitude of ways. With them, the dualities between culture over nature and public over private begin to crack. As women's perspectives are increasingly heard and thereby both reflect and construct the political world around us, as captured in our daily newspapers, we are left with the continuing edifice of western political thought and practice as developed through the centuries, but marbled through with feminism(s) constituting new, self-conscious and contested borderlands in both its foundations and its structure.

Notes

Chapter 1 Politics and Feminism: an Introduction

1 The focus of this book is on 'western' politics and how this concept has been constructed through the evolution of 'western' political theory. As will become clear through the development of the critiques in this book, it is critical that knowledge be situated or placed in its particular historical and geographical context, rather than an attempt being made to reach conclusions for some larger notion of universal or global 'politics'. Despite this caveat, it is also worth noting that western political thought, particularly in the modern period, has nevertheless held as its first premise the universality of its scope and understanding. Using a 'history of ideas' approach throughout, I attempt to analyse the development of such 'universal' ideas underpinning current understandings of 'politics' in the 'west'. From there it is possible to examine how these views have been challenged and deconstructed by those marginalized or excluded throughout the bulk of political theory's history by the very construction of 'politics' within this tradition.

2 *The Concise Oxford English Dictionary*, 7th edn, Oxford: Clarendon Press, 1982, p. 793.

3 It should be noted that such a definition of 'politics' would be challenged by some feminist theorists as well as postmodern thinkers; however, it reflects, as I will demonstrate, the western conceptualizations of 'politics' as it exists in contemporary parlance, including the dualities inherent between culture/nature and public/private. This definition is preliminary and will be deconstructed in the chapters to follow.

4 Vicky Randall, *Women and Politics*, London and Basingstoke: Macmillan Press, 1982.

5 This would include Machiavelli, and the early liberal thinkers.

6 This would include Marx and the postmodern thinkers respectively.
7 Again, having a single definition for feminism poses problems for those feminists who would disagree with the premises contained in this one. However, as a working definition of feminism as it is currently conceived, it provides a beginning point for critical analysis.

Chapter 2 Demarcating the Boundaries

1 This passage is taken from one of the speeches of Demosthenes, in an address to the Athenians, and quoted by Ernest Barker in his introduction to Aristotle's *Politics*, Oxford: Oxford University Press, 1980, pp. lxxi–lxxii.
2 Ibid., pp. xlviii–xlix.
3 Plato, *The Republic*, Harmondsworth: Penguin Books, 1963, pp. 62–87. All further references are to this edition, unless stated otherwise.
4 Plato, *The Republic*, translated by Allan Bloom, New York: Basic Books, 1968, p. 273.
5 Plato, *The Laws*, *The Dialogues of Plato*, edited by B. Jarrett, four volumes, 4th edn, Oxford: Clarendon Press, 1953, p. 781.
6 Ibid.
7 Plato, *The Republic*, p. 134.
8 Ibid., pp. 134–5.
9 Ibid., p. 179.
10 Ibid.
11 R. G. Collingwood, *The Idea of Nature*, cited in Aristotle, *Politics*, edited by Ernest Barker, p. xlix (note 1).
12 Aristotle, *The Politics*, p. 3.
13 Ibid., p. 4.
14 Barker, 'Introduction', Aristotle, *Politics*, p. lxxii.
15 Aristotle, *Politics*, p. 35.
16 Ibid.
17 Ibid., p. 5.
18 Ibid., p. 13.
19 Ibid., p. 35.
20 Ibid., p. 3.
21 Ibid. (note 3).
22 Ibid., p. 9.
23 Ibid., p. 12.
24 Aristotle, 'De generatione animalium', *History of Ideas on Women*, edited by Rosemary Agonito, New York: Perigree Books, 1978, pp. 43–56, at p. 47.
25 Ibid.
26 Francis Bacon, cited in Evelyn Fox Keller, 'Gender and science', in Sandra Harding and Merrill B. Hintikka (eds), *Discovering Reality:*

Feminists Perspectives on Epistemology, Metaphysics, Methodology, and Philosophy of Science, Boston: Reidel Publishing Company, 1983, pp. 187–205, at p. 190.

27 For a discussion of Hobbes's method see C. B. MacPherson's introduction to the Penguin Classics version of the *Leviathan*, pp. 25–30. Thomas Hobbes, *Leviathan*, Harmondsworth: Penguin Books, 1985.

28 Hobbes, *Leviathan*, p. 186.

29 John Locke, *Two Treatises of Government*, edited by Peter Laslett, Cambridge Texts in the History of Political Thought, Cambridge: Cambridge University Press, 1988, II, para. 124.

30 In chapter XV of the Second Treatise, John Locke distinguishes between paternal, political and despotical power: all are linked to the right of property: 'Paternal or Parental Power is nothing but that which Parents have over their children . . . where Minority makes the Child incapable to manage his property . . . Despotical power is an Absolute, Arbitaray Power one Man has over another . . . And thus Captives, taken in a just and lawful War and such only are subject to a Despotical power . . . Forfeiture gives . . . Despotical power to Lords for their own Benefit, over those who are stripp'd of all property.' Strangely, while Locke mentions conjugal power in other parts of the first and second treatise, it is not one of the powers included in the list he gives in this chapter, which comes towards the end of the second treatise. Like Hobbes, Locke seems to use the rights of 'wives' in the state of nature initially to challenge Filmer's patriarchal arguments but then to ignore them when he turns to discuss civil society in more depth.

31 I have written extensively on the role of colonialism and the Amerindian in Locke's theory of property: *John Locke and America: the Defence of English Colonialism*, Oxford: Clarendon Press, 1996.

32 Locke, *Two Treatises*, II, para. 28.

33 Ibid., I, para. 48 (emphasis added).

34 Ibid., I, para. 49.

35 Ibid., II, para. 24.

36 Ibid., II, para 172.

37 'The First Set of the Fundamental Constitutions of Carolina', *Historical Collections of South Carolina*, edited by B. R. Carroll, New York, 1836; Peter Laslett, 'John Locke, the Great Recoinage and the Board of Trade (1695–1698), *William and Mary Quarterly*, 3rd series, 14(3), July 1957; 'Temporary Laws to be added to Instructions to Ye Governor and Council of Carolina', *Collections of the South Carolina Historical Society*, V, Charleston, 1897, p. 367.

38 Karl Marx, 'The German ideology', in *Karl Marx: Selected Writings*, edited by David McClelland, Oxford: Oxford University Press, 1977, pp. 159–90, at p. 164.

39 Marx, 'Grundrisse', in McLelland, *Selected Writings*, p. 349; 'Wage, labour and capital', in McLelland, *Selected Writings*, p. 256.

40 Karl Marx, 'The German ideology', p. 167.
41 Ibid., p. 168. Marx repeatedly refers to the 'natural division' of labour within the family. In *Capital* Marx writes: 'Within a family . . . there springs up naturally a division of labour, caused by differences of sex and age, a division that is consequently based on a purely physiological foundation'. *Capital*, volume 1, in McLelland, *Selected Writings*, p. 476.
42 Marx, *Capital, volume I*, New York: International Publishers, 1967, p. 671, cited in Nancy Hartsock, 'The feminist standpoint: developing the ground for a specifically feminist historical materialism', in *Discovering Reality*, edited by Sandra Harding and Merrill B. Hintikka, Boston: D. Reidel Publishing, 1983, pp. 283–310, at p. 291.
43 Marx, 'Capital', p. 496.
44 Marx, 'Towards a critique of Hegel's *Philosophy of Right*', in *Selected Writings*, pp. 80–81. Marx states: 'The result we arrive at then [in capitalist society] is that man (the worker) only feels himself freely active in his animal functions of eating drinking, and procreating, at most also in his dwelling and dress, and feels himself an animal in his human functions [i.e. labour].'
45 Ibid., p. 88.
46 Friedrich Engels, *The Origin of the Family, Private Property and the State*, New York: International Publishers, 1985, p. 118.
47 Plato, 'Meno', *The Dialogues of Plato*, pp. 71–2.
48 Plato,*The Republic* (462), p. 219.
49 Ibid. (451), p. 204, (453) p. 206.
50 Ibid. (464), p. 221 (emphasis added).
51 Ibid. (549), p. 320.
52 Ibid. (454), p. 208.
53 Aristotle, *Politics*, p. 32.
54 Ibid., p. 35.
55 Ibid., p. 37.
56 Michel Foucault, 'What is Enlightenment?', based on an unpublished French manuscript in *The Foucault Reader*, New York: Pantheon Books, 1984, p. 36.
57 Ibid.
58 Immanuel Kant, *Observations on the Feeling of the Beautiful and Sublime*, translated by John T. Goldthwait, Berkeley: University of California Press, 1960, section 3.
59 Hobbes, *Leviathan*, chapter 20, p. 253.
60 Ibid., p. 254.
61 Ibid., p. 255.
62 Ibid., p. 256.
63 Ibid., p. 257.
64 Thomas Hobbes, *A Dialogue between a Philosopher and a Student of the Common Laws of England*, edited by Joseph Cropsey, Chicago, 1971, p. 159 (emphasis added); cited in Susan Moller Okin, *Women in Western Political Thought*, Princeton, NJ: Princeton University Press, p. 199.

65 Locke, *Two Treatises*, II, para. 78.
66 Ibid., II, para. 82 (emphasis added).
67 Hobbes, *Leviathan*, p. 257.
68 Locke, *Two Treatises*, II, para. 81.
69 Locke, *Two Treatises*, I, para. 47.
70 Locke, *Two Treatises*, II, para. 57.
71 Karl Marx, Article in *Rheinische Zeitung*, Marx and Engels, *Collected Works*, 1:236, cited in Jean Bethke Elshtain, *Public Man, Private Woman: Women in Social and Political Thought*, Princeton, NJ: Princeton University Press, 1981, p. 185.
72 Ibid., p. 186.
73 Friedrich Engels, *The Origins of the Family, Private Property and the State*, edited with an introduction by Eleanor Burke Leacock, New York: International Publishers, 1985, pp. 71–2.
74 Ibid., p. 138.
75 Ibid., p. 113.
76 Ibid., p. 120.
77 Ibid., p. 126.
78 Ibid., p. 221.
79 Ibid.
80 Marx, 'Communist Manifesto', in *Selected Writings*, p. 235.
81 Ibid., p. 246.
82 See, for example, Bernard Crick, *In Defence of Politics*, 2nd edn, Harmondsworth: Penguin Books, 1982; E. Hobsbawm, 'The idea of fraternity', *New Society*, November 1975; Carole Pateman, 'The fraternal social contract', in *The Disorder of Women: Democracy, Feminism and Political Theory*, Stanford, CA: Stanford University Press, 1989, pp. 33–57.

Chapter 3   Public versus Private: the Feminist Critique

1   After much thought, I have chosen to analyse the feminist response to the role of dualities in a historical fashion, meaning that I began, in the first two chapters, with traditional political theory (analysed in terms of the two dualities public/private and culture/nature), and now move to the early second wave feminist critiques of the duality of public and private and at the end of this chapter to the more recent critiques by lesbian feminists and feminists of colour. I will be doing the same in the next chapter with regard to the culture/nature divide. I considered integrating all the feminist critiques throughout this chapter and the next, but: (1) felt that the historical development of the ideas is critical; and (2) wanted to highlight the very real and central debate between those feminists who continue to believe in some kind of sameness and universality of women (often based around some notion of challenging the role of 'wife' or the private sphere), in the first part of this chapter, and those who critique this analysis as

suppressing difference by separating out the critiques, at the end of this chapter and in the next. In chapters 6 and 7, where I look at the development of feminism in its own terms, I integrate all the arguments and the mutliplicity of perspectives they encompass throughout both.

2 Michelle Zimbalist Rosaldo and Louise Lamphere (eds), *Woman, Culture and Society*, Stanford, CA: Stanford University Press, 1974, p. 23.

3 Linda Nicholson, *Gender and History: the Limits of Social Theory in the Age of the Family*, New York, 1986, p. 102.

4 Michelle Zimbalist Rosaldo, 'The use and abuse of anthropology: reflections on feminism and cross-cultural understanding', *Signs*, 5, Spring 1980, pp. 389–417.

5 Susan Reverby and Dorothy Helly 'Introduction', *Gendered Domains: Rethinking Public and Private in Women's History*, 1992, Ithaca, NY: Cornell University Press, p. 8.

6 Susan Moller Okin, *Women in Western Political Thought*, Princeton, NJ: Princeton University Press, 1978, p. 9. It must be noted that most of the feminist critiques of western political thought in the 1970s and 1980s, particularly those which adopted a critique based on the public/private divide, like Okin, Diana Coole, Carole Pateman and J. B. Elshtain, focused almost exclusively on the 'wives' in the family, seeming to assume that women and wives were synonymous. In fact, as was pointed out in chapter 2, women existed in these texts in many different categories in ancient and modern thought, including slave, servant, Indian, African, European and so on. By not taking into consideration in their analysis the roles of these different groups of women in political theory, these feminists excluded the historical and theoretical experience of any woman who is not a 'wife'. I have chosen therefore to use the word 'wife' as opposed to woman when discussing this group of women, a word which signifies a subset within political theory that excludes women who are servants or slaves within the private sphere.

7 Ibid., p. 41.

8 Jean Bethke Elshtain, *Public Man, Private Woman: Women in Social and Political Thought*, Princeton, NJ: Princeton University Press, 1981, p. 33.

9 Ibid., p. 39.

10 Diana Coole, *Women in Political Theory: from Ancient Misogyny to Contemporary Feminism*, Hemel Hempstead: Harvester Wheatsheaf, 1988, p. 25.

11 Ibid.

12 Aristotle's *Politics*, translated and edited by Ernest Barker, Oxford: Oxford University Press, 1980, p. 7.

13 Okin, *Women in Western Political Thought*, p. 81.

14 Aristotle, *Politics*, p. 54.

15 Okin, *Women in Western Political Thought*, p. 90.

16 Ibid., p. 92.
17 Elshtain, *Public Man, Private Woman*, p. 41.
18 Ibid., p. 53.
19 Ibid.
20 See, for example, Stanley I. Benn and Gerald F. Gaus (eds), *Public and Private in Social Life*, New York: St Martin's Press, 1983. This book, along with others, addressed issues facing the modern 'welfare state': the question of the size of the state, privacy and liberal conceptions of the public/private divide. There is one article in this collection by Carole Pateman on the feminist perspective.
21 Zillah Eisenstein, *The Radical Future of Liberal Feminism*, New York: Longman, 1981, p. 14.
22 Ibid., p. 223.
23 Ibid., p. 49.
24 Carole Pateman, 'Feminist critiques of the public private dichotomy', in Benn and Gaus (eds), *Public and Private in Social Life*, pp. 281303; *The Sexual Contract*, Cambridge: Polity Press, 1988; *The Disorder of Women*, Cambridge: Polity Press, 1989.
25 Pateman, *The Disorder of Women*, p. 120.
26 Once again, it must be noted that Pateman's theory of the 'sexual contract', her ground-breaking analysis of the implicit role of marital contracts in Hobbes's and Locke's social contracts, has an almost exclusive focus on women as wives in seventeenth-century political theory, leaving aside the role of women as servants or slaves within the household.
27 Pateman, *The Disorder of Women*, p. 121.
28 Elshtain, *Public Man, Private Woman*, p. 127.
29 Anne Phillips, 'Feminism, equality and difference', in Linda McDowell and Rosemary Pringle (eds), *Defining Women: Social Institutions and Gender Divisions*, Cambridge: Polity Press and the Open University, 1992, pp. 205–22, at pp. 215–16.
30 Pateman, *The Disorder of Women*, p. 130.
31 Ibid., p. 40.
32 Ibid., p. 52.
33 Phillips, 'Feminism, equality and difference', p. 216.
34 Ibid.
35 Anita L. Allen, 'Women and their privacy: what is at stake?', in Carol C. Gould (ed.), *Beyond Domination: New Perspectives on Women and Philosophy*, Totowa, NJ: Rowman and Allanheld Publishers, 1983, pp. 233–49, at p. 234.
36 Ruth Gavison, 'Privacy and the limits of the law', *Yale Law Journal*, 89(3), 1980, 421–71.
37 The recent legal challenge in Canada to the laws protecting the right of victims to keep private any notes taken during counselling, in medical examinations or at sexual assault victim centres is a case in point.

38 Allen, 'Women and their privacy', p. 241.
39 Elshtain, *Public Man, Private Woman*, p. 145.
40 Juliet Mitchell, *Psychoanalysis and Feminism*, New York: Vintage Books, 1975, p. 409. Cited in Iris Marion Young, 'Beyond the unhappy marriage: a critique of the dual systems theory', in Lydia Sargent (ed.), *Women and Revolution: a Discussion of the Unhappy Marriage of Marxism and Feminism*, Montreal: Black Rose Books, pp. 43–69, at p. 46.
41 Shulamith Firestone, *The Dialectic of Sex*, New York: Bantam Books, 1971.
42 Young, 'Beyond the unhappy marriage', p. 46.
43 Ibid., p. 60.
44 Mariarosa Dalla Costa, cited in Heidi Hartmann, 'The unhappy marriage of Marxism and feminism: towards a more progressive union', in Lydia Sargent (ed.), *Women and Revolution*, pp. 1–42, at p. 8.
45 See, for example, Ira Gerstein, 'Domestic work and capitalism' *Radical America*, 7, pp. 101–28; Lise Vogel, 'The earthly family' *Radical America*, 7(4/5), July–October 1973, pp. 9–50; Margaret Coulson, Branka Magas, and Hilary Wainwright, ' "The housewife and her labour under capitalism": a critique', *New Left Review*, 89 (January/February 1975), pp. 47–58; Jean Gardiner, Susan Himmelweit and Maureen Mackintosh, 'Women's domestic labour', *Bulletin of the Conference of Socialist Economists*, 4(2), 1975, pp. 85–96; Susan Himmelweit and Simon Mohn, 'Domestic labour and capital', *Cambridge Journal of Economics*, 1(1), March 1977, pp. 15–31; Diemut Elisabet Bubeck, *Care, Gender, and Justice*, Oxford: Clarendon Press, 1995; Tanis Day, *The Influence of Capital–Labour Substitution in the Home on the Processes and Value of Housework*, Toronto: University of Toronto, 1987.
46 Hartmann, 'The unhappy marriage of Marxism and feminism', p. 8.
47 Marilyn Waring, *If Women Counted*, London, Macmillan, 1989. Waring analyses women's labour in many different places in terms of hours spent, rather than wages earned, to get a more accurate and gender neutral picture of work.
48 Will Kymlicka, *Multicultural Citizenship*, Clarendon Press, Oxford, 1995, p. 2.
49 I have used the term 'mainstream' feminism, in this chapter, to represent early second wave feminism (Marxist, socialist and liberal feminism), which largely ignored the question of identity in their own assumptions about women, in contradistinction to other feminists, who challenged these assumptions. In using this term, I am arguing that, historically, the second group of feminists' arguments were initially 'marginal' to mainstream feminism. As we shall see in chapters 6 and 7 of this book, this is not to say that women of colour were not present throughout both first and second wave feminism, but that they were marginalized by a white middle-class heterosexual 'mainstream' feminism. Moreover, the questions they raised about 'differences' among women have now become central to, or the mainstream

of, current feminist debates. Thus, using the terms 'mainstream' and 'marginalized voice' is not to reinforce the 'centrality' of one voice over the other in current debates, but to recognize the historical reality of such exclusions within feminism.

50 Dating from the first wave, feminism's struggle for the vote in the late nineteenth century, African American suffragists and other feminists of colour from the beginning have challenged the conceptualization of what white suffragists and feminists meant by 'women' and the exclusion of certain groups from their definition of 'women's' emancipation.

51 bell hooks, *Feminist Theory: from Margin to Centre*, Boston, South End Press 1984, Introduction.

52 Diane Lewis, 'A response to inequality: black women, racism and sexism', *Signs*, 3(2), 1977.

53 In the USA, while white men were enfranchised from 1776, black men received the vote in the late nineteenth century, and white and black women received it at the beginning of the twentieth century. In Canada, groups of people from certain ethnic backgrounds were excluded from voting, based on provincial voting lists until after the Second World War, and aboriginal people, on reserve, did not receive the vote until 1960.

54 Aida Hurtado, 'Relating to privilege: seduction and rejection in the subordination of white women and women of color', *Signs*, 14(4), 1989, pp. 833–55, at p. 840. Quote of Stanton from: Elizabeth Cady Stanton, Susan B. Anthony and Matilda Joslyn Gage (eds), *History of Women's Suffrage*, Rochester, NY: Charles Mann, 1887, volume 2, p. 222.

55 Gloria Geller, 'The War-time Elections Act of 1917 and the Canadian women's movement', *Atlantis: a Women's Studies Journal*, 2(1), Autumn 1975, pp. 88–106, at p. 95.

56 bell hooks, *From Margin to Centre*, pp. 67, 68–9.

57 Donna Greschner, Rhonda Johnson, and Wanda Stevenson Peekiskwetan, *Canadian Journal of Women and the Law*, 6, 1993, pp. 161–75, at p. 171.

58 hooks, *From Margin to Center*, p. 67.

59 Sojourner Truth, 'Ain't I a Woman?', in Miriam Schneir (ed.), *Feminism: the Essential Historical Writings*, New York: Random House, 1972, pp. 94–5.

60 bell hooks, *Ain't I a Woman?: Black Women and Feminism*, Boston, South End Press, 1981, p. 48.

61 hooks, *From Margin to Centre*, pp. 133–4.

62 Ibid., p. 95.

63 Ibid., p. 134.

64 hooks, *Ain't I a Woman?*, p. 22.

65 Abigail B. Bakan and Daiva K. Stasiulis, 'Making the match: domestic placement agencies and the racialization of women's household work', *Signs*, 20(2), 1995, p. 303.

66 On the issue of the 'racialization of domestic labour', particularly in Canada, see Sedef Arat-Koc, 'In the privacy of our own home: foreign domestic workers as solution to the crisis in the domestic sphere in Canada', *Studies in Political Economy*, 28, 1989, pp. 33–58; Makeda Silvera, *Silenced: Talks with Working Class Caribbean Women about Their Lives and Struggles as Domestic Workers in Canada*, 2nd edn, Toronto: Sister Vision, 1989; Audrey Macklin, 'Foreign domestic worker: surrogate housewife or mail order servant?', *McGill Law Journal*, 37(3), 1992, pp. 681–760; Roxanna Ng, 'Immigrant women and institutionalized racism', in Sandra Burt, Lorraine Code and Lindsay Dorney (eds), *Changing Patterns: Women in Canada*, Toronto: McLelland & Stewart, 1988, pp. 184–203; Evelyn Nakano Glenn, 'From servitude to service work: historical continuities in the racial division of paid reproductive labor', *Signs*, 18(1), 1992, pp. 1–43.

67 Bakan and Staisilis, 'Making the match', pp. 303, 326.

68 It must be noted that those Canadian families who employ 'nannies' or 'domestic help' from poorer parts of the world are not necessarily white. The picture, needless to say, is more complicated and nuanced. The one factor which is common to employers is their ability to afford such 'care' or 'service'. Second, the group of women who serve as 'nannies' are not exclusively 'women of colour', but under the Live-in Caregiver Program, large numbers of women come, in particular, from the Caribbean and the Philippines.

69 Bakan and Stasiulis, 'Making the match', p. 304.

70 Kate Rogers, 'Aboriginal women and the feminist project: an uneasy alliance', Paper presented at the 1997 Learned Societies, Canadian Political Science Association, Memorial University, Newfoundland, June, p. 10.

71 Ibid.

72 Elshtain, 'The power and powerlessness of women', in G. Bock and S. James (eds), *Beyond Equality and Difference*, Routledge: New York, 1992.

73 Hurtado, 'Relating to privilege', p. 850.

74 Audre Lorde, *Sister Outsider*, New York: Crossing Press, 1984, pp. 118–19, cited in Hurtado, 'Relating to privilege', p. 845.

75 Nancy Henley, *Body Politics: Power, Sex and Nonverbal Communication*, New York: Simon and Schuster, 1986, p. 15.

76 Hurtado, 'Relating to privilege', p. 850.

77 Ibid.

78 Ibid., p. 851.

79 Gloria Joseph, 'The incompatible menage a trois: Marxism, feminism, and racism', in Sargent (ed.), *Women and Revolution*, pp. 91–107, at p. 93.

80 Angela Davis, 'Reflections on the black woman's role in the community of slaves', *The Black Scholar*, 3(4), December 1971, cited in Joseph, 'The incompatible menage a trois', p. 95.

81 Hurtado, 'Relating to privilege', p. 849.
82 Mary Daly, *Gyn/Ecology: the MetaEthics of Radical Feminism*. London: Women's Press, 1983; Adrienne Rich, 'Compulsory heterosexuality and lesbian existence', in *The Signs Reader: Women, Gender and Scholarship*, Chicago: University of Chicago Press, 1983, pp. 139–68.
83 Mark Blasius, *Gay and Lesbian Politics: Sexuality and the Emergence of a New Ethic*, Philadelphia: Temple University Press, 1994, p. 39. I am grateful to my student, Michelle Dwyer, for posing many of these questions in both her essay and our graduate seminar on gender and politics.
84 J. B. Elshtain, 'Aristotle, the public–private split and the case of the suffragists', in J. B. Elshtain (ed.), *The Family in Political Thought*, Amherst: The University of Massachusetts Press, 1982, p. 53.
85 Bat-Ami Bar On, 'The feminist sexuality debates and the transformation of the political', in Claudia Card (ed.), *Adventures in Lesbian Philosophy*, Indianapolis: Indiana University Press, 1994, p. 57.
86 Charlotte Bunch, 'Lesbians in revolt', in Nancy Myron and Charlotte Bunch (eds), *Lesbianism and the Women's Movement*, Baltimore, MD: Diana, 1975, p. 36; cited in Bat-Ami Bar On, 'The feminist sexuality debates and the transformation of the political', p. 55.
87 Paula Bennett, 'Dyke in academe (II)', in Margaret Cruikshank (ed.), *Lesbian Studies: Present and Future*, New York: The Feminists Press, City University of New York, 1982, p. 5.
88 See in particular chapter 3, 'The women-identified woman', in Shane Phelan, *Identity Politics: Lesbian Feminism and the Limits of Community*, Philadelphia: Temple University Press, 1989.
89 Rich, 'Compulsory heterosexuality and lesbian existence', p. 165.
90 Anne Koedt and Jo Freeman, *The Politics of Women's Liberation*, New York: Longman Press, 1975, p. 139; cited in Phelan, *Identity Politics*, p. 47.
91 Ibid.
92 Sidney Abbott and Barbara Love, *Sappho Was a Right-on Woman: a Liberated View of Lesbianism*, New York: Stein and Day, 1972, p. 112.

Chapter 4 Culture versus Nature: the Feminist Critique

1 Much of the early work done on the duality between culture and nature, like that between public and private, is by anthropologists. Unlike the public/private divide, which was primarily the subject matter for feminist analysis, 'nature/culture' can be traced back to other anthropologists, in particular Claude Lévi-Strauss. See, for example, *Structural Anthropology*, translated by C. Jacobson and B. G. Schoepf, New York: Basic Books, 1963; *The Savage Mind*, London: Weidenfeld and Nicolson, 1962.
2 Sherry B. Ortner, 'Is female to male as nature is to culture?', in Michelle Zimbalist Rosaldo and Louise Lamphere (eds), *Women,*

Culture, and Society, Stanford, CA: Stanford University Press, 1974, pp. 67–87, at p. 72.

3   In 1980, Cambridge University Press published a collection of essays which questioned the proposition set out in Ortner's article by providing ethnographic case studies where such a duality simply does not hold. Carol MacCormack and Marilyn Strathern (eds), *Nature, Culture and Gender*, Cambridge: Cambridge University Press, 1980.

4   Sherry B. Ortner, *Making Gender: the Politics and Erotics of Culture*, Boston: Beacon Press, 1996, pp. 173–80.

5   Simone de Beauvoir, *The Second Sex*, translated by H. M. Parshley, New York: Knopf, 1953, p. 96.

6   Ingrid Makus in her analysis of political theory distinguishes between feminism of difference and feminism of sameness. See Ingrid Makus, *Women, Politics, and Reproduction: the Liberal Legacy*, Toronto, University of Toronto Press, 1996, especially chapter 5.

7   Susan Moller Okin, *Women in Western Political Thought*, Princeton, NJ: Princeton University Press, 1978, p. 41.

8   Diana Coole, *Women in Political Theory: from Ancient Misogyny to Contemporary Feminism*, Hemel Hempstead: Harvester Wheatsheaf, 1988, p. 23.

9   Ibid., p. 25.

10   Ibid., p. 30.

11   Ibid., p. 19.

12   Okin, *Women in Western Political Thought*, pp. 92–3.

13   Coole, *Women in Political Theory*, p. 30.

14   Okin, *Women in Western Political Thought*, p. 81.

15   Simone de Beauvoir, *The Second Sex*, translated by H. M. Parshley, London: Picador Classics, 1988, p. 38. All further references to *The Second Sex* will be to this edition, unless stated otherwise.

16   Susan Griffin, cited in Lynda Birke, *Women, Feminism and Biology: the Feminist Challenge*, New York: Methuen, 1986, p. 118.

17   Carolyn Merchant, *Earthcare: Women and the Environment*, New York: Routledge, 1995, pp. 60–1.

18   Jean Bethke Elshtain, *Public Man, Private Woman: Women in Social and Political Thought*, Princeton, NJ: Princeton University Press, 1981, p. 53.

19   W. Leiss, *The Domination of Nature*, Boston: Beacon Press, 1974, cited in Evelyn Fox Keller, 'Gender and science', in Sandra Harding and Merrill B. Hintikka (eds), *Discovering Reality: Feminist Perspectives on Epistemology, Metaphysics, Methodology, and Philosophy of Science*, Boston: Reidel Publishing Company, 1983, pp. 187–205, at p. 190.

20   Keller, 'Gender and science', p. 190.

21   Birke, *Women, Feminism and Biology*, p. 107.

22   Keller, 'Gender and science', p. 191.

23   Nancy Chodorow, *The Reproduction of Mothering: Psychoanalysis and the Socialization of Gender*, Berkeley: University of California Press, 1978, p. 169.

24 Nancy C. M. Hartsock, 'The feminist standpoint: developing the ground for a specifically feminist historical materialism', in Harding and Hintikka (eds), *Discovering Reality*, pp. 283–310, at p. 299.

25 de Beauvoir, *The Second Sex*, p. 29.

26 B. Farrington, '*Temporus partus masculus*, an untranslated writing of Francis Bacon', *Centaurus*, 1, pp. 193–205, at p. 197, cited in Keller, 'Gender and science', p. 190.

27 Jane Flax, 'The patriarchal unconscious', in Harding and Hintikka (eds), *Discovering Reality*, pp. 245–81, at p. 260.

28 Maria Mies and Vandana Shiva, *Ecofeminism*, London: Zed Books, 1993, p. 6.

29 Merchant, *Earthcare*, pp. 10–11.

30 Ibid., p. 11.

31 Ortner, *Making Gender*, p. 179.

32 Shulamith Firestone, *The Dialectic of Sex: the Case for Feminist Revolution*, London: The Women's Press, 1979.

33 Susan Brownmiller, *Against Our Will: Men, Women and Rape*, London: Secker and Warburg, 1975; Susan Griffin, *Pornography and Silence: Culture's Revenge Against Women*, London: The Women's Press, 1981; Andrea Dworkin, *Pornography: Men Possessing Women*, London: Women's Press, 1981.

34 Robin Morgan, 'Introduction/planetary feminism: the politics of the 21st century', in Robin Morgan (ed.), *Sisterhood Is Global: the International Women's Movement Anthology*, New York: Doubleday, pp. 1–37, at p. 6; cited in Linda Nicholson, 'Interpreting gender', *Signs*, 20(1), Autumn 1994, pp. 79–105, at pp. 90–1.

35 Nancy Hartsock, *Money, Sex and Power*, London: Longman, 1983; Maggie Humm (ed.), *Feminisms: a Reader*, Hemel Hempstead: Harvester Wheatsheaf, 1992, p. 75.

36 Susan Griffin, *Women and Nature: the Roaring Insider Her*, London: The Women's Press, 1984; *Feminisms: a Reader*, p. 76; *Pornography and Silence: Culture's Revenge against Nature*, NewYork: Harper and Row, 1981, p. 28.

37 Dworkin, *Pornography*, p. 203.

38 Moira Gatens, 'Towards a feminist philosophy of the body', in B. Caine, E. A. Grosz and M. de Lepervanche (eds), *Crossing Boundaries: Feminism and the Critique of Knowledges*, Sydney: Allen and Unwin, 1988, pp. 59–70, at p. 64.

39 *Feminisms: a Reader*, p. 260.

40 Judith Butler, *Gender Trouble: Feminism and the Subversion of Identity*, New York: Routledge, 1990, p. 8.

41 Adrienne Rich, *Of Woman Born: Motherhood as Experience and Institution*, New York: W. W. Norton and Co. Inc., 1976, p. 285.

42 Elizabeth Gross, 'Philosophy, subjectivity and the body: Kristeva and Irigaray', in Carole Pateman and Elizabeth Gross (eds), *Feminist Challenges: Social and Political Theory*, pp. 125–43, at p. 136.

43 Helene Cixous, 'The laugh of the Medusa', in E. Abel and E. K. Abel (eds), *The Signs Reader: Women, Gender and Scholarship*, Chicago: University of Chicago Press, 1983, pp. 279, 285.

44 Gross, 'Philosophy, subjectivity and the body', pp. 137–8.

45 Simone de Beauvoir, 'An interview with Alice Schwartzer', in *Simone de Beauvoir Today*, translated by Marianne Howarth, London: Hogarth Press, 1984, p. 79; cited in Makus, *Women, Politics and Reproduction*, p. 164.

46 Mary O'Brien, *The Politics of Reproduction*, London: Routledge and Kegan Paul, 1981, p. 50.

47 Shulamith Firestone, *The Dialectic of Sex*, pp. 11–12.

48 See Simone de Beauvoir, *the Second Sex*, and for commentary on this subject, Catriona Mackenzie, 'Simone de Beauvoir: philosphy and/or the female body', in Carole Pateman and Elizabeth Gross (eds), *Feminist Challenges: Social and Political Theory*, Sydney: Allen and Unwin, 1986, pp. 144–56.

49 Linda Nicholson, 'Interpreting gender', p. 84.

50 Ibid., pp. 84–5.

51 Coole, *Women in Political Theory*, p. 56. See also Christine Di Stefano, 'Masculinity as ideology in political theory: Hobbesian man considered', *Women's Studies International Forum*, 6, 1983, pp. 633–44.

52 Rebecca Grant, 'Sources of gender bias in international relations theory', in R. Grant and K. Newland (eds),*Gender and International Relations*, Bloomington: Indiana University Press, 1991, pp. 9–26, at p. 10.

53 Flax, 'The patriarchal unconscious', p. 261.

54 See Melissa Butler, 'Early liberal roots of feminism: John Locke and the attack on patriarchy', *American Political Science Review*, 72(1), 1978, pp. 135–50.

55 Coole, *Women in Political Theory*, p. 56.

56 Merchant, *Earthcare*, pp. 31–3.

57 What Merchant leaves out is that there is not just a gender code with the 'fall', but there are colonial aspects of cultivation versus the 'waste' of nature. Locke is explicit in referring to America and 'American Indians' in his description of an Edenic state of nature. See my article, 'The *Wild Indian's* venison: John Locke's theory of property', *Political Studies*, 44(1), March 1996, pp. 60–74.

58 Gatens, 'Towards a feminist philosophy of the body', p. 61.

59 Coole, *Women in Political Theory*, pp. 54, 76.

60 Elena Lieven, 'If it's natural, we can't change it', in The Cambridge Women's Studies Group, *Women in Society: Interdisciplinary Essays*, London: Virago, 1981, pp. 203–23.

61 Gayle Rubin, 'The traffic in women', in Rayna Reiter (ed.), *Toward an Anthropology of Women*, New York: Monthly Review, pp. 157–210, at p. 159.

62 Makus, *Women, Politics and Reproduction*, p. 163.

63 Susan Okin, *Justice, Gender and the Family*, New York: Basic Books, 1989, p. 171.
64 Makus, p. 164.
65 Margaret Simons and Jessica Benjamin, 'Simone de Beauvoir: an interview', *Feminist Studies*, 5, Summer 1979, pp. 330–45, at p. 341; cited in Makus, *Women, Politics and Reproduction*, pp. 165–6.
66 Dorothy Dinnerstein, *The Mermaid and the Minotaur*, New York: Harper and Row, 1976.
67 Mary O'Brien, *The Politics of Reproduction*, London: Routledge and Kegan Paul, 1981, p. 8.
68 Rich, *Of Woman Born*, p. 13.
69 Catharine MacKinnon, 'Feminism, Marxism, method, and the state: an agenda for theory', in Abel and Abel (eds), *The Signs Reader*, pp. 227–256, at p. 255.
70 Hartsock, 'The feminist standpoint', p. 304.
71 Christin Di Stefano, 'Dilemmas of difference: feminism, modernity and postmodernism', in Linda J. Nicholson (ed.), *Feminism/Post-Modernism*, New York: Routledge, 1990, pp. 63–82, at pp. 73–4.
72 Merchant, *Earthcare*, pp. 52–3.
73 *Feminisms: a Reader*, p. 87.
74 Juliet Mitchell, *Women: the Longest Revolution. Essays in Feminism, Literature and Psychoanalysis*, London: Virago, 1984, p. 26.
75 Ibid.
76 Ibid., p. 54.
77 Nancy Hartsock, 'The feminist standpoint: developing the groundwork for a specifically feminist historical materialism', in Harding and Hintikka (eds), *Discovering Reality*, pp. 283–310, at p. 290.
78 Michelle Barrett, 'Women's oppression today: problems in Marxist feminist analysis', in *Feminisms: a Reader*, pp. 113–14.
79 Birke, *Women, Feminism and Biology*, p. 24.
80 Ibid., pp. 21–3.
81 Adrienne Rich, 'Compulsory heterosexuality and lesbian existence', in Abel and Abel (eds), *The Signs Reader*, pp. 139–68, at p. 156.
82 Ibid., p. 155.
83 Ibid., p. 145.
84 Shane Phelan, '(Be)Coming out: lesbian identity and politics', *Signs*, 18(4), 1993, pp. 765–90, at p. 769.
85 Birke, *Women, Feminism and Biology*, pp. 22–3.
86 Shane Phelan, *Identity Politics: Lesbian Feminism and the Limits of Community*, Philadelphia: Temple University Press, 1989, p. 21.
87 See Michel Foucault, *The Birth of the Clinic*, New York: Vintage Books, 1973; *Madness and Civilization*, New York: Vintage Books, 1973.
88 Phelan, *Identity Politics*, p. 30.
89 Claudia Card, 'What is lesbian philosophy? A new introduction', in Claudia Card (ed.), *Adventures in Lesbian Philosophy*, Bloomington: Indiana University Press, 1994, pp. ix–xxii, at p. x.

90 Phelan, *Identity Politics*, p. 17.

91 Monique Wittig, 'One is not born a woman', in Alison Jaggar and Paula Rothenberg (eds), *Feminist Frameworks: Alternative Theoretical Accounts of the Relations between Women and Men*, New York: McGraw-Hill, 1984.

92 Judith Butler, 'Sex and gender in Simone de Beauvoir's *Second Sex*', in Helen Vivienne Wenzel (ed.), *Simone de Beauvoir: Witness to a Century*, special issue of *Yale French Studies*, 72, 1986, pp. 35–49, at p. 46; cited in Margaret A. Simons, 'Lesbian connections: Simone de Beauvoir and feminism', in Card (ed.), *Adventures in Lesbian Philosophy*, pp. 217–40; Judith Butler, *Gender Trouble: Feminism and the Subversion of Identity*, New York: Routledge, 1989, p. 147.

93 Colette Guillaumin, *Racism, Sexism, Power and Ideology*, London: Routledge, 1995, p. 3. Judith Butler concurs: 'I follow those recent theories which have made the argument that the "race" is partially produced as an effect of the history of racism, that its boundaries and meanings are constructed over time not only in the service of racism, but also in the service of the contestation of racism': Judith Butler, *Bodies that Matter: on the Discursive Limits of 'Sex'*, New York: Routledge, 1993, p. 18.

94 Ibid., p. 150.

95 Ibid.

96 Ibid., p. 5.

97 Donna Haraway, 'Ecc homo, ain't (ar'n't) I a woman, and inappropriat'd others: the human in a post-humanist landscape', in Judith Butler and Joan W. Scott (eds), *Feminists Theorize the Political*, New York: Routledge, pp. 86–100, at pp. 93–4.

98 Hurtado, 'Relating to privilege', p. 841.

99 See Barbara Arneil, *John Locke and America: the Defence of English Colonialism*, Oxford: Clarendon Press, 1996. It is important to note that even in early modern political theory, ontological distinctions are made by Locke between Amerindians, who are considered to have potential capacity for reason and therefore may own property in limited amounts and exercise some power, and African slaves, who Locke seems to see as without reason and therefore subject to despotical power.

100 Haraway, 'Ecc homo . . .', p. 95.

101 bell hooks, *Feminist Theory: from Margin to Center*, Boston: South End Press, 1984, pp. 75, 68.

102 Gerder Lerner, *Black Women in White America*; cited in bell hooks, *Ain't I a Woman: Black Women and Feminism*, London: Pluto, 1981, p. 59.

103 See, for example, Rennie Simpson, 'The Afro-American female: the historical context of the construction of sexual identity', in Ann Snitow, Chrstine Stansell and Sharon Thompson (eds), *Desire: The Politics of Sexuality*, London: Virago, 1983; Susan Brownmiller, *Against*

Our Will: Men, Women and Rape, New York: Simon and Schuster, 1975; bell hooks, *Ain't I a Woman?*

104 hooks, *Ain't I a Woman?*, pp. 59, 52.
105 Angela Davis, cited in ibid., p. 72.
106 Ibid.
107 hooks, *Ain't I a Woman?*, p. 84.
108 Ibid., p. 85.
109 Bakan and Stasiulis, 'Making the match', pp. 318–19 (emphasis added).
110 Ibid., p. 320.
111 Ibid., p. 331 (emphasis added).
112 Avtar Brah, 'Re-framing Europe: engendered racisms, ethnicities and nationalism in contemporary Western Europe', *Feminist Review*, 45, Autumn 1993, p. 13.
113 Rogers, 'Aboriginal women and the feminist project: an uneasy alliance', Paper presented at the 1997 Canadian Learned Societies, Memorial University, Newfoundland, June.
114 bell hooks, *From Margin to Center*, p. 159.
115 The most recent debate occurs in the Winter 1997 issue of *Signs*, volume 22, number 2, with a lead off article by Susan Hekman and the responses by Nancy Hartsock, Patricia Hill Collins, Sandra Harding and Dorothy Smith. See also Donna Haraway, 'Situated knowledges: the science question in feminism and the privilege of partial perspective', *Feminist Studies*, 14, 1988, pp. 575–99, 'A manifesto for cyborgs: science, technology and socialist feminism in the 1980s', in Linda Nicholson (ed.), *Feminism/Postmodernism*, New York: Routledge, 1990, pp. 190–233.

Chapter 5   Politics and Feminism: Deconstructing the Theoretical Frameworks

1 J. S. Mill, *On Liberty*, Harmondsworth: Penguin Books, 1982, p. 68.
2 Robert Nozick, *Anarchy, State and Utopia*, Oxford: Basil Blackwell, 1974, p. ix.
3 See, for example, Carol McMillan, *Women, Reason and Nature: Some Philosophical Problems with Feminism*, Princeton, NJ: Princeton University Press, 1982.
4 Christine Di Stefano, 'Dilemmas of difference: feminism, modernity and postmodernism', in Linda Nicholson (ed.), *Feminism/Postmodernism*, New York: Routledge, 1990, pp. 63–82, at p. 67.
5 Anne Phillips, 'Universal pretensions in political thought', in Michele Barrett and Anne Phillips (eds), *Destabilizing Theory: Contemporary Feminist Debates*, Cambridge: Polity Press, 1992, pp. 10–30, at p. 26.
6 Nancy Hartsock, 'Foucault on power: a theory for women?', in Nicholson (ed.), *Feminism/Postmodernism*, p. 171.

7   John Locke, *Essay Concerning Human Understanding*, edited by Peter
    Nidditch, Oxford: Oxford University Press, 1975, book I, chapter 4,
    paras 10, 15.
8   John Locke, *Two Treatises of Government*, edited by Peter Laslett, Cam-
    bridge: Cambridge University Press, 1988, II, para. 34 (emphasis added).
9   Locke, *Two Treatises*, II, para. 174.
10 Genevieve Lloyd, *The Man of Reason: 'Male' and 'Female' in Western
    Philosophy*, 2nd edn, London: Routledge, 1993, p. 104.
11 Seyla Benhabib, 'Epistemologies of postmodernism: a rejoinder to Jean-
    Francois Lyotard', in Nicholson (ed.), *Feminism/Postmodernism*, pp. 107–
    30.
12 Ibid., p. 111.
13 See, for example, Michel Foucault, *Power/Knowledge: Selected Interviews
    and Other Writings, 1972–1977*, edited by Colin Gordon, New York:
    Random House, 1977.
14 Lloyd, *Man of Reason*, p. 104.
15 Susan Bordo, *The Flight to Objectivity: Essays on Cartesianism and Cul-
    ture*, Albany: State University of New York Press, 1987, p. 92.
16 Susan Bordo, 'Feminism, postmodernism, and gender-scepticism', in
    Nicholson (ed.), *Feminism/Postmodernism*, pp. 133–56, at pp. 143–4.
17 It must be noted that Pateman and many feminist critiques of liberal
    thought limit their gender analysis of the family in seventeenth-
    century thought to the 'wives' and the conjugal contract. In fact,
    as has been argued, women existed as both servants and slaves in
    these theories, not to mention in Locke's theories as African slaves
    and Amerindians. Thus, in focusing solely on the 'wives' of free men,
    feminist theorists exclude from their analysis many groups of women
    (both historically and theoretically). Thus when Pateman, Susan Moller
    Okin, Diana Coole and others talk about 'women', what they are
    really talking about is 'wives' of free men in these political theories.
18 Susan Moller Okin, *Women in Western Political Thought*, Princeton, NJ:
    Princeton University Press, 1979, p. 199.
19 Virginia Held, 'Noncontractual society: a feminist view', in Marsha
    Hanen and Kai Nielsen (eds), *Science, Morality and Feminist Theory*,
    Calgary: University of Calgary Press, 1987, p. 113.
20 Mary Astell, *Some Reflections upon Marriage*, New York: Source Book
    Press, 1970, p. 107; cited by Carole Pateman, *The Disorder of Women*,
    Stanford, CA: Stanford University Press, 1989.
21 Melissa Butler, 'Early liberal roots of feminism: John Locke and the
    attack on patriarchy', *American Political Science Review*, 73(1), 1978.
22 See Jean Hampton, 'Feminist contractarianism', in Louise Antony and
    Charlotte Witt (eds), *A Mind of One's Own: Feminist Essays on Reason
    and Objectivity*, Boulder, CO: Westview Press, 1993.
23 Carol Gilligan, *In a Different Voice: Psychological Theory and Women's
    Development*, Cambridge: Harvard University Press, 1982.
24 Anne Phillips, 'Universal pretensions', p. 26.

25 *Globe and Mail*, 8 November 1996, p. 2.

26 Ibid.

27 Marx, 'Economic and philosophic manuscripts', in *Selected Writings*, pp. 80–1.

28 Ibid., p. 82.

29 Marx, 'Grundrisse', in *Selected Writings*, p. 381.

30 Heidi Hartmann, 'The unhappy marriage of Marxism and feminism: towards a more progressive union', in Lydia Sargent (ed.), *Women and Revolution: a Discussion of the Unhappy Marriage of Marxism and Feminism*, Montreal: Black Rose Books, 1981, pp. 1–42, at p. 5.

31 Ibid.

32 Kate Millet, in the first section of her book *Sexual Politics*, develops the theory of patriarchy as the sexual politics through which men have established and maintained their power. Other feminists, including socialist feminists, incorporated this idea into their own theories. Kate Millet, *Sexual Politics*, London: Virago, 1977.

33 Juliet Mitchell, *Women's Estate*, Harmondsworth: Penguin Books, 1973, p. 88.

34 Hartmann, 'The unhappy marriage of Marxism and feminism', p. 14.

35 Iris Marion Young, 'Beyond the unhappy marriage: a critique of the dual system theory', in Sargent (ed.), *Women and Revolution*, p. 49.

36 Marx, 'The German ideology', *Selected Writings*, p. 169.

37 Margaret Benston, 'The political economy of women's liberation', *Monthly Review*, 21(4) September 1960, p. 16.

38 Marilyn Waring, *If Women Counted: a New Feminist Economics*, San Francisco: Harper & Row, 1988.

39 Alison Jaggar, *Feminist Politics and Human Nature*, Brighton: Harvester Press, 1983.

40 Jean Bethke Elshtain, *Public Man, Private Woman: Women in Social and Political Thought*, Princeton, NJ: University Press, 1981, p. 265.

41 Michael Sandel, 'Introduction', in Michael Sandel (ed.), *Liberalism and Its Critics*, New York: New York University Press, 1984, p. 5.

42 John Rawls, *Theory of Justice*, Oxford: University Press, 1971, p. 560.

43 Sandel, 'Introduction', p. 5.

44 Ronald Beiner, *What's the Matter with Liberalism?*, Berkeley: University of California Press, 1992, p. 16, emphasis added.

45 Alasdair MacIntyre, 'The virtues, the unity of a human life, and the concept of a tradition', in Sandel (ed.), *Liberalism and Its Critics*, pp. 125–48.

46 Alasdair MacIntrye, *After Virtue: a Study in Moral Theory*, London: Duckworth, 1981, p. 203.

47 Sandel, 'Introduction', p. 6.

48 Michael Sandel, 'Morality and the liberal ideal', *The New Republic*, 7 May 1985, p. 16.

49 Michael Walzer, 'Welfare, membership and need', in Sandel (ed.), *Liberalism and Its Critics*, p. 200.

50 Sandel, 'Introduction', pp. 6–7.
51 Elizabeth Frazer and Nicola Lacey, *The Politics of Community: a Feminist Critique of the Liberal–Communitarian Debate*, Hemel Hempstead: Harvester Wheatsheaf, 1993, p. 151.
52 See Michael Sandel, *Liberalism and the Limits of Justice*, Cambridge: Cambridge University Press, 1982, pp. 30–4; Amy Gutmann, 'Communitarian critics of liberalism', *Philosophy and Public Affairs*, 14(3), 1985, p. 309.
53 Iris Marion Young, 'The ideal of community and the politics of difference', in Nicholson (ed.), *Feminism/Postmodernism*, pp. 300–23, at p. 312.
54 Jean Bethke Elshtain, *Democracy on Trial*, The Massey Lecture Series, Concord, NH: House of Anansi Press Ltd, 1993.
55 See Frazer and Lacey, *The Politics of Community*, chapter 3; Lynn Segal, *Slow Motion: Changing Masculinities, Changing Men*, London: Virago Press, 1990; Sandel, *Liberalism and Its Critics*, p. 6.
56 Frazer and Lacey, *The Politics of Community*, p. 150.
57 Ibid., p. 155; Susan Moller Okin, *Justice, Gender and the Family*, New York: Basic Books, 1989.
58 Frazer and Lacey, *The Politics of Community*, p. 135.

Chapter 6   First and Second Wave Feminism: Challenging the Dualisms

1 It is interesting to note that the group of feminists who were not allied with any framework outside of themselves were labelled 'radical'.
2 Rebecca Walker writes: 'The . . . ideals of feminism can't help but leave young women and men struggling with the reality of who we are. Constantly measuring up to some cohesive fully down-for-the-feminist cause identity without contradictions and messiness . . . is not a fun or easy task': *To Be Real: Telling the Truth and Changing the Face of Feminism*, edited and with an introduction by Rebecca Walker, New York: Anchor Books, 1995, p. xxxi. Barbara Findlen writes: 'If there is a troublesome legacy from the feminism that has come before, it's the burden of high expectations': Barbara Findlen (ed.), *Listen Up: Voices from the Next Feminist Generation*, Seattle: Seal Press, 1995, p. xv.
3 If there is one aspect of the generational debate which is of great importance to the self-described 'third wave' younger feminist, it is the sense of coming at similar issues from the point of view of the individual's life and lived experience. Perspective, however contradictory and confusing, lies at the heart of both Walker's and Findlen's books and with it the demand that older feminists try to understand this new point of view, or rather, points of view.
4 Aida Hurtado writes: 'Recently, white feminist theorists have begun to recognize the theoretical implications of embracing diversity among

women . . . Rejecting the binary categorization of 'man' and 'woman' this new conceptualization opens up the possibility of diversity among women and men and the possibility of many feminisms': *The Color of Privilege: Three Blasphemies on Race and Feminism*, Ann Arbor: University of Michigan Press, 1996, p. 7.

5 There were many important women of colour, in particular African American suffragists, who fought for a larger goal than the one described in this opening sentence, as will be discussed shortly, but for the most part, first wave feminism was largely a racially and class bound project.

6 Mary Wollstonecraft, *A Vindication on the Rights of Women* (1792), Harmondsworth: Penguin Books, 1985, p. 263.

7 J. S. Mill, *Subjection of Women*, in John Gray (ed.), *On Liberty and Other Essays*, Oxford: Oxford University Press, 1991, p. 523.

8 Jean Bethke Elshtain, *Public Man, Private Woman: Women in Social and Political Thought*, Princeton, NJ: University Press, 1981, p. 231.

9 Elizabeth Stanton, Susan B. Anthony and Matilda Gage, *The History of Woman Suffrage*, three volumes, Rochester: Charles Mann, 1881–1891, volume II, pp. 351–2.

10 bell hooks, *Ain't I a Woman? Black Women and Feminism*, Boston, South End Press, 1981, pp. 31–2.

11 Ibid., pp. 31, 32.

12 Ibid., p. 127.

13 Sojourner Truth, 'Ain't I a Woman?', in Miriam Schneir (ed.), *Feminism: the Essential Historical Readings*, New York: Random House, 1972, p. 94.

14 Paula Giddings, 'Black feminism takes its rightful place', *Ms Magazine*, October 1985, pp. 25–6. There have been several works which discuss the historical role of women of colour in the fight for the vote and onwards in the USA. See, for example, Hurtado, *The Color of Privilege*; Barbara Omolade, 'Black women and feminism' in H. Eisenstein and Alice Jardine (eds), *The Future of Difference*, Boston: G. K. Hall, 1980, pp. 247–57; hooks, *Ain't I a Woman?*; Nancie Caraway, *Segregated Sisterhood: Racism and the Politics of American Feminism*, Knoxville: The University of Tennessee Press, 1991; Angel Davis, *Women, Race and Class*, New York: Random House, Vintage Books, 1983; Hazel Carby, *Reconstructing Womanhood: the Emergence of the Afro-American Woman Novelist*, Oxford: Oxford University Press, 1987.

15 Caraway, *Segregated Sisterhood*, p. 118.

16 Ibid., p. 119. For the revisiting of feminist history see: hooks, *Ain't I am Woman*; Carby, *Reconstructing Womanhood*; Davis, *Women Race and Class*; Paula Giddings, *When and Where I Enter: the Impact of Black Women on Race and Sex in America*, New York: William Morrow, 1984; Caraway, *Segregated Sisterhood*, especially chapter 5.

17 Anna Julia Cooper, 'Woman versus the Indian', cited in Carby, *Reconstructing Womanhood*, p. 106.

18   Women gained the vote at different times depending on a variety of factors, including most importantly their 'race' or 'ethncity', but also marital status, age and level of income or education. For example, in Canada in 1917, women whose husbands were with the Canadian Armed Forces were allowed to vote; in 1918, it was extended to women over the age of twenty-one except aboriginal women (and men), who eventually won the right to vote in 1960, and in British Columbia women (and men) of Indian, Chinese and Japanese descent, who had to wait until 1945.

19   Vera Brittain, 'Why feminism lives', in Maggie Humm (ed.), *Feminisms: a Reader*, Hemel Hempstead: Harvester Wheatsheaf, 1992, p. 40.

20   Vera Brittain and Winifred Holtby, 'Feminism divided', p. 42.

21   Virginia Woolf, 'A room of one's own', in *Feminisms: a Reader*, p. 26.

22   Naomi Black, 'Virginia Woolf: the life of natural happiness' in D. Spender (ed.), *Feminist Theorists*, London: Women's Press, 1983.

23   For a description of the evolving relationship between feminism and lesbianism in the USA in the 1960s, see Sidney Abbott and Barbara Love, *Sappho Was a Right-on Woman: a Liberated View of Lesbianism*, New York: Stein and Day, 1972, particularly chapters 5 and 6.

24   hooks, *Ain't I am Woman?*, p. 146.

25   Anne Phillips, 'Feminism, equality and difference', in Linda McDowell and Rosemary Pringle (eds), *Defining Women: Social Institutions and Gender Divisions*, Cambridge: Polity Press, 1992, pp. 205–22, at p. 214.

26   Juliet Mitchell, *Woman's Estate*, Harmondsworth: Penguin Books, 1973, pp. 88–9.

27   Ibid., p. 106.

28   Ibid., p. 107

29   Ibid., p. 158.

30   Sheila Rowbotham, *Woman's Consciousness: Man's World*, Harmondsworth: Penguin Books, 1974, p. 117.

31   Ibid., pp. 27, 30.

32   Heidi Hartmann, 'The unhappy marriage of Marxism and feminism: towards a more progressive union', in Lydia Sargeant (ed.), *Women and Revolution: a Discussion of the Unhappy Marriage of Marxism and Feminism*, Montreal: Black Rose Books, 1981, p. 2.

33   Ibid., p. 3.

34   See, for example, Christine Riddiough, 'Socialism, feminism and gay/ lesbian liberation' (pp. 71–90); and Gloria Joseph, 'The incompatible menage a trois: Marxism, feminism, and racism' (pp. 91–108) in Sargeant (ed.), *Women and Revolution*.

35   Catharine MacKinnon, 'Feminism, Marxism, method, and the state: an agenda for theory', in E. Abel and E. K. Abel (eds), *The Signs Reader: Women, Gender and Scholarship*, Chicago: University of Chicago Press, 1983, pp. 227–56, at p. 255.

36   Ibid.

37   Mitchell, *Woman's Estate*, p. 167.

38 Ibid.
39 Rosemarie Tong, *Feminist Thought: a Comprehensive Introduction*, Boulder, CO: Westview Press, 1989, p. 148. See Karen Horney, *Feminine Psychology*, New York: W. W. Norton, 1973; Clara Thompson, *Interpersonal Psychoanalysis: the Selected Papers of Clara Thompson*, edited by M. P. Green, New York: Basic Books, 1964.
40 Mitchell, *Women's Estate*, p. 167.
41 Dorothy Dinnerstein, The mermaid and the Minotaur, in *Feminisms: a Reader*, p. 236.
42 Dorothy Dinnerstein, *The Mermaid and the Minotaur*, New York: Harper Colophon Books, 1977, p. 5.
43 Nancy Chodorow, *The Reproduction of Mothering: Psychoanalysis and the Sociology of Gender*, Berkeley: University of California Press, 1978, p. 7.
44 Nancy Hirschmann, 'Freedom, recognition and obligation: a feminist approach to political theory', *American Poltiial Science Review*, 83(4), 1989, pp. 1227–44, at p. 1230.
45 Ibid., p. 1231.
46 Ibid., pp. 1240–1.
47 Jane Flax, 'Political philosophy and the patriarachal unconscious: a psychoanalytic perspective on epistemology and metaphysics', in Sandra Harding and Merrill B. Hintikka (eds), *Discovering Reality: Feminist Perspectives on Epistemology, Metaphysics, Methodology, and Philosophy of Science*, Boston: Reidel Publishing Company, 1983, pp. 245–81, at pp. 245, 247.
48 Ibid., p. 270.
49 Elizabeth Abel, 'Race, class, and pscyhoanalysis? opening questions', in Marianne Hirsch and Evelyn Fox Keller (eds), *Conflicts in Feminism*, New York: Routledge, 1990, pp. 184–204, at p. 184.
50 Elizabeth Spelman, *Inessential Woman: Problems of Exclusion in Feminist Thought*, Boston: Beacon Press, 1988; Toril Moi, 'Patriarchal thought and the drive for knowledge', in Teresa Brennan (ed.), *Between Feminism and Psychoanalysis*, London: Routledge, 1989, pp. 189–205.
51 Collette Guillaumin, *Racism, Sexism, Power and Ideology*, London: Routledge, 1995, pp. 90–2.
52 See, for example, Elizabeth Abel, 'Race, class, and pscyhoanalysis?', pp. 184–204. Abel incorporates two other texts: Hortense J. Spiller, 'Mama's baby, papa's maybe: an American grammer book' and Carolyn Kay Steedman's *Landscape for a Good Woman: a Story of Two Lives*.
53 Adrienne Rich, 'Compulsory heterosexuality and lesbian existence', p. 182.
54 Firestone, *Dialectic of Sex: the Case for Feminist Revolution*, New York: William Morrow and Co., 1970, p. 198.
55 H. Eisenstein, 'Shulamith Firestone', in Maggie Humm (ed.), *Modern Feminisms: Political, Literary, Cultural*, New York: Columbia University Press, 1992, p. 66.

56 Firestone, *Dialectic of Sex*, pp. 11–12.
57 Ibid., p. 47.
58 Linda Nicholson, 'Interpreting gender', *Signs*, 20(1), Autumn 1994, pp. 79–105, at p. 93. Nicholson identifies Mary Daly and Alison Jaggar as other examples of radical feminists who adopt a form of biological foundationalism.
59 Kate Millet, *Sexual Politics*, New York: Doubleday and Co. Inc., 1970, pp. 23, 25.
60 Ibid., p. 25.
61 Charlotte Bunch, 'Lesbians in revolt', in Nancy Myron and Charlotte Bunch (eds), *Lesbianism and the Women's Movement*, Baltimore, MD: Diana, 1975; cited in Bat-Ami Bar On, 'The feminist sexuality debates and the tranformation of the political', in Claudia Card (ed.), *Adventures in Lesbian Philosophy*, Bloomington: Indiana University Press, 1994.
62 Rich, 'Compulsory heterosexuality', p. 192.
63 Ruthann Robson, 'Mother; the legal domestication of lesbian existence', in Card (ed.), *Adventures in Lesbian Philosophy*.
64 Rich, *Of Woman Born*, p. 183.
65 Mary Daly, *Gyn/Ecology: the MetaEthics of Radical Feminism*, Boston: Beacon Press, 1978, p. xiii.
66 Audre Lorde, 'An open letter to Mary Daly', in *Sister Outsider*, Trumansburg: NY: The Crossing Press, 1984, pp. 66–71, at pp. 68, 69.

Chapter 7   Third Wave Feminism(s): the View at, of and from the Border

1 In using the term 'third wave feminism(s)', I will make the case, in this chapter, that there is a new body of thought, distinct from second wave feminism, which is characterized by notions of identity, difference, contradiciton and embodiment. It is not limited to either 'postmodern feminists', as some have claimed, or the new generation of young feminists who have described themselves as 'third wave', although each of these groups is important to its current expression. Rather, the roots of third wave feminism(s), as I hope to make clear, are to be found in the 1980s challenges by women of colour and lesbian/queer theorists.
2 Moira Gatens, 'Power, bodies and difference', in Michelle Barrett and Anne Phillips (eds), *Destabilizing Theories: Contemporary Feminist Debates*, Oxford: Polity Press, 1992.
3 E. A. Grosz, 'The in(ter)vention of feminist knowledges', in Barbara Caine, E. A. Grosz and Marie de Lepervanche (eds), *Crossing Boundaries: Feminisms and the Critique of Knowledges*, Sydney: Allen and Unwin, 1988, pp. 92–109, at p. 96.
4 Ibid.

5 Marilyn Frye concludes: 'The project of feminist theory is to write a new encyclopedia. Its title: *The World, According to Women*': Marilyn Frye, 'The possibility of feminist theory', in Deborah L. Rhode (ed.), *Theoretical Perspectives on Sexual Difference*, New Haven, CT: Yale University Press, 1990, p. 175.

6 Rebecca Walker co-founded a group called 'Third Wave': 'a national, multicultural organization devoted to facilitating and initiating young women's activism' in the United States.

7 *To Be Real: Telling the Truth and Changing the Face of Feminism*, edited and with an introduction by Rebecca Walker, New York: Anchor Books, 1995; Barbara Findlen (ed.), *Listen Up: Voices from the Next Feminist Generation*, Seattle: Seal Press, 1995. I want to thank my student, Laura Thomas, for introducing me to this new generation of feminisms. It should be noted that much of this generation-based third wave is coming from the United States, and is thus shaped by this particular political culture.

8 Jacquelyn N. Zita, 'Introduction', Special issue of *Hyptia: Third Wave Feminisms*, 12(3), Summer 1997, pp. 1–6, at pp. 1–2.

9 Walker, 'Introduction', p. xxxvii.

10 Findlen, 'Introduction', p. xiii.

11 Walker, 'Introduction', pp. xxxviii–xxxix.

12 Ibid., p. xxxix.

13 See Kate Roiphe, *The Morning After: Sex, Fear and Feminism*, Boston: Little Brown and Co., 1993; Naomi Wolf, *Fire with Fire: the New Female Power and How to Use It*, New York: Fawcett Combine, 1993; Rene Denfeld, *The New Victorians: a Young Woman's Challenge to the Old Feminist Order*, New York: Warner Books, 1995. Leslie Heywood and Jennifer Drake describe Roiphe, Denfeld and Wolf as 'postfeminists' rather than 'third wave feminists' – namely, 'a group of young, conservative feminists who explicitly define themselves against and criticize feminists of the second wave' ('Introduction', in Leslie Heywood and Jennifer Drake (eds), *Third Wave Agenda: Being Feminist, Doing Feminism*, Minneapolis: University of Minnesota Press, 1997, pp. 1–20, at p. 1). 'Third wave feminists', on the other hand, see themselves as 'keeping the faith' with second wave feminism, while simultaneously challenging some of its precepts. Heywood and Drake seem a little defensive on this point, for one can easily trace some of Roiphe, Denfeld and Wolf's ideas in third wave feminism. Indeed, they provide one of the many sides of the contradictory nature of third wave feminism, namely 'power feminism'. I prefer, like Catherine Orr, to think that the reason these feminists are not third wave feminists, and would not see themselves as such, is exactly because their worlds are without contradiction: 'Rather than navigating contradictions, these authors deny that feminism necessarily and inevitably holds contradictions', Orr, 'Charting the currents of the third wave', *Hypatia*, 12(3), Summer 1997, pp. 29–45,

p. 35. For more on this debate, see Carolyn Sorisio, 'A tale of two feminisms: power and victimization in contemporary feminist debate', in Heywood and Drake (eds), *Third Wave Agenda*, pp. 134–49.

14 On the alternative music scene and feminism see Melissa Klein, 'Duality and redefinition: young feminism and the alternative music community', in Heywood and Drake (eds), *Third Wave Agenda*, pp. 207–25. Klein writes: 'The underground music community has served as a particularly fertile breeding ground for redefining a feminism to fit our lives' (p. 208).

15 http://www.geocities.com/area51/vault/1363/riotgrrl.html. For the wide variety of websites which fall under the rubric 'riot grrl', check this term through any search engine. The anger of Riotgrrls is articulated in one site's welcome: 'You've come to the right place. A shrine to all girls who wish their gender started with a grrrrowl! And a tribute to all women who are too pissed off, unhappy, tough, geeky, or brainy to do and think what they're told.' http://garnet.berkeley.edu/~annaleen/riot.grrls.html.

16 'Thank heaven for little Girls', *The Globe and Mail*, Toronto, Monday 19 January 1998, p. A10.

17 Leslie Heywood and Jennifer Drake, 'Introduction', in Heywood and Drake (eds), *Third Wave Agenda*, pp. 1–20, at p. 4.

18 'Cybergrrls' and 'Webgrrls' are networks dedicated to putting women in touch with each other and empowering them to use information technology and communicate through the web. It was founded in 1995 by Aliza Sherman. http://www.folksonline.com/folks/ts/cybergirl.htm (cybergrrls/webgrrls website).

19 See note 89.

20 Orr, 'Charting the currents of the third wave', p. 29.

21 Rita Alfonso and Jo Trigilio, 'Surfing the third wave: a dialogue between two third wave feminists', *Hypatia*, 12(3), Summer 1997, pp. 7–16, at p. 9.

22 Orr, 'Charting the currents of the third wave', p. 37. Heywood and Drake make the same argument in their introduction to *Third Wave Agenda*. 'It was US third world feminism that modeled a language and a politics of hybridity that can account for our lives at the century's turn' (p. 13).

23 Heywood and Drake, 'Introduction', p. 13.

24 Maxine Zinn and Bonnie Thornton Dill, 'Theorizing difference from multiracial feminism', *Feminist Studies*, 22(2), Summer 1996, pp. 321–31, at p. 322.

25 Elizabeth Genovese-Fox, 'Difference, diversity and divsions in an agenda for the women's movement', in Gay Young and Bette J. Dickerson (eds), *Colour, Class, and Country: Experiences of Gender*, London: Zed Books, 1994, pp. 232–48, p. 232. For other recent studies on difference in feminist thought see Chirstina Crosby, 'Dealing with difference', in Judith Butler and Joan W. Scott (eds), *Feminists Theorize*

the Political, New York: Routledge, 1992, pp. 130–43; Anna Yeatman, 'A Feminist Theory of Social Differentiation' (pp. 281–99) and Iris Marion Young, 'The ideal of community and the politics of difference' (pp. 300–23), in Linda J. Nicholson (ed.), *Feminism/Postmodernism*, New York: Routledge, 1990.

26 Linda Nicholson, 'Interpreting gender', *Signs*, 20(1), Autumn 1994, pp. 79–105, at p. 93.

27 Carol Gilligan, *In a Different Voice*, Cambridge, MA: Harvard University Press, 1982.

28 See, for example, Carol Stack, 'The culture of gender: women and men of color', *Signs*, 11(2), Winter 1986, pp. 322–3.

29 Nancy Chodorow, *The Reproduction of Mothering: Psychoanalysis and the Sociology of Gender*, Berkeley: University of California Press, 1978, p. 169.

30 Jean Bethke Elshtain, *Public Man, Private Women: Women in Social and Political Thought*, Princeton, NJ: Princeton University Press, 1981, pp. 290–7; see also Judith Lorber, Rose Coser, Alice Rossi and Nancy Chodorow, 'On the *Reproduction of Mothering*: a methodological debate' *Signs*, 6(3), Spring 1981, pp. 482–515.

31 Helene Cixous, 'The laugh of the Medusa', in E. Abel and E. K. Abel (eds), *The Signs Reader: Women, Gender and Scholarship*, Chicago: University of Chicago Press, p. 285.

32 Luce Irigaray, 'The sex which is not one', in Lawrence Cahoone (ed.), *From Modernism to Postmodernism: an Anthology*, Oxford: Blackwell, 1996.

33 Luce Irigaray, *L'ethique de la difference sexuelle*, Paris: Minuit, 1984, p. 1; cited in Grosz, 'The in(ter)vention of feminist knowledges', p. 104.

34 Julia Kristeva, 'Desire in language: a semiotic approach to literature and art', in Maggie Humm (ed.), *Feminisms: a Reader*, Hemel Hempstead: Harvester Wheatsheaf, 1992, p. 214.

35 Julia Kristeva, cited in Rosemarie Tong, *Feminist Thought: a Comprehensive Introduction*, Boulder, CO: Westview Press, 1989, p. 230.

36 See, for example, Judith Butler, *Bodies that Matter: on the Discursive Limits of 'Sex'*, New York: Routledge, 1993; Alison Caddick, 'Feminism and the body', *Arena*, 74, 1985, pp. 60–88; Zillah Eisenstein, *The Female Body and the Law*, Berkeley: University of California Press, 1990; Moira Gatens, 'Towards a feminist philosophy of the body', in Caine et al. (eds), *Crossing Boundaries*, pp. 59–70; Elizabeth Grosz, 'Notes towards a corporeal feminism', *Australian Feminist Studies*, Summer 1995, pp. 1–16; Alison Jaggar and Susan Bordo (eds), *Gender/Body/Knowledge: Feminist Reconstructions of Being and Knowing*, New Brunswick, NJ: Rutgers University Press, 1989; Philippa Rothfield, 'Feminism, subjectivity, and sexual experience', in Sneja Gunew (ed.), *Feminist Knowledge: Critique and Construct*, London: Routledge, 1990; Iris Marion Young, *Throwing Like a Girl and Other Essays in Feminist Philosophy and Social Theory*, Bloomington: Indiana University Press, 1990.

37 Grosz, 'The in(ter)vention of feminist knowledges', p. 101.
38 Donna Haraway, 'Human in a post-humanist landscape', in Judith Butler and Joan Scott (eds), *Feminists Theorize the Political*, New York: Routledge, 1992, p. 96.
39 Ibid.
40 Nicholson, 'Interpreting gender', p. 81.
41 Jane Flax, 'Postmodernism and gender relations in feminist theory', in Nicholson (ed.), *Feminism/Postmodernism*, pp. 39–62, at p. 50.
42 Butler, *Bodies that Matter*, p. 2.
43 Avtar Brah, 'Re-framing Europe: engendered racisms, ethnicities and nationalism in contemporary Western Europe', *Feminist Review*, 45, Autumn 1993, p. 13.
44 Shane Phelan, '(Be)Coming out: lesbian identity and politics', *Signs*, 18(4), 1993, pp. 765–90, at p. 777.
45 Jeanine Lombard, 'Femmenism', in Rebecca Walker (ed.), *To Be Real*, New York: Anchor Books, 1995, pp. 21–33, at p. 21.
46 Moira Gatens, 'Towards a feminist philosophy of the body', p. 60.
47 Carole Pateman, *The Sexual Contract*, Cambridge: Polity Press, 1988, p. 216.
48 Carole Pateman, 'Feminism and paticipatory democrary', Unpublished paper present to the Meeting of the American Philosophical Association, St Louis, MO, May 1986, p. 24; cited in Chantal Mouffe, 'Feminism and radical politics', in Judith Butler and Joan W. Scott (eds), *Feminists Theorize the Political*, Routledge: New York, 1992, pp. 369–84, at p. 375.
49 Anne Phillips, 'Universal pretensions in political thought', in Michele Barrett and Anne Phillips (eds), *Destabilizing Theories: Contemporary Feminist Debates*, Cambridge: Polity Press, 1992, pp. 10–30, at p. 12.
50 Elshtain, *Public Man, Private Woman*, p. 336.
51 bell hooks, *Feminist Theory: from Margin to Center*, Boston: South End Press, 1984.
52 Allison Abner, 'Motherhood', in Walker (ed.), *To Be Real*, pp. 185–193, p. 193.
53 Sonja D. Curry-Johnson, 'Weaving an identity tapestry', in Findlen (ed.), *Listen Up*, pp. 221–9, at pp. 221–2, 228.
54 Stacy Alaimo, 'Cyborg and ecofeminist interventions: challenges for an environmental feminism', *Feminist Studies*, 20(1), Spring 1994, pp. 133–52, at p. 133.
55 Donna Haraway, *Primate Visions: Gender, Race, and Nature in the World of Modern Science*, New York: Routledge, 1989, p. 256.
56 Alaimo, 'Cyborg and ecofeminist interventions', p. 149.
57 Donna Haraway, 'A manifesto for cyborgs: science, technology and socialist feminism in the 1980s', in Nicholson (ed.), *Feminism/Postmodernism*, pp. 190–233, at p. 191.
58 Phelan, '(Be)Coming out', pp. 765–6.

59 Biddy Martin and Chadra Topade Mohanty, 'Feminist politics: what's home got to do with it?' in Teresa de Lauretis (ed.), *Feminist Studies/ Critical Studies*, Bloomington: Indiana University Press, 1986, pp. 191–212, at p. 203.

60 Haraway, 'A manifesto for cyborgs', p. 199.

61 Carraway, *Segregated Sisterhood*, p. 6.

62 Julia Kristeva, 'A question of subjectivity: an interview', in Mary Eagleton (ed.), *Feminist Literary Theory: a Reader*, Oxford: Blackwell, 1994, pp. 352, 351.

63 Haraway, 'A manifesto for cyborgs', p. 197.

64 Judith Butler, 'Gender trouble, feminist theory and psychonanlytic discourse', in Nicholson (ed.), *Feminism/Postmodernism*, pp. 324–40, at p. 325.

65 Zinn and Dill, 'Theorizing difference from multiracial feminism', p. 323.

66 Haraway, 'A manifesto for cyborgs', p. 197.

67 Judith Butler, *Gender Trouble: Feminism and the Subversion of Identity*, New York: Routledge, 1990, p. 148.

68 Patricia Hill Collins, *Black Feminist Thought: Knowledge, Consciousness and the Politics of Empowerment*, Boston: Unwin Hyman, 1990.

69 Young, 'The ideal of community', p. 319.

70 Haraway, 'A manifesto for cyborgs', p. 201. Haraway states: 'My complaint about socialist/Marxian standpoints is their unintended erasure of polyvocal, unassimilable, radical difference made visible in anti-colonial discourse and practice.'

71 Susan Hekman, 'Truth and method: feminist standpoint theory revisited', *Signs: Journal of Women in Culture and Society*, 22(2), 1997, pp. 341–65, at p. 342.

72 Ibid., p. 349.

73 Nancy Hartsock, 'Comment on Hekman's "Truth and method: feminist standpoint theory revisited": truth of justice?', *Signs: Journal of Women in Culture and Society*, 22(2), 1997, pp. 367–74, at p. 368.

74 Ibid., p. 373.

75 Patricia Hill Collins, 'Comment on Hekman's "Truth and method: feminist standpoint theory revisited": truth of justice?', *Signs*, 22(2), 1997, pp. 375–81, at p. 375.

76 Nancy Hartsock, 'Rethinking modernism: minority vs. majority theories', *Cultural Critique*, 7, pp. 187–206, at pp. 190–1; cited in Nicholson (ed.), *Feminism/Postmodernism*, p. 85.

77 bell hooks, 'Postmodern blackness', in Eagleton (ed.), pp. 280–3, at pp. 280, 282.

78 Patricia Hill Collins, 'Symposium: on West and Fenstermaker's "Doing difference"', *Gender and Society*, 9(4), August 1995, pp. 491–4, at pp. 493, 494.

79 Christine de Stefano, 'Dilemmas of difference: feminism, modernity, and postmodernism', *Feminism/Postmodernism*, pp. 63–82, at p. 78.

80   Jane Flax, 'Postmodernism and gender relations', in Nicholson (ed.), *Feminism/Postmodernism*, pp. 39–62, at p. 40.

81   Alfonso and Trigilio, 'Surfing the third wave', p. 8.

82   Ibid., p. 9.

83   Janine Brodie, 'Restructuring: the falling apart', Robarts Lecture, York Univesity, 1 March 1994, Robarts Centre for Canadian Studies, p. 43; For a similar position, see Donna Haraway, *Simians, Cyborgs and Women: the Reinvention of Nature*, New York: Routledge, 1991, p. 180.

84   Haraway, *Simians, Cyborgs and Women*, p. 190.

85   Ibid., p. 191.

86   Ibid., p. 192.

87   Ibid., p. 191.

88   Ibid., p. 212.

89   Japan Webgrrls site: http://www.iuj.ac.jp/webgrrls/about.htm.

90   Michelle Sidler, 'Living in McJobdom: third wave feminism and class inequality', in Heywood and Drake (eds), *Third Wave Agenda*, pp. 25–39, at p. 34.

91   Ibid., p. 38.

92   Trinh T. Minh-ha, *Woman, Native, Other: Writing Postcoloniality and Feminism*, Bloomington: Indiana University Press, 1989, p. 6.

93   Gloria Anzaldua, *Borderlands/La Frontera*, San Francisco: Aunt Lute Books, 1987, p. 2, preface.

94   Ibid., preface.

95   Ibid., p. 194.

96   Ibid., p. 195.

97   Gloria Anzaldua, 'Haciendo caras, una entrada', in Gloria Anzaldua (ed.), *Making Face, Making Soul, Haciendo Caras*, p. xxvi; cited in Patricia Clough, *Feminist Thought: Desire, Power, and Academic Discourse*, Oxford: Blackwell, 1994, p. 134.

98   Anzaldua, *Borderlands/La Frontera*, p. 80.

99   Zillah Eisenstein, *The Color of Gender: Reimaging Democracy*, Berkeley: University of California Press, 1994, p. 213.

100 Anzaldua, *Borderlands/La Frontera*, p. 80.

101 Quote from New York City magazine, *Outweek*, quoted by Steven Epstein, 'A queer encounter: sociology and the study of sexuality', *Sociological Theory*, 12, July 1994, p. 2.

102 Rosemary Hennesssy, 'Queer theory: a review of the *Differences* special issue and Wittig's *The Straight Mind*', *Signs*, 18(4), 1993, pp. 964–73, at p. 964.

103 Alice Walker, 'In the closet of the soul: Letter to an Afro-American friend', *Ms Magazine*, 15 November 1986, pp. 32–5; cited in Chela Sandoval, 'US third world feminism: the theory and method of oppositional consciousness in the postmodern world', *Genders*, 10, Spring 1991, pp. 1–24, at p. 19, note 12.

104 Rebecca Walker, 'Introduction', *To Be Real*, p. xxxiii.

105 Clough, *Feminist Thought*, pp. 115–16.

106 Sandoval, 'US third world feminism', p. 2.
107 Ibid., p. 15.
108 Haraway, 'A manifesto for cyborgs', p. 198.
109 Heywood and Drake, 'Introduction', in *Third Wave Agenda*, p. 3.
110 For example, the 'Third Wave' web page includes an article entitled 'Third wave shift' by Julie Carlson, Kathryn Starace and Alexandra Villano, who conclude: 'Third Wave theory suggests that the proscription . . . is synthesis, coalition and networking': http://www.feminist.com/third.htm (third wave website).
111 Anna Yeatman and Sneja Gunew, 'Introducation', in Sneja Gunew and Anna Yeatman (eds), *Feminism and the Politics of Difference*, Halifax: Fernwood Publishing, 1993, p. xxiii.
112 Brodie, 'Restructuring: the falling apart', pp. 40–1.
113 The web site is http://www.feminist.com/third.htm. Carlson, Starace and Villano 'Third wave shift'.
114 Elizabeth Frazer and Nichola Lacey, *The Politics of Community: a Feminist Critique of the Liberal–Communitarian Debate*, Hemel Hempstead: Harvester Wheatsheaf, 1993, p. 198.
115 Susan Stanford Friedman, 'Beyond white and other: relationality and narratives of race in feminist discourse', *Signs*, 21(1), Autumn 1995, pp. 1–49, at p. 17.
116 Ibid., p. 40.
117 R. Radhakrishnan, 'Post-structuralist politics: toward a theory of coalition', in Douglas Kellner (ed.), *Jameson/Postmodernism/Critique*, pp. 276–90, Washington, DC: Maisonneurve, 1989, cited in ibid., p. 40.
118 Walker, 'Introduction', in *To Be Real*, p. xxxv.
119 Heywood and Drake, 'Introduction', in *Third Wave Agenda*, p. 7.
120 Nicholson, 'Interpreting gender', p. 99.
121 Phelan, '(Be)Coming out', pp. 783–4.
122 Butler, 'Gender trouble, feminist theory and psychoanalytic discourse', p. 325.
123 Phillips, 'Universal pretensions in political thought', p. 28.
124 Butler, 'Gender trouble, feminist theory and psychoanalytic discourse', p. 339.

Chapter 8 Conclusion

1 For an interesting treatment of this subject I am indebted to the unpublished doctoral thesis of Julie Fieldhouse, 'Europe's mirror: civil society and the other', University of British Columbia, Doctoral dissertation, August 1997.

Bibliography

Abbott, Sidney and Love, Barbara (1972) *Sappho was a Right-on Woman: a Liberated View of Lesbianism*. New York: Stein and Day.

Abel, Elizabeth (1990) 'Race, class, and psychoanalysis: opening questions'. In Marianne Hirsch and Evelyn Fox Keller (eds), *Conflicts in Feminism*. New York: Routledge, pp. 184–204.

Agonito, Rosemary (ed.) (1978) *History of Ideas on Women*. New York: Perigree Books.

Alaimo, Stacy (1994) 'Cyborg and ecofeminist interventions: challenges for an environmental feminism'. *Feminist Studies*, 20(1), 133–52.

Alfonso, Rita and Trigilio, Jo (1997) 'Surfing the third wave: a dialogue between two third wave feminists'. *Hypatia* (special issue: *Third Wave Feminisms*), 12(3), 7–16.

Allen, Anita L. (1983) 'Women and their privacy: what is at stake?' In Carol C. Gould (ed.), *Beyond Domination: New Perspectives on Women and Philosophy*. Towota, NJ: Rowman and Allanheld Publishers, pp. 233–49.

Anzaldua, Gloria (1987) *Borderlands/La Frontera*. San Francisco: Aunt Lute, 1987.

Arat-Koc, Sedef (1989) 'In the privacy of our own home: foreign domestic workers as solution to the crisis in the domestic sphere in Canada'. *Studies in Political Economy*, 28, 33–58.

Aristotle (1978) 'De generatione animalium'. In Rosemary Agonito (ed.), *History of Ideas on Women*. New York: Perigree Books, pp. 43–56.

Aristotle (1980) *Politics*, translated with an introduction Ernest Barker). Oxford: Oxford University Press.

Arneil, Barbara (1996) 'The wild Indian's venison: John Locke's theory of property'. *Political Studies*, 44(1), 60–74.

Arneil, Barbara (1996) *John Locke and America: the Defence of English Colonialism*. Oxford: Clarendon Press.

Astell, Mary (1970) *Some Reflections upon Marriage*. New York: Source Book Press.

Bakan, Abigail B. and Stasiulis, Daiva K. (1995) 'Making the match: domestic placement agencies and the racialization of women's household work'. *Signs: Journal of Women in Culture and Society*, 20(2), 303–35.

Bar On, Bat-Ami (1982) 'The feminist sexuality debates and the transformation of the political'. In Margaret Cruikshank (ed.), *Lesbian Studies: Present and Future*. New York: The Feminists Press.

Bar On, Bat-Ami (1994) 'The feminist sexuality debates and the transformation of the political'. In Claudia Card (ed.), *Adventures in Lesbian Philosophy*. Indianapolis: Indiana University Press.

Barrett, Michelle (1992) 'Women's oppression today: problems in Marxist feminist analysis'. In Maggie Humm (ed.), *Feminisms: a Reader*. Hemel Hempstead: Harvester Wheatsheaf, pp. 112–15.

Beiner, Ronald (1992) *What's the Matter with Liberalism?* Berkeley: University of California Press.

Benhabib, Seyla (1990) 'Epistemologies of postmodernism: a rejoinder to Jean-François Lyotard'. In Linda Nicholson (ed.), *Feminism/Postmodernism*. New York: Routledge, pp. 107–30.

Benn, Stanley I. and Gaus, Gerald F. (eds) (1983) *Public and Private in Social Life*. New York: St Martin's Press.

Bennett, Paula (1982) 'Dyke in academe (II)'. In Margaret Cruikshank (ed.), *Lesbian Studies: Present and Future*. New York: The Feminists Press.

Benston, Margaret (1969) 'The political economy of women's liberation'. *Monthly Review*, 21(4), 13–27.

Birke, Lynda (1986) *Women, Feminism and Biology: the Feminist Challenge*. New York: Methuen Press.

Black, Naomi (1983) 'Virginia Woolf: the life of natural happiness'. In D. Spender (ed.), *Feminist Theorists: Three Centuries of Women's Intellectual Traditions*. London: Women's Press.

Blasius, Mark (1994) *Gay and Lesbian Politics: Sexuality and the Emergence of a New Ethic*. Philadelphia: Temple University Press.

Bordo, Susan (1987) *The Flight to Objectivity: Essays on Cartesianism and Culture*. Albany: State University of New York Press.

Bordo, Susan (1990) 'Feminism, postmodernism, and gender-scepticism'. In Linda J. Nicholson (ed.), *Feminism/Postmodernism*. New York: Routledge, pp. 133–56.

Brah, Avtar (1993) 'Re-framing Europe: engendered racisms, ethnicities and nationalism in contemporary Western Europe'. *Feminist Review*, 45, Autumn, 9–29.

Brittain, Vera (1992) 'Why feminism lives'. In Maggie Humm (ed.), *Feminisms: a Reader*. Hemel Hempstead: Harvester Wheatsheaf, pp. 40–1.

Brittain, Vera and Holtby, Winifred (1992) 'Feminism divided'. In Maggie Humm (ed.), *Feminisms: a Reader*. Hemel Hempstead: Harvester Wheat-sheaf, pp. 42–3.

Brodie, Janine (1994) 'Restructuring: the falling apart'. Robarts Lecture, York University, Robarts Centre for Canadian Studies, 1 March.

Brownmiller, Susan (1975) *Against Our Will: Men, Women and Rape*. London: Secker and Warburg.

Bubeck, Diemut Elisabet (1995) *Care, Gender, and Justice*. Oxford: Clarendon Press.

Bunch, Charlotte (1975) 'Lesbians in revolt'. In Nancy Myron and Charlotte Bunch (eds), *Lesbianism and the Women's Movement*. Baltimore, MD: Diana.

Butler, Judith (1986) 'Sex and gender in Simone de Beauvoir's *Second Sex*'. In Helen Vivienne Wenzel (ed.), *Simone de Beauvoir: Witness to a Century*. Yale French Studies (special issue), 72, 35–49.

Butler, Judith (1989) *Gender Trouble: Feminism and the Subversion of Identity*. New York: Routledge.

Butler, Judith (1990) 'Gender trouble, feminist theory and psychoanalytic discourse'. In Linda J. Nicholson (ed.), *Feminism/Postmodernism*. New York: Routledge.

Butler, Judith (1992) 'Sexual inversions'. In Donna Stanton (ed.), *Discourses of Sexuality: from Aristotle to AIDS*. Ann Arbor: University of Michigan Press.

Butler, Judith (1993) *Bodies that Matter: on the Discursive Limits of 'Sex'*. New York: Routledge.

Butler, Judith and Scott, Joan W. (eds) (1992) *Feminists Theorize the Political*. New York: Routledge.

Butler, Melissa (1978) 'Early liberal roots of feminism: John Locke and the attack on patriarchy'. *American Political Science Review*, 72(1), 135–50.

Caddick, Alison (1985) 'Feminism and the body'. *Arena*, 74, 60–88.

Caraway, Nancie (1991) *Segregated Sisterhood: Racism and the Politics of American Feminism*. Knoxville: The University of Tennessee Press.

Carby, Hazel (1987) *Reconstructing Womanhood: the Emergence of the Afro-American Woman Novelist*. Oxford: Oxford University Press.

Card, Claudia (ed.) (1994) *Adventures in Lesbian Philosophy*. Bloomington: Indiana University Press.

Card, Claudia (1994) 'What is lesbian philosophy? A new introduction'. In Claudia Card (ed.), *Adventures in Lesbian Philosophy*. Bloomington: Indiana University Press.

Chodorow, Nancy (1978) *The Reproduction of Mothering: Psychoanalysis and the Socialization of Gender*. Berkeley: University of California Press.

Cixous Helene (1983) 'The laugh of the Medusa'. In E. Abel and E. K. Abel (eds), *The Signs: Journal of Women in Culture and Society. Reader: Women, Gender and Scholarship*. Chicago: University of Chicago Press.

Clough, Patricia (1994) *Feminist Thought: Desire, Power, and Academic Discourse*. Oxford: Blackwell.

Collins, Patricia Hill (1990) *Black Feminist Thought: Knowledge, Consciousness and the Politics of Empowerment*. Boston: Unwin Hyman.

Collins, Patricia Hill (1995) 'Symposium: on West and Fenstermaker's "Doing difference"'. *Gender and Society*, 9(4), 491–4.

Collins, Patricia Hill (1997) 'Comment on Hekman's "Truth and method: feminist standpoint theory revisited": truth of justice?' *Signs: Journal of Women in Culture and Society*, 22(2), 375–81.

Coole, Diana (1988) *Women in Political Theory: from Ancient Misogyny to Contemporary Feminism* Hemel Hempstead: Harvester Wheatsheaf.

Coulson, Margaret, Magas, Branka and Wainwright, Hilary (1975) 'The housewife and her labour under capitalism: a critique' *New Left Review*, 89, January/February, 47–58.

Crick, Bernard (1982) *In Defence of Politics*. Harmondsworth: Penguin Books.

Crosby, Christina (1992) 'Dealing with difference'. In Judith Butler and Joan W. Scott (eds), *Feminists Theorize the Political*. New York: Routledge, pp. 130–43.

Daly, Mary (1978) *Gyn/Ecology: The Metaethics of Radical Feminism*. Boston: Beacon Press.

Davis, Angela (1971) 'Reflections on the black woman's role in the community of slaves'. *The Black Scholar*, 3(4).

Davis, Angela (1983) *Women, Race and Class*. New York: Random House.

Day, Tanis (1987) *The Influence of Capital–Labour Substitution in the Home on the Processes and Value of Housework*. Toronto: University of Toronto Press.

de Beauovir, Simone (1953) *The Second Sex*, translated by H. M. Parshley. New York: Knopf.

de Beauvoir, Simone (1984) 'An interview with Alice Schwartzer'. In *Simone de Beauvoir Today*, translated by Marianne Howarth. London: Hogarth Press.

de Beauvoir, Simone (1988) *The Second Sex*. translated by H. M. Parshley. London: Picador Classics.

Denfeld, Rene (1995) *The New Victorians: a Young Woman's Challenge to the Old Feminist Order*. New York: Warner Books.

Di Stefano, Christine (1983) 'Masculinity as ideology in political theory: Hobbesian man considered'. *Women's Studies International Forum*, 6, 633–44.

Di Stefano, Christine (1990) 'Dilemmas of difference: feminism, modernity and postmodernism'. In Linda J. Nicholson (ed.), *Feminism/Postmodernism*. New York: Routledge, pp. 63–82.

Dinnerstein, Dorothy (1976) *The Mermaid and the Minotaur*. New York: Harper and Row.

Dworkin, Andrea (1981) *Pornography: Men Possessing Women*. London: Women's Press.

Eisenstein, Zillah (1981) *The Radical Future of Liberal Feminism*. New York: Longman.

Eisenstein, Zillah (1990) *The Female Body and the Law*. Berkeley: University of California Press.

Eisenstein, Zillah (1994) *The Color of Gender: Reimaging Democracy*. Berkeley: University of California Press.

Elshtain, Jean Bethke (1981) *Public Man, Private Woman: Women in Social and Political Thought*. Princeton, NJ: Princeton University Press.

Elshtain, Jean Bethke (1982) 'Aristotle, the public–private split and the case of the suffragists'. In J. B. Elshtain (ed.), *The Family in Political Thought*. Amherst: The University of Massachusetts Press.

Elshtain, Jean Bethke (1992) 'The power and powerlessness of women'. In G. Bock and S. James (eds), *Beyond Equality and Difference*. Routledge: New York.

Elshtain, Jean Bethke (1993) *Democracy on Trial*. The Massey Lecture Series, Concord, NH: House of Anansi Press Ltd.

Engels, Friedrich (1985) *The Origin of the Family, Private Property and the State*. New York: International Publishers.

Epstein, Steven (1994) 'A queer encounter: sociology and the study of sexuality'. *Sociological Theory*, 12, July, 188–202.

Findlen, Barbara (ed.) (1995) *Listen Up: Voices from the Next Feminist Generation*. Seattle: Seal Press.

Firestone, Shulamith (1979) *The Dialectic of Sex: the Case for Feminist Revolution*. London: The Women's Press.

Flax, Jane (1983) 'The Patriarchal Unconscious'. In Sandra Harding and Merrill B. Hintikka (eds), *Discovering Reality: Feminists' Perspectives on Epistemology, Metaphysics, Methodology, and Philosophy of Science*. Boston: Reidel Publishing Company, pp. 245–81.

Flax, Jane (1990) 'Postmodernism and gender relations'. In Linda Nicholson (ed.), *Feminism/Postmodernism*. New York: Routledge, pp. 39–62.

Foucault, Michel (1973) *Madness and Civilization*. New York: Vintage Books.

Foucault, Michel (1973) *The Birth of the Clinic*. New York: Vintage Books.

Foucault, Michel (1977) *Power/Knowledge: Selected Interviews and Other Writings (1972–1977)*, edited by Colin Gordon. New York: Random House.

Foucault, Michel (1980) *History of Sexuality*. New York: Vintage Books.

Foucault, Michel (1984) 'What is enlightenment?' In *The Foucault Reader*. New York: Pantheon Books.

Frazer, Elizabeth and Lacey, Nicola (1993) *The Politics of Community: a Feminist Critique of the Liberal–Communitarian Debate*. Hemel Hempstead: Harvester Wheatsheaf.

Friedman, Susan Stanford (1995) 'Beyond white and other: relationality and narratives of race in feminist discourse'. *Signs: Journal of Women in Culture and Society*, 21(1), 1–49.

Frye, Marilyn (1990) 'The possibility of feminist theory'. In Deborah L. Rhode (ed.), *Theoretical Perspectives on Sexual Difference*. New Haven, CT: Yale University Press.

Gatens, Moira (1988) 'Towards a feminist philosophy of the body'. In B. Caine, E. A. Grosz, M. de Lepervanche (eds), *Crossing Boundaries: Feminism and the Critique of Knowledges*. Sydney: Allen and Unwin, pp. 59–70.

Gatens, Moira (1992) 'Power, bodies and difference'. In Michele Barrett and Anne Phillips (eds), *Destabilizing Theories: Contemporary Feminist Debates*. Cambridge: Polity Press.

Gavison, Ruth (1980) 'Privacy and the limits of the law'. *Yale Law Journal*, 89(3), 421–71.

Geller, Gloria (1975) 'The War-time Elections Act of 1917 and the Canadian women's movement'. *Atlantis: a Women's Studies Journal*, 2(1), 88–106.

Genovese-Fox, Elizabeth (1994) 'Difference, diversity and divisions in an agenda for the women's movement'. In Gay Young and Bette J. Dickerson (eds), *Colour, Class, and Country: Experiences of Gender*. London: Zed Books, pp. 232–48.

Gerstein, Ira (1973) 'Domestic work and capitalism'. *Radical America*, 7(4/5), 101–28.

Giddings, Paula (1984) *When and Where I Enter: the Impact of Black Women on Race and Sex in America*. New York: William Morrow.

Giddings, Paula (1985) 'Black feminism takes its rightful place'. *Ms. Magazine*, October, 25–6.

Gilligan, Carol (1982) *In a Different Voice: Psychological Theory and Women's Development*. Cambridge, MA: Harvard University Press.

Glenn, Evelyn Nakano (1992) 'From servitude to service work: historical continuities in the racial division of paid reproductive labor'. *Signs: Journal of Women in Culture and Society*, 18(1), 1–43.

Grant, Rebecca (1991) 'Sources of gender bias in international relations theory'. In R. Grant and K. Newland (eds), *Gender and International Relations*. Bloomington: Indiana University Press, pp. 9–26.

Greschner, Donna, Johnson, Rhonda and Stevenson, Wanda (1993) 'Peekiskwetan'. *Canadian Journal of Women and the Law*, 6, 161–75.

Griffin, Susan (1981) *Pornography and Silence: Culture's Revenge against Women*. London: The Women's Press.

Griffin, Susan (1984) *Women and Nature: the Roaring Insider Her*. London: The Women's Press.

Gross, Elizabeth (1986) 'Philosophy, subjectivity and the body: Kristeva and Irigaray'. In Carole Pateman and Elizabeth Gross (eds), *Feminist Challenges: Social and Political Theory*. Sydney: Allen and Unwin, pp. 125–43.

Grosz, E. A. (1988) 'The in(ter)vention of feminist knowledges'. In Barbara Caine, E. A. Grosz and Marie de Lepervanche (eds), *Crossing Boundaries: Feminisms and the Critique of Knowledges*. Sydney: Allen and Unwin, pp. 92–109.

Grosz, Elizabeth (1995) 'Notes towards a corporeal feminism'. *Australian Feminist Studies*, Summer, 1–16.

Guillaumin, Colette (1995) *Racism, Sexism, Power and Ideology*. London: Routledge.

Gutmann, Amy (1985) 'Communitarian critics of liberalism'. *Philosophy and Public Affairs*, 14(3), 308–22.

Hampton, Jean (1993) 'Feminist contractarianism'. In Louise Antony and Charlotte Witt (eds), *A Mind of One's Own: Feminist Essays on Reason and Objectivity*. Boulder, CO: Westview Press.

Haraway, Donna (1988) 'Situated knowledges: the science question in feminism and the privilege of partial perspective'. *Feminists Studies*, 14, 575–599.

Haraway, Donna (1989) *Primate Visions: Gender. Race. and Nature in the World of Modern Science*. New York: Routledge.

Haraway, Donna (1990) 'A manifesto for cyborgs: science, technology and socialist feminism in the 1980s'. In Linda Nicholson (ed.), *Feminism/ Postmodernism*. New York: Routledge, pp. 190–233.

Haraway, Donna (1991) *Simians. Cyborgs and Women: The Reinvention of Nature*. New York: Routledge.

Haraway, Donna (1992) 'Ecc homo, ain't (ar'n't) I a Woman, and inappropriat'd others: the human in a post-humanist landscape'. In Judith Butler and Joan W. Scott (eds), *Feminists Theorize the Political*. New York: Routledge, pp. 86–100.

Harding, Sandra and Hintikka, Merrill (eds) (1983) *Discovering Reality*, Boston: D. Reidel Publishing.

Hartmann, Heidi (1981) 'The unhappy marriage of marxism and feminism: towards a more progressive union'. In Lydia Sargent (ed.), *Women and Revolution: a Discussion of the Unhappy Marriage of Marxism and Feminism*. Montreal: Black Rose Books, pp. 1–42.

Hartsock, Nancy C. M. (1983) 'The feminist standpoint: developing the ground for a specifically feminist historical materialism'. In Sandra Harding and Merrill B. Hintikka (eds), *Discovering Reality: Feminists Perspectives on Epistemology. Metaphysics. Methodology. and Philosophy of Science*. Boston: Reidel Publishing Company, pp. 283–310.

Hartsock, Nancy (1983) *Money, Sex and Power*. London: Longman.

Hartsock, Nancy (1990) 'Foucault on power: a theory for women?' In Linda Nicholson (ed.), *Feminism/Postmodernism*. New York: Routledge, pp. 157–75.

Hartsock, Nancy (1997) 'Comment on Hekman's "Truth and method: feminist standpoint theory revisited": truth of justice?' *Signs: Journal of Women in Culture and Society*, 22(2), 367–74.

Hartsock, Nancy (1983) 'Rethinking modernism: minority vs. majority theories'. *Cultural Critique*, 7, 187–206.

Hekman, Susan (1997) 'Truth and method: feminists standpoint theory revisited'. *Signs: Journal of Women in Culture and Society*, 22(2), 341–65.

Held, Virginia (1987) 'Noncontractual society: a feminist view'. In Marsha Hanen and Kai Nielsen (eds), *Science, Morality and Feminist Theory*. Calgary: University of Calgary Press.

Henley, Nancy (1986) *Body Politics: Power. Sex and Nonverbal Communication*. New York: Simon and Schuster.

Hennessy, Rosemary (1993) 'Queer theory: a review of the *Differences* special issue and Wittig's *The Straight Mind*'. *Signs: Journal of Women in Culture and Society*, 18(4), 964–73.

Heywood, Leslie and Drake, Jennifer (eds) (1997) *Third Wave Agenda: Being Feminist, Doing Feminism*. Minneapolis: University of Minnesota Press.

Himmelweit Susan and Mohn, Simon (1977) 'Domestic labour and capital'. *Cambridge Journal of Economics*, 1(1), 15–31.

Hirschmann, Nancy (1989) 'Freedom, recognition and obligation: a feminist approach to political theory'. *American Political Science Review*, 83(4), 1227–44.

Hobbes, Thomas (1985) *Leviathan*, edited by C. B. MacPherson. Harmondsworth: Penguin Books.

Hobsbawm, E. (1975) 'The idea of fraternity'. *New Society*, November.

hooks, bell (1981) *Ain't I a Woman? Black Women and Feminism*. Boston: South End Press.

hooks, bell (1984) *Feminist Theory: from Margin to Center*. Boston: South End Press.

hooks, bell (1994) 'Postmodern blackness'. In Mary Eagleton (ed.), *Feminist Literary Theory: a Reader*. Oxford: Blackwell, pp. 280–3.

Horney, Karen (1973) *Feminine Psychology*. New York: W. W. Norton.

http://www.feminist.com/third.htm (third wave website)

http://www.folksonline.com/folks/ts/cybergirl.htm (cybergrrls/webgrrls website)

http://www.geocities.com/area51/vault/1363/riotgrrl.html. (riotgrrl website)

http://www.iuj.ac.jp/webgrrls/about.htm (Japan chapter of webgrrls website)

Humm, Maggie (ed.) (1992) *Feminisms: a Reader*. Hemel Hempstead: Harvester Wheatsheaf.

Hurtado, Aida (1989) 'Relating to privilege: seduction and rejection in the subordination of white women and women of color'. *Signs: Journal of Women in Culture and Society*, 14(4), 833–55.

Hurtado, Aida (1996) *The Color of Privilege: Three Blasphemies on Race and Feminism*. Ann Arbor: University of Michigan Press.

Irigaray, Luce (1996) 'The sex which is not one'. In Lawrence Cahoone (ed.), *From Modernism to Postmodernism: an Anthology*. Oxford: Blackwell.

Jaggar, Alison (1983) *Feminist Politics and Human Nature*. Brighton: Harvester Press.

Jaggar, Alison and Bordo, Susan (eds) (1989) *Gender/Body/Knowledge: Feminist Reconstructions of Being and Knowing*. New Brunswick, NJ: Rutgers University Press.

Joseph, Gloria (1981) 'The incompatible menage a trois: Marxism, feminism, and racism'. In Lydia Sargent (ed.), *Women and Revolution: A Discussion of the Unhappy Marriage of Marxism and Feminism*. Montreal: Black Rose Books, pp. 91–107.

Keller, Evelyn Fox (1983) 'Gender and science'. In Sandra Harding and Merrill B. Hintikka (eds), *Discovering Reality: Feminists Perspectives on Epistemology*.

Metaphysics. Methodology. and Philosophy of Science. Boston: Reidel Publishing Company, pp. 187–205.

Koedt, Anne and Freeman, Jo (1975) *The Politics of Women's Liberation*. New York: Longman Press.

Kristeva, Julia (1994) 'A question of subjectivity: an interview'. In Mary Eagleton (ed.), *Feminist Literary Theory: a Reader*. Oxford: Blackwell.

Kymlicka, Will (1995) *Multicultural Citizenship*. Oxford: Clarendon Press.

Laslett, Peter (1957) 'John Locke, the Great Recoinage and the Board of Trade (1695–1698)'. *William and Mary Quarterly*, third series, 14(3), 370–402.

Leiss, W. (1974) *The Domination of Nature*. Boston: Beacon Press.

Lévi-Strauss, Claude (1962) *The Savage Mind*. London: Weidenfeld and Nicolson.

Lévi-Strauss, Claude (1963) *Structural Anthropology*, translated by C. Jacobson and B. G. Schoepf. New York: Basic Books.

Lewis, Diana K. (1977) 'A response to inequality: black women, racism, and sexism'. *Signs: Journal of Women in Culture and Society*, 3(2), 339–80.

Lieven, Elena (1981) 'If it's natural, we can't change it'. In *Women in Society: Interdisciplinary Essays*. London: Virago, pp. 203–23.

Lloyd, Genevieve (1993) *The Man of Reason: 'Male' and 'Female' in Western Philosophy*, 2nd edn. London: Routledge.

Locke, John (1836) 'The First Set of the Fundamental Constitutions of Carolina' In B. R. Carroll (ed.), *Historical Collections of South Carolina*. New York.

Locke, John (1897) 'Temporary Laws to be added to Instructions to Ye Governor and Council of Carolina'. *Collections of the South Carolina Historical Society*, V. Charleston.

Locke, John (1975) *Essay Concerning Human Understanding*, edited by Peter Nidditch. Oxford: Oxford University Press.

Locke, John (1988) *Two Treatises of Government*, edited by Peter Laslett. Cambridge Texts in the History of Political Thought. Cambridge: Cambridge University Press.

Lorde, Audre (1984) 'An open letter to Mary Daly'. In *Sister Outsider*. New York: The Crossing Press.

Lorde, Audre (1984) *Sister Outsider*. New York: Crossing Press.

MacCormack, Carol and Strathern, Marilyn (eds) (1980) *Nature. Culture and Gender*. Cambridge: Cambridge University Press.

MacIntyre, Alasdair (1984) 'The virtues, the unity of a human life, and the concept of a tradition'. In *Liberalism and Its Critics*. New York: New York University Press, pp. 125–48.

MacIntyre, Alasdair (1981) *After Virtue: a Study in Moral Theory*. London: Duckworth.

Mackenzie, Catriona (1986) 'Simone de Beauvoir: philosophy and/or the female body'. In Carole Pateman and Elizabeth Gross (eds), *Feminist Challenges: Social and Political Theory*. Sydney: Allen and Unwin, pp. 144–56.

MacKinnon, Catharine (1983) 'Feminism, Marxism, method, and the state: an agenda for theory'. In E. Abel and E. K. Abel (eds), *The Signs: Journal of Women in Culture and Society. Reader: Women, Gender and Scholarship*. Chicago: University of Chicago Press, pp. 227–56.

Macklin, Audrey (1992) 'Foreign domestic worker: surrogate housewife or mail order servant?' *McGill Law Journal*, 37(3), 681–760.

Makus, Ingrid (1996) *Women, Politics, and Reproduction: the Liberal Legacy*. Toronto: University of Toronto Press.

Martin, Biddy and Mohanty, Chandra (1986) 'Feminist politics: what's home got to do with it?' In Teresa de Lauretis (ed.), *Feminist Studies/Critical Studies*. Bloomington: Indiana University Press, pp. 191–212.

Marx, Karl (1977) *Karl Marx: Selected Writings*, edited by David McClelland, Oxford: Oxford University Press.

Merchant, Carolyn (1995) *Earthcare: Women and the Environment*. New York: Routledge.

Mies, Maria and Shiva, Vandana (1993) *Ecofeminism*. London: Zed Books.

Mill, John Stuart (1982) *On Liberty*. Harmondsworth: Penguin Books.

Mill, John Stuart (1991) 'Subjection of women'. In *On Liberty and Other Essays*, edited by John Gray. Oxford: Oxford University Press.

Millett, Kate (1970) *Sexual Politics*. New York: Doubleday and Co.

Minh-ha, Trinh T. (1989) *Woman, Native, Other: Writing Postcoloniality and Feminism*. Bloomington: Indiana University Press.

Mitchell, Juliet (1973) *Woman's Estate*. Harmondsworth: Penguin Books.

Mitchell, Juliet (1975) *Psychoanalysis and Feminism*, New York: Vintage Books.

Mitchell, Juliet (1984) *Women: the Longest Revolution. Essays in Feminism. Literature and Psychoanalysis*. London: Virago.

Moi, Toril (1989) 'Patriarchal thought and the drive for knowledge'. In Teresa Brennan (ed.), *Between Feminism and Psychoanalysis*. London: Routledge, pp. 189–205.

Morgan, Robin (1996) 'Introduction/planetary feminism: the politics of the 21st century'. In Robin Morgan (ed.), *Sisterhood Is Global: the International Women's Movement Anthology*. New York: Doubleday, pp. 1–37.

Mouffe, Chantal (1992) 'Feminism and radical politics'. In Judith Butler and Joan W. Scott (eds), *Feminists Theorize the Political*. Routledge: New York, pp. 369–84.

Ng, Roxana (1988) 'Immigrant women and institutionalized racism'. In Sandra Burt, Lorraine Code and Lindsay Dorney (eds), *Changing Patterns: Women in Canada*. Toronto: McLelland & Stewart, pp. 184–203.

Nicholson, Linda (1986) *Gender and History: the Limits of Social Theory in the Age of the Family*. New York: Columbia University Press.

Nicholson, Linda (1994) 'Interpreting gender'. *Signs: Journal of Women in Culture and Society*, 20(1), 79–105.

Nozick, Robert (1974) *Anarchy, State and Utopia*. Oxford: Basil Blackwell.

O'Brien, Mary (1981) *The Politics of Reproduction*. London: Routledge, Kegan and Paul.

Okin, Susan Moller (1978) *Women in Western Political Thought*. Princeton, NJ: Princeton University Press.

Omolade, Barbara (1980) 'Black women and feminism'. In H. Eisenstein and Alice Jardine (eds), *The Future of Difference*. Boston: G. K. Hall, pp. 247–57.

Orr, Catherine (1997) 'Charting the currents of the third wave'. *Hypatia* (special issue: *Third Wave Feminisms*), 12(3), 29–45.

Ortner, Sherry B. (1974) 'Is female to male as nature is to culture?' In Michelle Zimbalist Rosaldo and Louise Lamphere (eds), *Women, Culture, and Society*. Stanford, CA: Stanford University Press, pp. 67–87.

Ortner, Sherry B. (1996) *Making Gender: the Politics and Erotics of Culture*. Boston: Beacon Press.

Pateman, Carole (1983) 'Feminist critiques of the public private dichotomy' In Stanley I. Benn and Gerald F. Gaus (eds), *Public and Private in Social Life*. New York: St Martin's Press, pp. 281–303.

Pateman, Carole (1988) *The Sexual Contract*. Oxford: Polity Press.

Pateman, Carole (1989) 'The fraternal social contract'. In *The Disorder of Women: Democracy. Feminism and Political Theory*. Stanford, CA: Stanford University Press.

Pateman, Carole (1989) *The Disorder of Women*. Stanford, CA: Stanford University Press.

Phelan, Shane (1989) *Identity Politics: Lesbian Feminism and the Limits of Community*. Philadelphia: Temple University Press.

Phelan, Shane (1993) '(Be)Coming Out: lesbian identity and politics'. *Signs: Journal of Women in Culture and Society*, 18(4), 765–90.

Phelan, Shane (1993) 'Lesbian identity and politics'. *Signs: Journal of Women in Culture and Society*, 18(4), 765–90.

Phillips, Anne (1992) 'Feminism, equality and difference'. In Linda McDowell and Rosemary Pringle (eds), *Defining Women: Social Institutions and Gender Divisions*. Cambridge: Polity Press, pp. 205–22.

Phillips, Anne (1992) 'Universal pretensions in political thought'. In Michele Barrett and Anne Phillips (eds), *Destabilizing Theory: Contemporary Feminist Debates*. Cambridge: Polity Press, pp. 10–30.

Plato (1953) *The Dialogues of Plato*, edited by B. Jarrett, four volumes, 4th edn. Oxford: Clarendon Press.

Plato (1963) *The Republic*. Harmondsworth: Penguin Books.

Plato (1968) *The Republic*, translated by Allan Bloom. New York: Basic Books.

Radhakrishnan, R. (1989) 'Post-structuralist poltiics: toward a theory of coalition'. In Douglas Kellner (ed.), *Jameson/Postmodernism/Critique*. Washington, DC: Maisonneuve, pp. 276–90.

Randall, Vicky (1982) *Women and Politics*. London: Macmillan Press.

Rawls, John (1971) *Theory of Justice*. Oxford: University Press.

Reverby, Susan and Helly, Dorothy (1992) 'Introduction'. In *Gendered Domains: Rethinking Public and Private in Women's History*. Ithaca, NY: Cornell University Press, p. 8.

Rich, Adrienne (1976) *Of Woman Born: Motherhood as Experience and Institution*. New York: W. W. Norton and Co. Inc.

Rich, Adrienne (1983) 'Compulsory heterosexuality and lesbian existence'. In E. Abel and E. K. Abel (eds), *The Signs Reader: Women, Gender and Scholarship*. Chicago: University of Chicago Press, pp. 139–68.

Riddiough, Christine (1981) 'Socialism, feminism and gay/lesbian liberation'. In Lydia Sargeant (ed.), *Women and Revolution: a Discussion of the Unhappy Marriage of Marxism and Feminism*. Montreal: Black Rose Books, pp. 71–90.

Robson, Ruthann (1994) 'Mother; the legal domestication of lesbian existence'. In Claudia Card (ed.), *Adventures in Lesbian Philosophy*. Bloomington: Indiana University Press.

Rogers, Kate (1997) 'Aboriginal women and the feminist project: an uneasy alliance'. Paper Presented at the 1997 Learned Societies, Canadian Political Science Association, Memorial University, Newfoundland, June.

Roiphe, Kate (1993) *The Morning After: Sex, Fear and Feminism*. Boston: Little Brown and Co.

Rosaldo, Michelle Zimbalist (1980) 'The use and abuse of anthropology: reflections on feminism and cross-cultural understanding'. *Signs: Journal of Women in Culture and Society*, 5, Spring, 389–417.

Rosaldo, Michelle Zimbalist and Lamphere, Louise (eds) (1974) *Woman, Culture and Society*. Stanford, CA: Stanford University Press.

Rothfield, Philippa (1990) 'Feminism, subjectivity, and sexual experience'. In Sneja Gunew (ed.), *Feminist Knowledge: Critique and Construct*. London: Routledge.

Rowbotham, Sheila (1972) *Women, Resistance and Revolution*. Harmondsworth: Penguin Books.

Rowbotham, Sheila (1974) *Woman's Consciousness: Man's World*. Harmondsworth: Penguin Books.

Rubin, Gayle 'The traffic in women'. In Rayna Reiter (ed.), *Toward an Anthropology of Women*. New York: Monthly Review, pp. 157–210.

Ruddick, Sara (1984) 'Preservative love and military destruction: some reflections of mothering and peace'. In J. Trebilcot (ed.), *Mothering: Essays in Feminist Theory*. Totowa, NJ: Rowman and Allenheld.

Sandel, Michael (1982) *Liberalism and the Limits of Justice*. Cambridge: Cambridge University Press.

Sandel, Michael (1984) *Liberalism and Its Critics*. New York: New York University Press.

Sandel, Michael (1985) 'Morality and the liberal ideal'. *The New Republic*, 7 May.

Sandoval, Chela (1991) 'US Third World feminism: the theory and method of oppositional consciousness in the postmodern world'. *Genders*, 10, Spring, 1–24.

Segal, Lynn (1990) *Slow Motion: Changing Masculinities, Changing Men*. London: Virago Press.

Silvera, Makeda (1989) *Silenced: Talks with Working Class Caribbean Women about Their Lives and Struggles as Domestic Workers in Canada*, 2nd edn. Toronto: Sister Vision.

Simons, Margaret A. (1994) 'Lesbian connections: simone de beauvoir and feminism'. In Claudia Card (ed.), *Adventures in Lesbian Philosophy*. Bloomington: Indiana University Press, pp. 217–40.

Simons, Margaret and Benjamin, Jessica (1979) 'Simone de Beauvoir: an interview'. *Feminist Studies*, 5, Summer, 330–45.

Simpson, Rennie (1983) 'The Afro-American female: the historical context of the construction of sexual identity'. In Ann Snitow, Christine Stansell and Sharon Thompson (eds), *Desire: the Politics of Sexuality*. London: Virago.

Spelman, Elizabeth (1989) *Inessential Woman: Problems of Exclusion in Feminist Thought*. Boston: Beacon Press.

Spiller, Hortense J. (1987) 'Mama's baby, papa's maybe: an American grammer book'. *Mediacritics*, Summer, 65–81.

Stack, Carol (1986) 'The culture of gender: women and men of color'. *Signs: Journal of Women in Culture and Society*, 11(2), 322–3.

Stanton, Elizabeth Cady, Anthony, Susan B. and Gage, Matilda Joslyn (eds) (1887) *History of Women's Suffrage*. Rochester: Charles Mann.

Thompson, Clara (1964) *Interpersonal Psychoanalysis: The Selected Papers of Clara Thompson*, edited by M. P. Green. New York: Basic Books.

Tong, Rosemarie (1989) *Feminist Thought: a Comprehensive Introduction*. Boulder, CO: Westview Press.

Truth, Sojourner (1972) 'Ain't I a Woman'. In Miriam Schneir (ed.), *Feminism: the Essential Historical Readings*. New York: Random House, pp. 94–5.

Walker, Alice (1986) 'In the closet of the soul: letter to an Afro-American friend'. *Ms. Magazine*, 15, November, 32–5.

Walker, Rebecca (ed.) (1995) *To Be Real: Telling the Truth and Changing the Face of Feminism*. New York: Anchor Books.

Walzer, Michael (1984) 'Welfare, membership and need'. In *Liberalism and Its Critics*. New York: New York University Press.

Waring, Marilyn (1988) *If Women Counted: a New Feminist Economics*. San Francisco: Harper & Row.

Wittig, Monique (1984) 'One is not born a woman'. In Alison Jaggar and Paula Rothenberg (eds), *Feminist Frameworks: Alternative Theoretical Acounts of the Relations between Women and Men*. New York: McGraw-Hill.

Wolf, Naomi (1993) *Fire with Fire: the New Female Power and How to Use It*. New York: Fawcett Combine.

Yeatman, Anna (1992) 'A feminist theory of social differentiation'. In Judith Butler and Joan W. Scott (eds), *Feminists Theorize the Political*. New York: Routledge, pp. 281–99.

Yeatman, Anna and Gunew, Sneja (eds) (1993) *Feminism and The Politics of Difference*, Halifax: Fernwood Publishing, 228–45.

Young, Iris Marion (1981) 'Beyond the unhappy marriage: a critique of the dual systems theory'. In Lydia Sargent (ed.), *Women and Revolution: a Discussion of the Unhappy Marriage of Marxism and Feminism*. Montreal: Black Rose Books, pp. 43–69.

Young, Iris Marion (1990) 'The ideal of community and the politics of difference'. In Linda J. Nicholson (ed.), *Feminism/Postmodernism*. New York: Routledge, pp. 300–23.

Young, Iris Marion (1990) *Throwing Like a Girl and Other Essays in Feminist Philosophy and Social Theory*. Bloomington: Indiana University Press.

Zinn, Maxine Baca and Dill, Bonnie Thornton (1996) 'Theorizing difference from multiracial feminism'. *Feminist Studies*, 22(2), 321–31.

Zita, Jacquelyn N. (1997) 'Introduction'. *Hypatia* (special issue: *Third Wave Feminisms*), 12(3), pp. 1–6.

Index